BY CARL T. BERGSTROM
AND JEVIN D. WEST

Calling Bullshit

BY CARL T. BERGSTROM

Evolution (with Lee Alan Dugatkin)

CALLING BULLSHIT

CALLING BULLSHIT

The Art of Skepticism in a Data-Driven World

CARL T. BERGSTROM
& JEVIN D. WEST

RANDOM HOUSE | NEW YORK

Published in the United States by Random House,
an imprint and division of Penguin Random House LLC, New York.

RANDOM HOUSE and the HOUSE colophon are
registered trademarks of Penguin Random House LLC.

LIBRARY OF CONGRESS CATALOGING-IN-PUBLICATION DATA

NAMES: Bergstrom, Carl T., author. | West, Jevin D. (Jevin Darwin),
author.

TITLE: Calling bullshit : the art of skepticism in a data-driven world /
Carl T. Bergstrom and Jevin D. West.

DESCRIPTION: First edition. | New York : Random House, 2020. |
Includes bibliographical references.

IDENTIFIERS: LCCN 2020003592 (print) | LCCN 2020003593 (ebook) |
ISBN 9780525509189 (hardcover acid-free paper) | ISBN 9780593229767
(international edition acid-free paper) | ISBN 9780525509196 (ebook)

SUBJECTS: LCSH: Skepticism.

CLASSIFICATION: LCC B837 .B47 2020 (print) | LCC B837 (ebook) |
DDC 149/.73—dc23

LC record available at https://lccn.loc.gov/2020003592

LC ebook record available at https://lccn.loc.gov/2020003593

Printed in the United States of America on acid-free paper

randomhousebooks.com

987654321

First Edition

Book design by Barbara M. Bachman

To our wives, Holly and Heather,
for calling us on our bullshit when we need it—
but especially for not, when we don't.

Contents

PREFACE

THE WORLD IS AWASH WITH BULLSHIT, AND WE'RE DROWNING IN IT. Politicians are unconstrained by facts. Science is conducted by press release. Silicon Valley startups elevate bullshit to high art. Colleges and universities reward bullshit over analytic thought. The majority of administrative activity seems to be little more than a sophisticated exercise in the combinatorial reassembly of bullshit. Advertisers wink conspiratorially and invite us to join them in seeing through all the bullshit. We wink back—but in doing so drop our guard and fall for the second-order bullshit they are shoveling at us. Bullshit pollutes our world by misleading people about specific issues, and it undermines our ability to trust information in general. However modest, this book is our attempt to fight back.

The philosopher Harry Frankfurt recognized that the ubiquity of bullshit is a defining characteristic of our time. His classic treatise *On Bullshit* begins as follows:

> One of the most salient features of our culture is that there is so much bullshit. Everyone knows this. Each of us contributes his share. But we tend to take the situation for granted [yet] we have no clear understanding of what bullshit is, why there is so much of it, or what functions it serves. And we lack a conscientiously developed appreciation of what it means to us. In other words, we have no theory.

To eradicate bullshit, it is helpful to know precisely what it is. And here things get tricky.

First of all, "bullshit" is both a noun and a verb. Not only can I get tired of listening to your bullshit (*n.*), I can turn around and bullshit (*v.*) you myself. This is straightforward enough. To bullshit is, at a first approximation, the act of producing bullshit.

But what does the noun "bullshit" refer to anyway? As with many attempts to match philosophical concepts to everyday language, it would be a fool's errand to attempt a definition that incorporates and excludes everything it should. Instead, we will start with a few examples and then try to describe some things that would qualify as bullshit.

Most people think they're pretty good at spotting bullshit. That may be true when bullshit comes in the form of rhetoric or fancy language, what we call *old-school bullshit*. For example:

- Our collective mission is to functionalize bilateral solutions for leveraging underutilized human resource portfolio opportunities. (In other words, we are a temp agency.)
- We exist as transmissions. To embark on the myth is to become one with it. (We might call this new-age old-school bullshit.)
- Just as our forefathers before us, we look to the unending horizons of our great nation with minds fixed and hearts aflame to rekindle the dampened sparks of our collective destiny. (Spare us. How are you going bring jobs back to the district?)

Old-school bullshit doesn't seem to be going away, but it may be overshadowed by the rise of what we call *new-school bullshit*. New-school bullshit uses the language of math and science and statistics to create the impression of rigor and accuracy. Dubious claims are given a veneer of legitimacy by glossing them with numbers, figures, statistics, and data graphics. New-school bullshit might look something like this:

- Adjusted for currency exchange rates, our top-performing global fund beat the market in seven of the past nine years.

(How exactly were returns adjusted? How many of the company's funds failed to beat the market and by how much? For that matter, was there a single fund that beat the market in seven of nine years, or was it a different fund that beat the market in each of those seven years?)

   • While short of statistical significance ($p = 0.13$), our results underscore the clinically important effect size (relative
   odds of survival at five years = 1.3) of our targeted oncotherapy
   and challenge the current therapeutic paradigm.

(What does it mean for a result to be clinically important if it is not statistically significant? Is five-year survival a relevant measure for this particular cancer, or are most patients deceased within three years? Why should we imagine that any of this "challenges the current therapeutic paradigm"?)

   • The team's convolutional neural net algorithm extracts
   the underlying control logic from a multiplex network composed of the human metabolome, transcriptome, and pro-
   teome.

(What is a multiplex network? Why are connections among these various -omes meaningful, and how are they measured? What does the author mean by "control logic"? How do we know there *is* an underlying control logic linking these systems, and if there is, how do we know that this approach can actually capture it?)

   • Our systematic screening revealed that 34 percent of behaviorally challenged second graders admit to having sniffed
   Magic Markers at least once in the past year.

(Why does it matter? And if it does, is marker-sniffing a cause or a consequence of being "behaviorally challenged"? What fraction of nonchallenged second graders admit to sniffing Magic Markers? Perhaps that fraction is even higher!)

New-school bullshit can be particularly effective because many of us don't feel qualified to challenge information that is presented in quantitative form. That is exactly what new-school bullshitters are counting on. To fight back, one must learn when and how to question such statements.

WE HAVE DEVOTED OUR careers to teaching students how to think logically and quantitatively about data. This book emerged from a course we teach at the University of Washington, also titled "Calling Bullshit." We hope it will show you that you do not need to be a professional statistician or econometrician or data scientist to think critically about quantitative arguments, nor do you need extensive data sets and weeks of effort to see through bullshit. It is often sufficient to apply basic logical reasoning to a problem and, where needed, augment that with information readily discovered via search engine.

We have civic motives for wanting to help people spot and refute bullshit. It is not a matter of left- or right-wing ideology; people on both sides of the aisle have proven themselves skilled at creating and spreading misinformation. Rather (at the risk of grandiosity), we believe that adequate bullshit detection is essential for the survival of liberal democracy. Democracy has always relied on a critically thinking electorate, but never has this been more important than in the current age of fake news and international interference in the electoral process via propaganda disseminated over social media. In a December 2016 *New York Times* op-ed, Mark Galeotti summarized the best defense against this form of information warfare:

> Instead of trying to combat each leak directly, the United States government should teach the public to tell when they are being manipulated. Via schools and nongovernmental organizations and public service campaigns, Americans should be taught the basic skills necessary to be savvy media consumers, from how to fact-check news articles to how pictures can lie.

As academics with decades of experience teaching data science, statistics, and related subjects at a public university, we know how to teach this sort of thinking. We believe that it can be done without taking sides, politically. You may not agree with us about the optimal size of the federal government, about what constitutes an acceptable degree of government involvement in our private lives, or how the country should conduct itself on the world stage—but we're good with that. We simply want to help people of all political perspectives resist bullshit, because we feel that a democracy is healthiest when voters can see through the bullshit coming from all sides.

We are not setting up a platform from which we can call bullshit on things that we don't like. For that reason, the examples in this book are seldom the most egregious ones we know, let alone the instances that anger us the most. Rather, our examples are chosen to serve a pedagogical purpose, drawing out particular pitfalls and highlighting appropriate strategies for responding. We hope you'll read, think, and go call bullshit yourself.

OVER A CENTURY AGO, the philosopher John Alexander Smith addressed the entering class at Oxford as follows:

> Nothing that you will learn in the course of your studies will be of the slightest possible use to you [thereafter], save only this, that if you work hard and intelligently you should be able to detect when a man is talking rot, and that, in my view, is the main, if not the sole, purpose of education.

For all of its successes, we feel that higher education in STEM disciplines—science, technology, engineering, and medicine—has dropped the ball in this regard. We generally do a good job teaching mechanics: students learn how to manipulate matrices, transfect cells, run genomic scans, and implement machine learning algorithms. But this focus on facts and skills comes at the expense of training and practice in the art of critical thinking. In the humanities and the social sciences, students are taught to smash conflicting ideas up against one another and grapple with discordant arguments. In STEM fields, students seldom are given paradoxes that they need to resolve, conflicting forms of evidence that they must reconcile, or fallacious claims that they need to critique. As a result, college graduates tend to be well prepared to challenge verbal arguments and identify logical fallacies but surprisingly acquiescent in the face of quantitative claims. Of course, the same holds true for secondary education. If STEM education incorporated the interrogatory teaching practices already common in the humanities, schools could shape a generation of students prepared to call bullshit on statistical statements and artificial intelligence analyses just as comfortably as current students can on political, ethical, artistic, and philosophical claims.

For a number of reasons, we draw heavily on examples from research in science and medicine in the chapters that follow. We love science and this is where our expertise lies. Science relies on the kinds of quantitative arguments we address in this book. Of all human institutions, science seems as though it ought to be free from bullshit—but it isn't. We believe that public understanding of science is critical for an informed electorate, and we want to identify the many obstacles that interfere with that understanding.

But we want to stress that nothing we say undermines science as a successful, institutionalized means to understand the physical world. For all our complaints, for all the biases we identify, for all the problems and all the bullshit that creeps in, at the end of the day *science works*. With science on our side, we fly in airplanes, talk on videophones, transplant organs, eradicate infectious diseases, and apprehend phenomena ranging from the early moments after the Big Bang to the molecular basis of life.

New forms of information technology have changed the way we communicate in both science and society. As access has improved, information overload has worsened. We hope this book will help you face the onslaught and separate fact from fiction.

CALLING BULLSHIT

CHAPTER 1

Bullshit Everywhere

This is a book about bullshit. It is a book about how we are inundated with it, about how we can learn to see through it, and about how we can fight back. First things first, though. We would like to understand what bullshit is, where it comes from, and why so much of it is produced. To answer these questions, it is helpful to look back into deep time at the origins of the phenomenon.

Bullshit is not a modern invention. In one of his Socratic dialogues, *Euthydemus,* Plato complains that the philosophers known as the Sophists are indifferent to what is actually true and are interested only in winning arguments. In other words, they are bullshit artists. But if we want to trace bullshit back to its origins, we have to look a lot further back than any human civilization. Bullshit has its origins in deception more broadly, and animals have been deceiving one another for hundreds of millions of years.

CHEATING CRUSTACEANS AND DEVIOUS RAVENS

The oceans are full of fierce and wonderful creatures, but few are as badass as the marine crustaceans known as the mantis shrimp or, in more technical circles, stomatopods. Some specialize in eating marine snails, which are protected by hard, thick shells. To smash through these calcite defenses, mantis shrimp have evolved a spring-loading mechanism in their forelimbs that allows them to punch with enormous force. Their hammer-like claws travel 50 mph when they strike. The punch is so powerful that it creates an underwater phenomenon known as cavitation bubbles, a sort of literal Batman "KAPOW!" that results in a loud noise and a flash of light. In captivity they sometimes punch right through the glass walls of their aquariums.

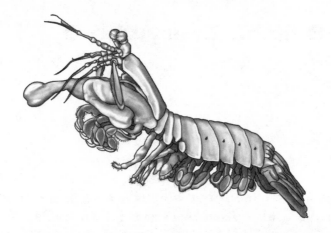

This punching power serves another purpose. Mantis shrimp live on shallow reefs, where they are vulnerable to moray eels, octopi, sharks, and other predators. To stay safe, they spend much of their time holed up in cavities in the reef, with just their powerful foreclaws exposed. But suitable cavities are in short supply, and this can lead to fights. When an intruder approaches a smaller resident, the resident typically flees. But if the resident is big enough, it waves its claws in a fierce display, demonstrating its size and challenging its opponent.

Like any superhero, however, mantis shrimp have an Achilles' heel. They have to molt in order to replace the hard casings of their hammer claws—which as you can imagine take more than their share of abuse. During the two or three days that the animal is molting, it is extremely vulnerable. It can't punch, and it lacks the hard shell that normally defends it against predators. Pretty much everything on the reef eats everything else, and mantis shrimp are essentially lobster tails with claws on the front.

So if you're a molting mantis shrimp holed up in a discreet crevice, the last thing you want to do is flee and expose yourself to the surrounding dangers. This is where the deception comes in. Normally, big mantis shrimp wave their claws—an honest threat—and small mantis shrimp flee. But during molting, mantis shrimp of any size perform the threat display, even though in their current state they can't punch any harder than an angry gummy bear. The threat is completely empty—but the danger of leaving one's hole is even greater than the risk of getting into a fight. Intruders, aware that they're facing the mantis shrimp's fierce punch, are reluctant to call the bluff.

Stomatopods may be good bluffers, and bluffing does feel rather like a kind of bullshit—but it's not very sophisticated bullshit. For one thing, this behavior isn't something that these creatures think up and decide to carry out. It is merely an evolved response, a sort of instinct or reflex.

A sophisticated bullshitter needs a *theory of mind*—she needs to be able to put herself in the place of her mark. She needs to be able to think about what the others around her do and do not know. She needs to be able to imagine what impression will be created by what sort of bullshit, and to choose her bullshit accordingly.

Such advanced cognition is rare in the animal kingdom. We have it. Our closest primate relatives, chimpanzees and gorillas, may have it as well. Other apes and monkeys do not seem to have this capacity. But one very different family does: Corvidae.

We know that corvids—ravens, crows, and jays—are remarkably intelligent birds. They manufacture the most sophisticated tools of any nonhuman species. They manipulate objects in their environment to solve all manners of puzzle. The Aesop's fable about the crow putting pebbles into an urn to raise the water level is probably based on a real observation; captive crows can figure out how to do this sort of thing. Ravens plan ahead for the future, selecting objects that may be useful to them later. Crows recognize human faces and hold grudges against those who have threatened or mistreated them. They even pass these grudges along to their fellow crows.

We don't know exactly why corvids are so smart, but their lifestyle does reward intelligence. They live a long time, they are highly social, and they creatively explore their surroundings for anything that might be edible. Ravens in particular may have evolved alongside pack-hunting species such as wolves and ourselves, and are excellent at tricking mammals out of their food.

Because food is sometimes plentiful and other times scarce, most corvid species cache their food, storing it in a safe place where it can be recovered later. But caching is a losing proposition if others are watching. If one bird sees another cache a piece of food, the observer often steals it. As a result, corvids are cautious about caching their food in view of other birds. When being watched, ravens cache quickly, or move out of sight before hiding their food. They also "fake-cache," pretending to stash a food item but actually keeping it safely in their beak or crop to be properly cached at a later time.

So when a raven pretends to cache a snack but is actually just faking, does that qualify as bullshitting? In our view, this depends on why the raven is faking and whether it thinks about the impression its fakery will create in the mind of an onlooker. Full-on bullshit is intended to distract, confuse, or mislead—which means that the bullshitter needs to have a mental model of the effect that his actions have on an observer's mind. Do corvids have a theory of mind? Do they understand that other birds can see them caching and are likely to steal from them? Or do they merely follow some simple rule of thumb—such as "cache only when no other ravens are around"—without knowing *why* they are doing so? Researchers who study animal behavior have been hard-pressed to demonstrate that any nonhuman animals have a theory of mind. But recent studies suggest that ravens may be an exception. When caching treats, they do think about what other ravens know. And not only do ravens act to deceive other birds sitting right there in front of them; they recognize that there might be other birds out there, unseen, who can be deceived as well.* That is pretty close to what we do when we bullshit on the In-

---

* One experiment worked as follows. A first raven was given food to cache, while a second raven in an adjacent room watched through a large window. Knowing that it was being watched, the raven with the food would cache hastily and avoid revisiting the cache lest it give away the location. If the investigators placed a wooden screen over the window so that the ravens could not see each other, the raven with the food took its time to cache its food and unconcernedly revisited the cache to adjust it.

Then the investigators added a small peephole to the screen covering the window, and gave the ravens time to learn that they could see each other by peering into the peephole. Then they removed the watching raven from the cage, so that no one was watching through the peephole. The key question was, what will a raven do when the peephole is open, but it cannot directly see whether or not there is a bird watching from within the cage? If the ravens use a simple rule of thumb like "when you can see the other bird, behave as though you are being watched," they should ignore the peephole. If ravens have a theory of mind, they would realize that they might be under observation through the peephole even if they don't see another bird, and would behave as if they were being watched. This is exactly what the ravens did. The researchers concluded that the ravens were generalizing from their own experience of watching through the peephole, and recognized that when the peephole was open, an unseen bird could be watching them.

ternet. We don't see anyone out there, but we hope and expect that our words will reach an audience.

Ravens are tricky creatures, but we humans take bullshit to the next level. Like ravens, we have a theory of mind. We can think in advance about how others will interpret our actions, and we use this skill to our advantage. Unlike ravens, we also have a rich system of language to deploy. Human language is immensely expressive, in the sense that we can combine words in a vast number of ways to convey different ideas. Together, language and theory of mind allow us to convey a broad range of messages and to model in our own minds what effects our messages will have on those who hear them. This is a good skill to have when trying to communicate efficiently—and it's equally useful when using communication to manipulate another person's beliefs or actions.

That's the thing about communication. It's a two-edged sword. By communicating we can work together in remarkable ways. But by paying attention to communication, you are giving other people a "handle" they can use to manipulate your behavior. Animals with limited communication systems—a few different alarm calls, say—have just a few handles with which they can be manipulated. Capuchin monkeys warn one another with alarm calls. On average this saves a lot of capuchin lives. But it also allows lower-ranking monkeys to scare dominant individuals away from precious food: All they have to do is send a deceptive alarm call in the absence of danger. Still, there aren't all that many things capuchins can say, so there aren't all that many ways they can deceive one another. A capuchin monkey can tell me to flee, even if doing so is not in my best interest. But it can't, say, convince me that it totally has a girlfriend in Canada; I've just never met her. Never mind getting me to transfer $10,000 into a bank account belonging to the widow of a mining tycoon, who just happened to ask out of the blue for my help laundering her fortune into US currency.

So why is there bullshit everywhere? Part of the answer is that everyone, crustacean or raven or fellow human being, is trying to sell you something. Another part is that humans possess the cognitive tools to figure out what kinds of bullshit will be effective. A third part is that our complex language allows us to produce an infinite variety of bullshit.

WEASEL WORDS AND LAWYER LANGUAGE

We impose strong social sanctions on liars. If you get caught in a serious lie, you may lose a friend. You may get punched in the nose. You may get sued in a court of law. Perhaps worst of all, your duplicity may become the subject of gossip among your friends and acquaintances. You may find yourself no longer a trusted partner in friendship, love, or business.

With all of these potential penalties, it's often better to mislead without lying outright. This is called *paltering*. If I deliberately lead you to draw the wrong conclusions by saying things that are technically not untrue, I am paltering. Perhaps the classic example in recent history is Bill Clinton's famous claim to Jim Lehrer on *Newshour* that "there is no sexual relationship [with Monica Lewinsky]." When further details came to light, Clinton's defense was that his statement was true: He used the present-tense verb "is," indicating no *ongoing* relationship. Sure, there *had been* one, but his original statement hadn't addressed that issue one way or the other.

Paltering offers a level of plausible deniability—or at least deniability. Getting caught paltering can hurt your reputation, but most people consider it less severe an offense than outright lying. Usually when we get caught paltering, we are not forced to say anything as absurdly lawyerly as Bill Clinton's "It depends upon what the meaning of the word 'is' is."

Paltering is possible because of the way that we use language. A large fraction of the time, what people are literally saying is not what they intend to communicate. Suppose you ask me what I thought of David Lynch's twenty-fifth-anniversary *Twin Peaks* reboot, and I say, "It wasn't terrible." You would naturally interpret that to mean "It wasn't very good either"—even though I haven't said that. Or suppose when talking about a colleague's recreational habits I say, "John doesn't shoot up when he is working." Interpreted literally, this means only that John doesn't do heroin when he is working and gives you no reason to suspect that John uses the drug after hours either. But what this sentence implies is very different. It implies that John is a heroin user with a modicum of restraint.

Within linguistics, this notion of implied meaning falls under the area of *pragmatics*. Philosopher of language H. P. Grice coined the term *implicature* to describe what a sentence is being used to mean, rather than what it means literally. Implicature allows us to communicate efficiently. If you ask where you can get a cup of coffee and I say, "There's a diner just down the block," you interpret my response as an answer to your question. You assume that the diner is open, that it serves coffee, and so forth. I don't have to say all of that explicitly.

But implicature is also what lets us palter. The implicature of the claim "John doesn't shoot up when working" is that he *does* shoot up at other times. Otherwise, why wouldn't I have just said that John doesn't shoot drugs, period?

Implicature provides a huge amount of wiggle room for people to say misleading things and then claim innocence afterward. Imagine that John tried to take me to court for slandering him by my saying he doesn't shoot up at work. How could he possibly win? My sentence is true, and he has no interest in claiming otherwise. People all too often use this gulf between literal meaning and implicature to bullshit. "He's not the most responsible father I've ever known," I say. It's true, because I know one dad who is even better—but you think I mean that he's a terrible father. "He will pay his debts if you prod him enough." It's true, because he's an upright guy who quickly pays his debts without prompting, but you think I mean that he's a cheapskate. "I got a college scholarship and played football." It's true, though my scholarship was from the National Merit society and I played touch football with my buddies on Sunday mornings. Yet you think I was a star college athlete.

An important genre of bullshit known as *weasel wording* uses the gap between literal meaning and implicature to avoid taking responsibility for things. This seems to be an important skill in many professional domains. Advertisers use weasel words to suggest benefits without having to deliver on their promises. If you claim your toothpaste reduces plaque "by up to" 50 percent, the only way that would be false is if the toothpaste worked *too* well. A politician can avoid slander litigation if he hedges: "People are saying" that his opponent has ties to organized crime. With the classic "mistakes were made," a manager goes through the motions of apology without holding anyone culpable.

Homer Simpson understood. Defending his son, Bart, he famously implored "Marge, don't discourage the boy. Weaseling out of things is important to learn. It's what separates us from the animals. . . . Except the weasel."

Homer's joking aside, corporate weaselspeak diffuses responsibility behind a smoke screen of euphemism and passive voice. A 2019 NBC News report revealed that many global manufacturers were likely using materials produced by child labor in Madagascar. A spokesperson for Fiat Chrysler had this to say: Their company "engages in collaborative action with global stakeholders across industries and along the value chain to promote and develop our raw material supply chain." Collaborative action? Global stakeholders? Value chain? We are talking about four-year-olds processing mica extracted from crude mines. Entire families are working in the blazing sun and sleeping outside all night for forty cents a day. This is bullshit that hides a horrible human toll behind the verbiage of corporate lingo.

Some bullshitters actively seek to deceive, to lead the listener away from truth. Other bullshitters are essentially indifferent to the truth. To explain, let's return from weasels back to the animal-signaling stories with which we began this chapter. When animals communicate, they typically send *self-regarding signals*. Self-regarding signals refer to the signaler itself rather than to something in the external world. For example, "I'm hungry," "I'm angry," "I'm sexy," "I'm poisonous," and "I'm a member of the group" are all self-regarding signals because they convey something about the signaler.

Other-regarding signals refer to elements of the world beyond the signaler itself. Such signals are uncommon among animal signals, with the notable exception of alarm calls. Most nonhuman animals simply don't have ways to refer to external objects. Humans are different. One of the novel or nearly novel features of human language is that human language gives us the vocabulary and grammar to talk about not only ourselves but also other people and other external objects in the world.

But even when humans are ostensibly communicating about elements of the external world, they may be saying more about themselves than it seems. Think about meeting someone for the first time at a party or other social event and falling into conversation. Why do you tell the stories that you do? Why do you talk at all, for that matter? Your stories don't just inform the other person about aspects of the world. They convey things about whom you are—or at least about whom you want to be. Maybe you're trying to come off as brave and adventurous. Or maybe sensitive and troubled. Maybe you're iconoclastic. Maybe you're a master of self-deprecating humor. We tell stories to create impressions of ourselves in the eyes of others.

This impulse drives a lot of bullshit production. When you're talking about a crazy adventure you had on a backpacking trip through Asia, your story doesn't actually need to be true to create the impression you are seeking. You often don't care one way or the other. Your story just needs to be interesting, impressive, or engaging. One need only to sit around with friends and a shared pitcher of beer to see this firsthand. This kind of bullshit has become an art form in the so-called attention economy. Think about the stories that go viral on social media: funny things that kids say, horrible first dates, trouble that pets get into. These may or may not be true, and to most people who read them, it doesn't matter.

Just because people can spew bullshit doesn't mean that they will, nor does it mean that bullshit will not be quickly eradicated by the force of truth. So why is bullshit ubiquitous?

FALSEHOOD FLIES AND THE TRUTH
COMES LIMPING AFTER

Perhaps the most important principle in bullshit studies is Brandolini's principle. Coined by Italian software engineer Alberto Brandolini in 2014, it states:

"The amount of energy needed to refute bullshit is an order of magnitude bigger than [that needed] to produce it."

Producing bullshit is a lot less work than cleaning it up. It is also a lot simpler and cheaper to do. A few years before Brandolini formulated his principle, Italian blogger Uriel Fanelli had already noted that, loosely translated, "an idiot can create more bullshit than you could ever hope to refute." Conspiracy theorist and radio personality Alex Jones need not be an evil genius to spread venomous nonsense such as his Sandy Hook denialism and Pizzagate stories; he could be an evil idiot—or even a misguided one.

Within the field of medicine, Brandolini's principle is exemplified by the pernicious falsehood that vaccines cause autism. After more than twenty years of research, there is no evidence that vaccines cause autism; indeed there is overwhelming evidence that they do not. Yet misinformation about vaccines persists, due in large part to a shockingly poor 1998 study published in *The Lancet* by British physician Andrew Wakefield and colleagues. In that article, and in numerous subsequent press conferences, Wakefield's research team raised the possibility that a syndrome involving autism paired with inflammatory bowel disease may be associated with the measles-mumps-rubella (MMR) vaccine.*

Wakefield's paper galvanized the contemporary "antivax" movement, created a remarkably enduring fear of vaccines, and contributed to the resurgence of measles around the world. Yet seldom in the history of science has a study been so thoroughly discredited. Millions of dollars and countless research hours have been devoted to checking and rechecking this study. It has been utterly and incontrovertibly discredited.†

As the evidence against the MMR-autism hypothesis piled up and as Wakefield's conflicts of interest came to light, most of Wakefield's co-authors started to lose faith in their study. In 2004, ten of them

---

* One of the immediately apparent problems with Wakefield's study was the tiny sample size. His study looked at only twelve children, most of whom reportedly developed the purported syndrome shortly after receiving the MMR vaccine. It is very difficult, if not impossible, to draw meaningful conclusions about rare phenomena from such a tiny sample.

Yet the small sample size of his study was the least of his problems. A subsequent investigation revealed that for many of the twelve patients, the *Lancet* paper described ailments and case histories that did not match medical records or reports from the parents. In a scathing article for the *British Medical Journal,* journalist Brian Deer enumerated a host of issues, including: Three of twelve patients listed as suffering from regressive autism did not have autism at all; in several cases the timing of onset of symptoms was not accurately reported; and five of the children reported as normal prior to the vaccine had case histories reflecting prior developmental issues.

† Wakefield's claims came under scrutiny almost immediately after his paper was published. Within a year of Wakefield's publication, *The Lancet* published another study investigating a possible vaccination-autism link. This study used careful statistical analysis on a much larger sample—498 autistic children—and found no association whatsoever.

This was only the beginning. On the mechanistic side, other researchers were unable to replicate the original claims that the measles virus persists in the gut of Crohn's disease patients. On the epidemiological side, numerous studies were conducted and found no association between the vaccine and autism. For example, in 2002, *Pediatrics* published a study of over half a million Finnish children, and *The New England Journal of Medicine* published a study of over half a million Danish children. Neither found any connection, and the conclusion of the Danish study states bluntly, "This study provides strong evidence against the hypothesis that MMR vaccination causes autism."

A natural experiment took place in Japan when the MMR vaccine was replaced by monovalent (single-disease) vaccines in 1993. If Wakefield's hypothesis—that the combined MMR vaccine can cause autism whereas giving three vaccines, one for each disease, should be safe—we would have seen a decrease in autism rates in Japan. That did not happen. More recently, a meta-analysis combining data from multiple studies looked at 1.3 million children and again found no relation between vaccination and autism.

formally retracted the "interpretations" section of the 1998 paper. Wakefield did not sign on to the retraction. In 2010, the paper was fully retracted by *The Lancet*.

The same year, Wakefield was found guilty of serious professional misconduct by Britain's General Medical Council. He was admonished for his transgressions surrounding the 1998 paper, for subjecting his patients to unnecessary and invasive medical procedures including colonoscopy and lumbar puncture, and for failure to disclose financial conflicts of interest.* As a result of this hearing, Wakefield's license to practice medicine in the UK was revoked. In 2011, *British Medical Journal* editor in chief Fiona Godlee formally declared the original study to be a fraud, and argued that there must have been intent to deceive; mere incompetence could not explain the numerous issues surrounding the paper.

These ethical transgressions are not the strongest evidence against Wakefield's claim of an autism-vaccine link. Wakefield's evidence may have been insufficient to justify his conclusions. His handling of the data may have been sloppy or worse. His failure to follow the ethics of his profession may have been egregious. The whole research paper may have indeed been an "elaborate fraud" rife with conflicts of interest and fabricated findings. In principle Wakefield's claim could still have been correct. *But he is not correct.* We know this because of the careful scientific studies carried out on a massive scale. It is not the weaknesses in Wakefield's paper that prove there is no autism-vaccine link: *it is the overwhelming weight of subsequent scientific evidence.*

To be clear, there was nothing inappropriate about looking to see if there is a connection between autism and vaccination. The problem is

---

* Investigative work by journalist Brian Deer revealed that Wakefield was concealing massive conflicts of interest. At the time he was working on the 1998 paper, Wakefield's research was being funded by a lawyer who was putting together a lawsuit against a vaccine manufacturer. Wakefield's purported vaccine-autism link was to be a major feature of the lawsuit. Over the course of a decade, Wakefield ultimately received well over £400,000 from the UK Legal Services Commission for his work on this lawsuit. Professional ethics require that an author disclose any financial interest he or she has in a published paper, but Wakefield did not do so in his *Lancet* report. Moreover, his co-authors were reportedly unaware that he was being paid for this work. There was another financial conflict of interest. Prior to publishing his paper Wakefield had filed at least two patent applications, one for a diagnostic test for Crohn's disease and ulcerative colitis by the presence of the measles virus in the bowel, and a second one for the production of a "safer" measles vaccine. The commercial value of each hinged upon proving his theory that the MMR vaccine was associated with autism and inflammatory bowel disorders. According to Deer, Wakefield also helped to launch, and held a substantial equity stake in, startup companies in this domain.

that the original study was done irresponsibly at best—and that when its frightening conclusions were definitively disproven, antivaxxers invented a story about a Big Pharma conspiracy to hide the truth. Wakefield eventually directed a documentary titled *Vaxxed,* which alleged that the Centers for Disease Control and Prevention (CDC) was covering up safety problems surrounding vaccines. The film received a large amount of press attention and reinvigorated the vaccine scare. Despite all the findings against Wakefield and the crushing avalanche of evidence against his hypothesis, Wakefield retains credibility with a segment of the public and unfounded fears about a vaccine-autism link persist.

TWO DECADES LATER, WAKEFIELD'S hoax has had disastrous public health consequences. Vaccine rates have risen from their nadir shortly after Wakefield's paper was published, but remain dangerously lower than they were in the early 1990s. In the first six months of 2018, Europe reported a record high 41,000 measles cases. The US, which had nearly eliminated measles entirely, now suffers large outbreaks on an annual basis. Other diseases such as mumps and whooping cough (pertussis) are making a comeback. Particularly in affluent coastal cities, many Americans are skeptical that vaccines are safe. One recent trend is for parents to experiment with delayed vaccination schedules. This strategy has no scientific support and leaves children susceptible for a prolonged period to the ravages of childhood diseases. Children with compromised immune systems are particularly vulnerable. Many of them cannot be vaccinated, and rely for their safety on the "herd immunity" that arises when those around them are vaccinated.

So here we have a hypothesis that has been as thoroughly discredited as anything in the scientific literature. It causes serious harm to public health. And yet it will not go away. Why has it been so hard to debunk the rumors of a connection between vaccines and autism? This is Brandolini's principle at work. Researchers have to invest vastly more time to debunk Wakefield's arguments than he did to produce them in the first place.

This particular misconception has a number of characteristics that make it more persistent than many false beliefs. Autism is terrifying to parents, and as yet we do not know what causes it. Like the most successful urban legends, the basic narrative is simple and gripping: "A child's vulnerable body is pierced with a needle and injected with a foreign substance. The child seems perfectly fine for a few days or even weeks, and then suddenly undergoes severe and often irreversible behavioral regression." This story taps into some of our deepest fears—in this case, fears about hygiene and contamination, and anxiety about the health and safety of our children. The story caters to our desire for explanations, and to our tendency to ascribe cause when we see two events occurring in succession. And it hints at a way we might protect ourselves. Successfully refuting something like this is a decidedly uphill battle.

Bullshit is not only easy to create, it's easy to spread. Satirist Jonathan Swift wrote in 1710 that "falsehood flies, and truth comes limping after it."* This saying has many different incarnations, but our favorite is from Franklin D. Roosevelt's secretary of state, Cordell Hull: "A lie will gallop halfway round the world before the truth has time to pull its breeches on." We envision hapless Truth half-running and half-tripping down the hallway, struggling to pull its pants up from around its ankles, in hopeless pursuit of a long-departed Lie.

Taken together, Brandolini's principle, Fanelli's principle, and Swift's observation tell us that (1) bullshit takes less work to create than to clean up, (2) takes less intelligence to create than to clean up, and (3) spreads faster than efforts to clean it up. Of course, they are just aphorisms. They sound good, and they feel "truthy," but they could be just more bullshit. In order to measure bullshit's spread, we need an environment where bullshit is captured, stored, and packaged for large-scale analysis. Facebook, Twitter, and other social media platforms provide such environments. Many of the messages sent on these platforms are rumors being passed from one person to the next. Rumors are not exactly the same as bullshit, but both can be products of intentional deception.

Retracing the path of a rumor's spread is largely a matter of looking at who shared what with whom and in what order, all information that is readily available given adequate access to the system. Tweets

---

* The full quotation is: "Falsehood flies, and truth comes limping after it, so that when men come to be undeceived, it is too late; the jest is over, and the tale hath had its effect: like a man, who hath thought of a good repartee when the discourse is changed, or the company parted; or like a physician, who hath found out an infallible medicine, after the patient is dead."

about crises are particularly consequential. The concentration of attention during these events creates both the incentive to generate misinformation, and a vital need to refute it.

One such crisis was the terrorist bombing of the Boston Marathon in 2013. Shortly after the attack, a tragic story appeared on Twitter. An eight-year-old girl was reported to have been killed in the bombing. This young girl had been a student at Sandy Hook Elementary School, and she was running the marathon in memory of her classmates who were killed in the horrific mass shooting that had occurred there a few months prior. The terrible irony of her fate, surviving Sandy Hook only to die in the Boston Marathon bombing, propelled her story to spread like wildfire across the Twitter universe. The girl's picture—bib #1035 over a fluorescent pink shirt, ponytail streaming behind her—led thousands of readers to respond with grief and compassion.

But other readers questioned the story. Some noted that the Boston Marathon does not allow kids to run the race. Others noticed that her bib referred to a different race, the Joe Cassella 5K. Rumor-tracking website Snopes.com quickly debunked the rumor, as did other fact-checking organizations. The girl hadn't been killed; she hadn't even run the race. Twitter users tried to correct the record, with more than two thousand tweets refuting the rumor. But these were vain efforts. More than ninety-two thousand people shared the false story of the girl. Major news agencies covered the story. The rumor continued to propagate despite the many attempts to correct it. Brandolini was right yet again.

Researchers at Facebook have observed similar phenomena on their platform. Tracing rumors investigated by Snopes, the researchers found that false rumors spread further than true rumors, even after the claim had been debunked by Snopes. Posts that spread false rumors are more likely to be deleted after being "Snoped," but they are seldom taken down quickly enough to stop the propagation of false information.

Other researchers have looked at what drives these rumor cascades. When comparing conspiracy theory posts to posts on other subjects, conspiracy theories have much larger reach. This makes it especially difficult to correct a false claim. Jonathan Swift's intuition about bullshit has been well corroborated. People who clean up bullshit are at a substantial disadvantage to those who spread it.

Truth tellers face another disadvantage: The ways that we acquire and share information are changing rapidly. In seventy-five years we've gone from newspapers to news feeds, from *Face the Nation* to Facebook, from fireside chats to firing off tweets at four in the morning. These changes provide fertilizer for the rapid proliferation of distractions, misinformation, bullshit, and fake news. In the next chapter, we look at how and why this happened.

CHAPTER 2

Medium, Message, and Misinformation

I F IN 1990 YOU HAD TOLD US THAT BY 2020 NEARLY HALF OF THE people on the planet would carry a wallet-size machine that could instantly look up any fact in the world—a "smartphone"—we would have predicted an end to bullshit. How could you bullshit someone who could check your claims easily, immediately, and costlessly?

Apparently people have neither the time nor the inclination to use smartphones this way. Instead, smartphones have become just one more vehicle for spreading bullshit. On the positive side, you can have a decent dinner conversation without being fact-checked thirty times. On the negative side, bullshit goes largely unchallenged.

Technology didn't eliminate our bullshit problem, it made the problem worse. In this chapter, we will explore how that happened. In short, the rise of the Internet changed what kinds of information get produced, how information is shared, and the ways in which we find the information that we want. While much good has come of the Internet revolution, there have been major drawbacks as well. Fluff and glitter have overtaken serious, in-depth, thoughtful content. News coverage has become increasingly partisan. Misinformation, disinformation, and fake news abound. We will consider these issues in turn.

THE BROTHEL OF THE PRINTING PRESS

Pity the soul who hopes to hold back a revolution in information technology. Priest and scribe Filippo de Strata lived through one such revolution. In 1474, he railed against the damage wrought by the invention of the printing press. Printers, de Strata argued, "shamelessly print, at a negligible price, material which may, alas, inflame impressionable youths, while a true writer dies of hunger. . . ." By massively lowering the cost of manufacturing books, the printing press was bound to reduce the value and authority of text. When every book had to be written by hand, only royalty and the clergy could commission a well-trained scribe like de Strata to produce a copy of a book. The great expense of hiring scribes served as a filter on the kind of information committed to paper. There was little demand for books that served only as trivial entertainment; most new books were copies of the Bible and other documents of huge importance. But the advent of the printing press opened a spillway through which less serious content could flood the market. Publicly, Filippo de Strata fretted that that the "brothel of the printing press" would lead readers to cheap, salacious entertainment—the works of Ovid, even. Privately, he may have been more concerned about his own job security.

Others worried about a proliferation of fluff that would obscure important information. Pioneers in cataloging human knowledge, such as Conrad Gessner in the sixteenth century and Adrien Baillet in the seventeenth century, cautioned that the printing press would bring scholarship to a halt as readers became overwhelmed by the range of options for study. They were wrong. With the advantage of a few centuries' hindsight, we can see that Gutenberg's revolution brought vastly more good than harm. The printing press—later coupled with public libraries—democratized the written word. In the year 1500, German writer Sebastian Brant described this change:

> In our time . . . books have emerged in lavish numbers. A book that once would've belonged only to the rich—nay, to a king—can now be seen under a modest roof. . . . There is nothing nowadays that our children . . . fail to know.

Still, Filippo de Strata was right that when the cost of sharing information drops dramatically, we see changes in both the nature of the information available and the ways that people interact with that information.*

Roughly five hundred years after Filippo de Strata sounded the alarm about the printing press, sociologist Neil Postman echoed his sentiments:

> The invention of new and various kinds of communication has given a voice and an audience to many people whose opinions would otherwise not be solicited, and who, in fact, have little else but verbal excrement to contribute to public issues.

If we wanted to condemn blogs, Internet forums, and social media platforms, we could scarcely say it better. But Postman was not referring to social media or even the Internet. He delivered this line a half century ago. In a 1969 lecture, he lamented the lowbrow programming on television, the vacuous articles in newspapers and magazines, and the general inanity of mass media. This kind of infotainment, he maintained, distracts consumers from the information that does matter—and distraction can itself be a form of disinformation. If religion is the opiate of the masses, *Jersey Shore* and *Temptation Island* are the spray canisters from which the masses huff metallic paint fumes.

Since Postman's lecture, we've undergone another revolution. The Internet has changed the way we produce, share, and consume information. It has altered the way we do research, learn about current events, interact with our peers, entertain ourselves, and even think. But why has the Internet also triggered a bullshit pandemic of unprecedented proportions?

Let's begin by looking at what gets published. Through the 1980s, publishing required money—a lot of it. Typesetting was expensive, printing required substantial overhead, and distribution involved getting physical paper into the hands of readers. Today, anyone with a personal computer and an Internet connection can produce professional-looking documents and distribute them around the world without cost. And they can do so in their pajamas.

This is the democratizing promise of the Internet: endless new

---

* Eörs Szathmary and John Maynard Smith make a similar point, applied to living systems, in their 1995 book *The Major Transitions in Evolution*. Their ideas about biological transitions in information use have been instrumental to us in developing this section.

voices brought into a worldwide conversation. Members of marginalized groups, who previously might have lacked the financial and social capital to publish and publicize their work, can now make their stories heard. At the same time, the new technology captures the long tail of interests and creates communities around even the rarest of obsessions. Want to build your own air calliope? Explore the Scooby-Doo cartoons from a critical theory perspective? Learn the complex dice games played by the protagonists of *The Canterbury Tales*? The Internet has you covered.

This democratization has a dark side as well. Aided by viral spread across social media, amateur writers can reach audiences as large as those of professional journalists. But the difference in the reporting quality can be immense. A typical Internet user lacks the journalistic training, let alone the incentives to report accurately. We can access more information than ever, but that information is less reliable.

Prior to the Internet, mass media filled our living rooms with voices from afar—but these voices were familiar to us. We listened to Ed Murrow; we read the words of familiar newspaper columnists; we watched Walter Cronkite, "the most trusted man in America"; and we dove into the fictional worlds created by famous authors. In today's social media world, our friends treat us to saccharine drivel about their latest soul mates, square-framed snapshots of their locally sourced organic brunches, and tiresome boasts about their kids' athletic, artistic, or academic accomplishments. But our homes are also filled with the voices of strangers—often anonymous strangers—that our friends have seen fit to share. We don't know these people. What they write is seldom written with the attention to accuracy we would expect from a commercial media outlet. And some of the "authors" are paid human agents or computer programs spreading disinformation on behalf of corporate interests or foreign powers.

Back when news arrived at a trickle, we might have been able to triage this information effectively. But today we are confronted with a deluge. As we are writing this chapter, we both have multiple browser windows open. Each window has roughly ten open tabs, and each of those tabs contains a news story, journal article, blog post, or other information source that we intend to revisit but never will. Additional stories and tidbits are scrolling across our social media feeds faster than we could track, even if we did nothing else. Because there is so much more volume and so much less filtering, we find ourselves like the Sorcerer's Apprentice: overwhelmed, exhausted, and losing the will to fight a torrent that only flows faster with every passing hour.

THE INADEQUACY OF THE UNVARNISHED TRUTH

Filippo de Strata feared that the works of Ovid might crowd out the Bible. We fear that the mindless lists, quizzes, memes, and celebrity gossip that proliferate on social media might crowd out thoughtful analyses of the sort you see in *The New York Times* or *The Wall Street Journal*. Every generation thinks that its successor's lazy habits of mind will bring on a cultural and intellectual decline. It may be a stodgy lament that has been repeated for thousands of years, but it's our turn now, and we're not going to miss the opportunity to grumble.

Prior to the Internet, newspapers and magazines made money by selling subscriptions.* Subscribing to a periodical, you embarked on a long-term relationship. You cared about the quality of information a source provided, its accuracy, and its relevance to your daily life. To attract subscribers and keep them, publishers provided novel and well-vetted information.

The Internet news economy is driven by clicks. When you click on a link and view a website, your click generates advertising revenue for the site's owner. The Internet site is not necessarily designed to perpetuate a long-term relationship; it is designed to make you click, now. Quality of information and accuracy are no longer as important as *sparkle*. A link needs to catch your eye and pull you in. Internet publishers are not looking for Woodward and Bernstein. Instead, they want "Seven Cats That Look Like Disney Princesses," "Eight Amazing Nutrition Secrets Your Personal Trainer Doesn't Want You to Know," "Nine Never-Before-Published Photos of Elvis Found in Retiree's Attic," and "Ten Ways That Experts Spot Quantitative Bullshit."

Publishers produce this fluff because we click on it. We might aspire to patronize quality news sources that provide nuanced analysis.

---

* A considerable fraction of the revenue to most newspaper and magazine publishers has always come from advertising, but advertising revenue scaled with the subscription base, so again publishers needed to maximize subscriptions.

But faced with the temptation to click on the informational equivalent of empty calories, the mental junk food usually wins.

You can see this trend toward fluff in headlines. Headlines draw our attention—and in the social media environment, where many people never read any further, they are a significant source of information. A satirical website published a headline proclaiming that "70% of Facebook Users Only Read the Headline of Science Stories before Commenting." The story began by noting that most people don't read stories before sharing them on social media either. After a couple of sentences, the text gave way to paragraph after paragraph of the standard "*lorem ipsum dolor* . . ."—random text used as filler for webpage layouts. The post was shared tens of thousands of times on social media, and we don't know how many of those who did so were in on the joke.

Headlines, written by editors rather than journalists, have always been somewhat inconsistent with the stories they announce. But within a single issue of *The New York Times,* for example, the articles aren't competing with one another for your attention. The newspaper is trying to create a package of stories that together provide as much value as possible. Click-driven media, on the other hand, drives an arms race among headlines. On social media sites and news feeds, headlines from competing media outlets are presented side by side. Readers rarely read everything—there is simply too much content available. Instead they click on the most tantalizing or titillating headlines that they see.

How do you win an arms race to come up with catchy headlines? Sensationalism works. Tabloids have long used sensational headlines to draw attention at the newsstand, but major subscription papers largely eschewed this practice. But sensationalism is not the only way. Entrepreneur Steve Rayson looked at 100 million articles published in 2017 to determine what phrases were common in the headlines of articles that were widely shared. Their results will make you gasp in surprise—unless you've spent a few minutes on the Internet at some point in the past few years.

The study found that the most successful headlines don't convey facts, *they promise you an emotional experience.* The most common phrase among successful Facebook headlines, by nearly twofold, is "will make you," as in "will break your heart," "will make you fall in love," "will make you look twice," or "will make you gasp in surprise" as above. This phrase is also highly successful on Twitter. Other top phrases include "make you cry," "give you goosebumps," and "melt your heart." Intellectual experiences cannot compete. Pause for a moment and think about what a huge shift this represents. Can you imagine *The New York Times* or your local newspaper with headlines that told you how you'd feel about each story, but not what the story actually entailed?

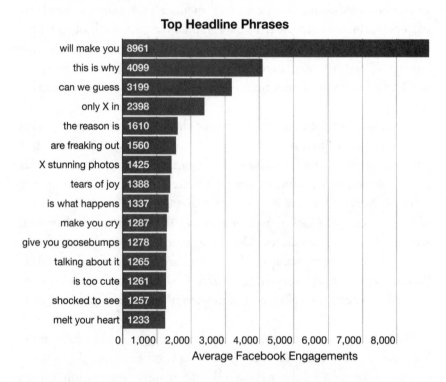

Top Headline Phrases

Phrase	Value
will make you	8961
this is why	4099
can we guess	3199
only X in	2398
the reason is	1610
are freaking out	1560
X stunning photos	1425
tears of joy	1388
is what happens	1337
make you cry	1287
give you goosebumps	1278
talking about it	1265
is too cute	1261
shocked to see	1257
melt your heart	1233

Average Facebook Engagements

Headlines once aimed to concisely convey the essence of a story: "Kennedy Is Killed by Sniper as He Rides in Car in Dallas; Johnson Sworn In on Plane." "Men Walk on Moon. Astronauts Land on Plain; Collect Rocks, Plant Flag." "East Germany Opens Wall and Borders, Allowing Citizens to Travel Freely to the West."

With click-driven advertising, if a headline tells too much, there is little incentive to click on the story. Headlines now go through contortions *not* to tell you what the story says. While these so-called forward reference headlines are most commonly used by Internet media companies, traditional media are getting into the game as well. "One-Fifth of This Occupation Has a Serious Drinking Problem," announces *The Washington Post*. "How to Evade the Leading Cause of Death in the United States," CNN promises to inform you. "Iceland Used to Be the Hottest Tourism Destination. What Happened?" asks *USA Today*. (So as not to leave you in suspense: lawyers; don't get in a car accident; and nobody knows.)

Headlines also lure us in by making the story about *us*. In the world of social media, news is a two-way street in which everyone is both a consumer and a producer. As we were writing this section, the following headlines were coming across our social media feeds.

- "*People Are Freaking Out* About This Photo That Might Show That Amelia Earhart Survived Her Crash" (*BuzzFeed*)
- " 'This is a huge bombshell.' *Twitter reacts* to NCAA arrests by FBI" (*IndyStar*)
- "McDonald's Invented 'Frorks' and *the Internet Can't Stop Talking* About Them" (*HuffPost*)

What we are saying becomes more interesting than what is happening.

All of this fluff and glitter does more than just dumb down the national conversation: It opens the door for bullshit. *The unvarnished truth is no longer good enough.* Straight-up information cannot compete in this new marketplace.

PARTISANSHIP, PERSONALIZATION, AND POLARIZATION

Much as the invention of the printing press allowed for a more diverse array of books, the advent of cable television allowed people to select specialized media outlets that closely reflected their views. Prior to 1987, the Fairness Doctrine of the US Federal Communications Commission (FCC) strived to ensure balanced coverage of controversial issues in news programming. But it was repealed under President Ronald Reagan. Hastened by the advent of the 24-hour news cycle, cable news channels proliferated and specialized in delivering specific political perspectives. In the United States, mainstream news has become increasingly partisan over the past twenty years. The figure below illustrates the diverging ideological positions of three prominent cable news channels, as estimated from broadcast transcripts.

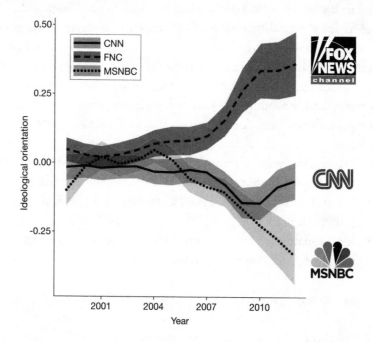

Online, it's the same story, only more so. Even mainstream outlets deliver news with a partisan slant. We find ourselves isolated in separate echo chambers. Publishers such as Breitbart News Network and The Other 98% go one step further, pushing what is known as hyperpartisan news. Their stories may be based in fact, but they are so strongly filtered through an ideological lens that they often include significant elements of untruth.

Publishers churn out partisan and hyperpartisan content because it pays to do so. Social media favors highly partisan content. It is shared more than mainstream news, and once shared, it is more likely to be clicked on. Deepening the ideological divide has become a lucrative business.

MIT professor Judith Donath has observed that even when people appear to be talking about other things, they're often talking about themselves. Suppose I log on to Facebook and share a false—even absurd—story about how airplane contrails are endocrine-disrupting chemicals being sprayed as part of a liberal plot to lower the testosterone levels of America's youth. I may not be as interested in having you believe my claims about contrails as I am in signaling my own political affiliations. Sharing an article like this signals that I belong to a group of people who believe in conspiracy theories and distrust the "liberal agenda" in America. And if that's my aim, it doesn't matter to me whether the story is true or false. I may not have read it, I may not care if you read it, but I want you to know that I am a fellow tinfoil hatter.

The signal itself becomes the point. If I share a story about how the IRS is investigating Donald Trump's business dealings prior to the 2016 election, my political affiliation is unclear. But if I share a story that says Donald Trump has sold the Washington Monument to a Russian oligarch, it's clear that I hate Trump. And I'm demonstrating a political allegiance so strong that I can suspend disbelief when it comes to stories of Trump's treachery.

Professor Donath's insight springs from a broader tradition in the field known as *communication theory*. We often think of communication solely as the transmission of information from sender to receiver. But this ignores a second, broader social aspect of communication, one that is revealed by its origins in the Latin verb *communicare,* "to make shared or common."

Communication is how we establish, reinforce, and celebrate a shared framework for thinking about the world. Think about a religious mass, or even the scripted, ordered regularity of the nightly news. Communication over social media does the same thing: It creates and structures social communities. When we send out a tweet or Facebook post or Instagram image, we are affirming our commitment to the values and beliefs of our particular online community. As the community responds, these common values are reaffirmed through likes, shares, comments, or retweets.

Blindfolded and submerged in a pool, I shout "Marco!" If I do so correctly, my network of acquaintances sends back an encouraging chorus. "Polo! Polo! Polo!" Participating on social media is only secondarily about sharing new information; it is primarily about maintaining and reinforcing common bonds. The danger is that, in the process, what was once a nationwide conversation fragments beyond repair. People begin to embrace *tribal epistemologies* in which the truth itself has less to do with facts and empirical observation than with who is speaking and the degree to which their message aligns with their community's worldview.

Algorithms only make matters worse. Facebook, Twitter, and other social media platforms use algorithms to find "relevant" posts and stories for you, personalizing your feed. These algorithms are not designed to keep you informed; they are designed to keep you active on the platform. The aim is to feed you content that is sufficiently compelling to prevent you from wandering elsewhere on the Web or, Lord forbid, going to bed at a decent hour. The problem is that the algorithms create a vicious cycle, giving you more of what they think you want to hear, and fewer opportunities to read divergent points of view. The actual details of these algorithms are hidden from view; but what you like and what you read, whom your friends are, your geolocation, and your political affiliations all influence what you see next. The algorithms amplify content that aligns with their guesses about your sociopolitical orientation, and they suppress alternative viewpoints.

On the Web, we are all test subjects. Commercial websites are continually running large-scale experiments to see what keeps us online and engaged. Online media companies experiment with different variations on a headline, different accompanying images, even different fonts or "click to continue" buttons. At the same time, Facebook and other platforms offer advertisers—including political advertisers—the ability to target specific consumers with messages designed to cater to their interests. These messages may not even be clearly identified as advertisements.

Think about what YouTube can learn as they experiment by recommending different videos and observing what users select to watch. With billions of videos viewed every day and vast computational resources, they can learn more about human psychology in a day than an academic researcher could learn in a lifetime. The problem is, their computer algorithms have learned that one way to retain viewers is to recommend increasingly extreme content over time. Users who watch left-leaning videos are quickly directed to extreme-left conspiracy theories; users who enjoy right-leaning material soon get recommendations for videos from white supremacists or Holocaust deniers. We've seen this ourselves. As Jevin and his six-year-old son watched real-time video from the International Space Station 254 miles above spherical Earth, YouTube filled the sidebar of their screen with videos claiming that the earth is actually flat.

Riffing on Allen Ginsberg, tech entrepreneur Jeff Hammerbacher complained in 2011 that "the best minds of my generation are thinking about how to make people click ads. That sucks." The problem is not merely that these "best minds" could have been devoted to the artistic and scientific progress of humankind. The problem is that all of this intellectual firepower is devoted to hijacking our precious attention and wasting *our* minds as well. The Internet, social media, smartphones—we are exposed to increasingly sophisticated ways of diverting our attention. We become addicted to connectivity, to meaningless checking, to a life of fragmented attention across myriad streams of digital information. In short, the algorithms driving social media content are bullshitters. They don't care about the messages they carry. They just want our attention and will tell us whatever works to capture it.

MISINFORMATION AND DISINFORMATION

Social media facilitates the spread of *misinformation*—claims that are false but not deliberately designed to deceive. On social media platforms, the first outlet to break a story receives the bulk of the traffic. In the race to be first, publishers often cut any fact-checking out of the publication process. You can't beat your competitors to press if you pause to rigorously fact-check a story. Being careful is admirable, but it doesn't sell ads.

Social media is also fertile ground for *disinformation,* falsehoods that are spread deliberately.

A study in 2018 found that about 2.6 percent of US news articles were false. This might not seem like a big percentage, but if every American read one article per day, it would mean that nearly eight million people a day were reading a false story.

Sometimes false information is just a nuisance. One satirical news site claimed that musician Taylor Swift was dating notorious anticommunist senator Joseph McCarthy—who died forty-two years before she was born. Predictably, some fans were unable to realize the absurdity of the story and reacted with disgust. But no businesses were undermined, no lives were at stake, and even Ms. Swift is unlikely to suffer any serious harm to her reputation.

But misinformation and disinformation can be far more serious. As more of the world comes online, the problem multiplies. For example, nearly half a billion Indian citizens received access to the Internet for the first time between 2010 and 2020. Overall, the rapid expansion of connectivity benefits both those coming online and those already there. Unfortunately, new Internet users tend to be more susceptible.

In addition to basic social messaging functions, WhatsApp serves as a news source to its 1.5 billion users worldwide. It is also a potent vector for spreading misinformation. In early 2018, Indian users widely shared a series of fake videos that purported to illustrate children being kidnapped by organized gangs. A fear of strangers spread, with disastrous consequences. Visiting a temple in Tamil Nadu, one family stopped to ask for directions. Locals became suspicious that they might be the type of kidnappers seen in the WhatsApp videos. A crowd gathered; the family was pulled from their car; the mob stripped them naked and beat them brutally with metal bars and sticks. One was killed and the others permanently disfigured. Motivated by the same false story, mobs attacked dozens of other innocent people, beating and often killing them.

Police tried to counter the online misinformation and put a stop to the killings. But the rumors traveled too fast. In some regions, authorities had to shut down the Internet completely to slow them down. WhatsApp tried its own interventions, changing how many times a message could be shared. Previously a message could be forwarded 250 times. They dropped this to five. Still the mob attacks continued.

It is not only new Internet users who are fooled. In December 2016, a website called AWD News published a frightening headline: "Israeli Defense Minister: If Pakistan Send Ground Troops to Syria on Any Pretext, We Will Destroy This Country with a Nuclear Attack."

The story contained several cues that should have tipped off a careful reader. The headline contained grammatical errors ("send" instead of "sends"). The story named the wrong person as the Israeli defense minister.* The article sat next to other implausible headlines such as "Clinton Staging Military Coup against Trump." But it still fooled the person you would least want it to: Khawaja Muhammad Asif, defense minister of Pakistan. Asif responded with a threat of his own via Twitter: "Israeli def min threatens nuclear retaliation presuming pak role in Syria against Daesh . . . Israel forgets Pakistan is a Nuclear state too."

A single fake news piece led one major power to threaten another with a nuclear attack. It is one thing to mislead the infinitely gullible about Taylor Swift's latest romance. It is another to tip the globe toward nuclear war.

And then there is political propaganda. Social media is a more effective medium for spreading propaganda than leaflets dropped from airplanes or high-powered radio transmissions directed into enemy territory. Social media posts are unconstrained by most borders. And they are shared organically. When social media users share propaganda they have encountered, they are using their own social capital to back someone else's disinformation. If I come across a political leaflet or poster on the street, I am immediately skeptical. If my dear uncle forwards me a story on Facebook that he "heard from a friend of a friend," my guard drops. Disinformation flows through a network of trusted contacts instead of being injected from outside into a skeptical society.

In 2017, Facebook admitted that over the past two years, 126 million US users—half of the adult population and about three-quarters of its US user base—had been exposed to Russian propaganda on the site. More than one hundred thirty thousand messages from these accounts were designed to deepen preexisting ideological divides within the US, and to seed mistrust between neighbors. They focused on emotionally charged issues such as race relations, gun rights, border security, welfare, and abortion, and played both sides of each topic to reach the largest possible audience. The goal was to amplify the loudest and most extreme voices in each political camp, while drowning out the more reasonable and productive discussants. When the divide

---

* The defense minister at the time was Avigdor Lieberman, but the story attributed the quotation to Moshe Yaalon, who had previously served in that role.

between political factions grows deep enough, conversations between them stop. Our trust in people and institutions erodes. We lose faith in our ability to make collective decisions. Ultimately we start to question the democratic process itself.

While we think of propaganda as designed to convince people of specific untruths, much modern propaganda has a different aim. The "firehose strategy" is designed to leave the audience disoriented and despairing of ever being able to separate truth from falsehood. Social media makes it easy to broadcast large volumes of disinformation at high rates across multiple channels. This is part of the firehose strategy. The other part is to deliberately eschew consistency. Rather than being careful to convey only a single cohesive story, the aim is to confuse readers with a large number of mutually contradictory stories. In 2016, chess grand master Garry Kasparov summarized this approach in a post on Twitter: "The point of modern propaganda isn't only to misinform or push an agenda. It is to exhaust your critical thinking, to annihilate truth."

Meanwhile, authoritarian governments have embraced social media. They were originally fearful of this medium and prone to censor its use. But more recently, governments such as those of China, Iran, and Russia have discovered that social media offers an ideal platform on which to monitor public sentiment, track dissent, and surreptitiously manipulate popular opinion.

Still, fake news is not *primarily* a propaganda tool. Most fake and hyperpartisan news is created for a different reason: to generate advertising revenue. Anyone, anywhere can get in on the action. In the final days of the 2016 US election, Barack Obama talked extensively about the fake news factories in Macedonia. The people running these factories—often teenagers—created at least 140 popular fake news websites during the election. When a story went viral, it generated huge advertising revenues for the site owners. Some of them were making in excess of $5,000 per month, compared with the average Macedonian monthly salary of $371. The teens writing these stories didn't care whether Trump or Clinton won; they cared only about clicks. The most shared fake news story in that whole election proclaimed that "Pope Francis Shocks the World, Endorses Donald Trump for President." This story was created by a group of teenagers in Macedonia, under the aegis of WT05 News, and received nearly a million engagements on Facebook. To put that in perspective, the top *New York Times* article during this same period received 370,000 engagements.

Pope Francis was not happy about this story. He issued the following statement about the salacious reporting in general and about fake news in particular. "I think the media have to be very clear, very transparent, and not fall into—no offence intended—the sickness of coprophilia, that is, always wanting to cover scandals, covering nasty things, even if they are true," he said. "And since people have a tendency towards the sickness of coprophagia, a lot of damage can be done."

Fake news purveyors, take note. When the pope himself says you eat shit, it is time to reevaluate your life choices.

THE NEW COUNTERFEITERS

Since the advent of money, governments have had to deal with counterfeiting. Precious-metal coins came into use in the Mediterranean world in the sixth century B.C.E.; soon after counterfeiters started to produce facsimiles with gold or silver plating over a cheaper base metal. They've been at it ever since. Conducted on a sufficiently large scale, counterfeiting can undermine public trust in a currency, devalue the currency, and drive runaway inflation. Counterfeiting has often been used this way during wartime—by the British in the American Revolutionary War, by the Union in the American Civil War, and by the Nazis in the Second World War, to list just a few examples.

In an Internet-connected world, governments have to worry about a new kind of counterfeiting—not of money, but of *people*. Researchers estimate that about half of the traffic on the Internet is due not to humans, but rather "bots," automated computer programs designed to simulate humans. The scale of the problem is staggering. By 2018, Facebook had over two billion legitimate users—but in the same year deleted even more fake accounts: nearly three billion. Some bots act as information providers, pushing out their messages, usually for advertising purposes but occasionally in service of propaganda aims. Others emulate information consumers. "Click farms" use massive banks of cell phones to generate webpage views or YouTube video views for a fee.

For a representative democracy to function, constituents must be able to share their views with their elected officials. The ability to counterfeit people threatens to swamp real voices with fake ones. In mid-2017, the FCC solicited public comments on a proposal to eliminate "net neutrality," the requirement that Internet service providers treat all information that they transmit the same, regardless of source or content. The FCC received a staggering 21.7 million citizen comments in response—but a large fraction of these appeared to be fraudulent. Over half came from throwaway email addresses or from addresses used to send multiple comments. A strong signature of bot activity is the simultaneous transmission of huge numbers of messages. At 2:57:15 P.M. EDT on July 19, 2017, half a million similar comments were sent at the exact same second. One bot submitted over a million different anti–net neutrality comments following the same basic structure, using a MadLibs approach of plugging in synonyms for various words. Half a million comments on net neutrality came directly from Russian email addresses. The New York State attorney general estimated that nearly 10 million of the comments were sent using stolen identities of people who had no idea their names were being used. In the end, the vast majority of the twenty-one million comments the FCC received were in favor of abandoning net neutrality—even though there is reason to believe public opinion ran strongly in the opposite direction.

The most influential fake accounts are run not by bots but by real people pretending to be someone else. All-American girl Jenna Abrams was an Internet celebrity who spent a lot of time commenting on pop culture, but also broadcast provocative right-wing views to her seventy thousand Twitter followers. The problem is, Jenna Abrams wasn't real. She was a creation of a Moscow propaganda outfit known as the Internet Research Agency. Still, she was very effective. Her tweets were retweeted extensively and covered by top news outlets including *The New York Times* and *The Washington Post*. She fooled the magazine *Variety* into posting a fake news story about CNN airing pornography. Once exposed, she turned around and mocked the media for covering her: "Don't blame the media for including my tweets in their articles. If you pull the right strings a puppet will dance any way you desire."

Until recently, creating fake personalities on the Internet was tricky because in a social media world, we want to see the pictures of the people we follow. Without a picture, a user account on the Internet could be anyone. The computer security professional posting to a tech forum could be a kid in his mom's basement. A fourteen-year-old girl in a chat room could be an undercover cop. The oil heiress in your in-box is undoubtedly a scam artist. But if we can see a picture, we tend to be less suspicious. Fake accounts sometimes use stock photos or images scraped from the Internet—but these were easily tracked down by savvy users using tools such as Google's reverse image search.

No longer. A new class of algorithms, collectively known as adversarial machine learning, can fashion photorealistic faces of nonexistent people out of whole cloth. The fabricated images are stunningly good. This is a dangerous period for a technology: It is widely available but few people know it's being used. To raise public awareness, we developed a website called WhichFaceIsReal.com. A real photograph of a real person is paired with a computer-generated image of someone who does not exist. Your aim is to guess which is which. More than a million people have played the game on our website and the results show just how good the fakes are. People do not do much better than chance when they start playing, and even with lots of practice people still are fooled one time in five.

Similar machine learning algorithms are able to "voiceshop," generating fake audio and video that are nearly indistinguishable from the real thing. By synthesizing audio from previous recordings and grafting expressions and facial movements from a person acting as model onto the visage of a target, these so-called deepfake videos can make it look like anyone is doing or saying anything.

Director and comedian Jordan Peele created a public service announcement about fake news using this technology. Peele's video depicts Barack Obama addressing the American people about fake news, misinformation, and the need for trusted news sources. Midway through the video, however, the face of Jordan Peele appears next to Obama, speaking the same words in perfect time, clearly the model from which Obama's facial movements and expressions have been derived. Obama concludes, in his own voice but with Peele's words:

"How we move forward in the age of information is going to be the difference between whether we survive or whether we become some kind of fucked-up dystopia."

Confronted with all of these technologies for fabricating reality, one might lose hope of getting to the truth about anything. We are not so pessimistic. Our society adjusted to the anonymity afforded by an Internet on which "nobody knows you're a dog." And we adjusted to a Photoshop world in which pictures do lie. How? In a word, we triangulate. We no longer trust a single message, a single image, a single claim. We look for independent witnesses who can confirm testimony. We seek multiple images from multiple vantage points. Society will adjust similarly to a world of deepfakes and whatever reality-bending technologies follow.

There are three basic approaches for protecting ourselves against misinformation and disinformation online. The first is technology. Tech companies might be able to use machine learning to detect online misinformation and disinformation. While this is a hot area for research and development, we are not optimistic. Tech companies have been trying to do this for years, but the problem shows no signs of abating. Microsoft, Facebook, and others have recently started to release large data sets to academic researchers working on this problem; that suggests to us that the tech companies know that they need help. And economically, it's not clear that Internet companies have sufficient incentives. After all, extreme content is highly effective at drawing an audience and keeping users on a platform. Technologically, the same artificial intelligence techniques used to detect fake news can be used to get around detectors, leading to an arms race of production and detection that the detectors are unlikely to win.

A second approach is governmental regulation. Some countries have already passed laws against creating or spreading fake news, but we worry about this approach for two reasons. First, it runs afoul of the First Amendment to the US Constitution, which guarantees freedom of speech. Second, who gets to determine what is fake news? If a leader doesn't like a story, he or she could declare it fake news and pursue criminal charges against the perpetrators. That has happened already in some parts of the world. A lighter regulatory touch might help. We have long advocated a legislative ban on targeted political advertising online, and are heartened by Twitter's self-imposed moratorium. We would like to see users control the information that comes across their social media feeds, rather than being forced to rely on a hopelessly opaque algorithm. The justification for the FCC's Fairness Doctrine was one of democratic necessity. For a democracy to function properly, a country needs an informed populace with access to reliable information. Similar arguments could justify governmental regulation of social media.

A third and most powerful approach is education. If we do a good job of educating people in media literacy and critical thinking, the problem of misinformation and disinformation can be solved from the bottom up. That is our focus in this book, and in much of our professional lives.

Every generation has looked back on the past with nostalgia for a simpler and more honest time. We may have greater than usual cause for nostalgia. The Internet has brought about a sea change in the way that information is created, sorted, discovered, spread, and consumed. While this has had a decentralizing effect on the dissemination of information, it has come with a cost. Bullshit spreads more easily in a massively networked, click-driven social media world than in any previous social environment. We have to be alert for bullshit in everything we read.

CHAPTER 3

The Nature of Bullshit

So what is bullshit, exactly? People sometimes use the term the same way that little kids use the word "unfair": to describe anything they don't like. Used in this way, the term can apply to a close but correct call at home plate, or a parking ticket written two minutes after your meter expires. Other times the term applies to injustice: a corrupt process of granting government contracts, an unwarranted acquittal, or legislation denying people basic civil liberties.

Then there is language to soften bad news and more generally grease the wheels of social interaction. "I just loved your turnip lasagna. You absolutely must give me the recipe." "What a beautiful baby!" "It's not you, it's me." "Your haircut looks great." "Your call is important to us." "I had a lovely evening." These are often bullshit, but they're not really the kind of bullshit we're concerned with here.

Insincere promises and outright lies get a bit closer to the mark. "Honey, I'm going to have to work late again tonight"; "I didn't inhale"; "I'd love to give you a better deal if I could"; "I have read and agreed to the above terms and conditions"; "Read my lips: No new taxes." Still, we tend to think of these claims as outright lies rather than bullshit.

But lies are often most persuasive when dressed in superfluous details; these details come quite close to what we mean by "bullshit." A friend leaves you waiting for twenty-five minutes at the local café because he got distracted watching YouTube videos and left his house half an hour late. "I'm sorry I'm late, traffic was terrible. You know that bridge down by Fifteenth? A bus had stalled right where it goes down to two lanes each way, and some idiot had rear-ended it, blocking the other lane. So by the time I got through all that mess . . ." The first sentence is a lie; the subsequent ones are bullshit.

Harry Frankfurt, the philosopher we introduced in the preface, refined this notion a bit further. He described bullshit as what people create when they try to impress you or persuade you, without any concern for whether what they are saying is true or false, correct or incorrect. Think about a high school English essay you wrote without actually reading the book, a wannabe modernist painter's description of his artistic vision, or a Silicon Valley tech bro co-opting a TED Talk invitation to launch his latest startup venue. The intention may be to mislead, but it need not be. Sometimes we are put on the spot and yet have nothing to say. The bullshit we produce under those circumstances is little more than the "filling of space with the inconsequential."

Bullshit can be total nonsense. Another philosopher to take up the issue of bullshit, G. A. Cohen, notes that a lot of bullshit—particularly of the academic variety—is meaningless and so cloaked in rhetoric and convoluted language that no one can even critique it. Thus for Cohen, bullshit is "unclarifiable unclarity." Not only is the bullshitter's prose unclear, but the ideas underlying it are so ill-formed that it cannot possibly be clarified. Cohen suggests a test for unclarity: If you can negate a sentence and its meaning doesn't change, it's bullshit. "Shakespeare's Prospero is ultimately the fulcrum of an epistemic tragedy, precisely because of his failure to embrace the hermeneutics of the transfinite."

What these notions of bullshit have in common is that the speaker aims to persuade or impress, rather than to lead the listener toward the truth. The speaker may do this with active obfuscation, or simply by talking nonsense to conceal the fact that he or she doesn't actually know anything about the subject at hand. Some authors distinguish between *persuasive bullshit* and *evasive bullshit*. The former aims to convey an exaggerated sense of competence or authority, while the latter avoids directly answering a question that the speaker would prefer not to address.

When someone is bullshitting, he and his audience are not allies in the process of communication. Rather, the speaker is aiming to manipulate the listener with rhetorical flair, superfluous detail, or statistical snake oil. For us:

> *Bullshit* involves language, statistical figures, data graphics, and other forms of presentation intended to persuade or impress an audience by distracting, overwhelming, or intimidating them with a blatant disregard for truth, logical coherence, or what information is actually being conveyed.

The key elements of this definition are that bullshit bears no allegiance to conveying the truth, and that the bullshitter attempts to conceal this fact behind some type of rhetorical veil. Sigmund Freud illustrated the concept about as well as one could imagine in a letter he wrote his fiancée, Martha Bernays, in 1884:

> So I gave my lecture yesterday. Despite a lack of preparation, I spoke quite well and without hesitation, which I ascribe to the cocaine I had taken beforehand. I told about my discoveries in brain anatomy, all very difficult things that the audience certainly didn't understand, but all that matters is that they get the impression that I understand it.

While he has not written about bullshit directly, the sociologist of science Bruno Latour has had a formative effect on our thinking about how people bullshit their audiences. Latour looks at the power dynamics between an author and a reader. In Latour's worldview, a primary objective of nonfiction authors is to appear authoritative. One good way to do this is to be correct, but that is neither necessary nor sufficient. Correct or not, an author can adopt a number of tactics to make her claims unassailable by her readers—who in turn strive not to be duped. For example, the author can line up a phalanx of allies by citing other writers who support her point, or whose work she builds upon. If you question me, she implies, you have to question all of us. She can also deploy sophisticated jargon. Jargon may facilitate technical communication within a field, but it also serves to exclude those who have not been initiated into the inner circle of a discipline.

BULLSHIT AND BLACK BOXES

According to Latour, scientific claims are typically built upon the output of metaphorical "black boxes," which are difficult if not impossible for the reader to penetrate. These black boxes often involve the use of specialized and often expensive equipment and techniques that are time-consuming and unavailable, or are so broadly accepted that to question them represents a sort of scientific heresy.* If I were to write a paper claiming that specific genetic variants are associated with susceptibility to bullshit, a skeptic might reasonably argue my choice of sample population, the way I measure bullshit susceptibility, or the statistical method I use to quantify associations. But the biotechnology used to derive the DNA sequences from blood samples would typically be treated as a black box. In principle a skeptic could question this as well, but to do so she would be challenging the scientific establishment and, more important for our purposes, she would need access to advanced equipment and extensive technical expertise in molecular genetics.

Latour is not saying that these aspects of academic science make the entire enterprise bullshit, and neither are we. He is saying only that science is more than a dispassionate search for the truth, a theme to which we will return in chapter 9. The important thing about Latour's black box idea is that we see a powerful analogy here to what speakers do when they bullshit effectively. Outright lies are often straightforward to catch and refute. But effective bullshit is difficult to fact-check. Bullshit can act like one of Latour's black boxes, shielding a claim from further investigation.

Suppose a friend tells you, "You know, on average, cat people earn higher salaries than dog people." It's easy to call bullshit on that statement when it stands by itself. And when you do so, perhaps your friend will simply laugh and admit, "Yeah, I made that up."

---

* For Latour, aspects of technology or experimental procedure are "black-boxed" when they are so thoroughly accepted by the relevant scientific community that they become generally agreed upon standards and are no longer open to question. In Latour's *Pandora's Hope: Essays on the Reality of Science,* he explains: "When a machine runs efficiently, when a matter of fact is settled, one need focus only on its inputs and outputs and not on its internal complexity. Thus, paradoxically, the more science and technology succeed, the more opaque and obscure they become."

Here our analogy begins to break down somewhat. For the purposes of thinking about quantitative bullshit, consider a technique to be black-boxed once it requires expertise beyond that of the typical reader, irrespective of whether it is accepted by the scientific community.

But suppose instead she doubles down and starts filling out—or making up—details to support her claim. "No, really, it's true. I saw this TED Talk about it. They explained how cat owners value independence whereas dog owners value loyalty. People who value independence are more likely to have NVT . . . no . . . NVS . . . I can't remember, but some kind of personality. And that makes them better able to rise in the workplace."

This is full-on bullshit, and it functions like one of Latour's black boxes. If you want to dispute your friend's claims, you now have substantial work to do. This is where lies and bullshit come together: In our view, a lie becomes bullshit when the speaker attempts to conceal it using various rhetorical artifices.

Now imagine that she points you to a research study that makes this claim. Suppose you track down the study, and read something like the following:

> We observe a statistically significant difference in cat- and dog-lovers' earnings, based on an ANCOVA using log-transformed earnings data ($F = 3.86$).

If you don't have a professional background in statistics, you've just slammed head-on into a particularly opaque black box. You probably don't know what an ANCOVA is or what the F value means or what a log transformation is or why someone would use it. If you do know some of these things, you still probably don't remember all of the details. We, the authors, use statistics on a daily basis, but we still have to look up this sort of stuff all the time. As a result, you can't unpack the black box; you can't go into the details of the analysis in order to pick apart possible problems. Unless you're a data scientist, and probably even then, you run into the same kind of problem you encounter when you read about a paper that uses the newest ResNet algorithm to reveal differences in the facial features of dog and cat owners. Whether or not this is intentional on the part of the author, this kind of black box shields the claim against scrutiny.

But it doesn't need to. The central theme of this book is that you usually don't have to open the analytic black box in order to call bullshit on the claims that come out of it. Any black box used to generate bullshit has to take in data and spit results out, like the diagram on page 43.

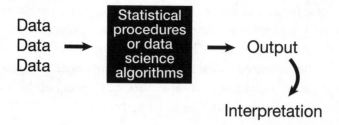

Most often, bullshit arises either because there are biases in the data that get fed into the black box, or because there are obvious problems with the results that come out. Occasionally the technical details of the black box matter, but in our experience such cases are uncommon. This is fortunate, because you don't need a lot of technical expertise to spot problems with the data or results. You just need to think clearly and practice spotting the sort of thing that can go wrong. In the pages that follow, we will show you how to do precisely this.

RETURNING TO OUR CAT and dog example, instead of digging into the details of the statistical analysis, you might ask how the samples were collected. Maybe the study looked at pet ownership and merged data from people in living in New York City—where salaries are high and keeping a dog is difficult—with data from upstate New York, where salaries are lower and dogs are far more practical. Maybe dog-lover salaries are assumed to be the US average whereas cat-lover salaries were solicited from visitors to a website for startup founders who cohabitate with cats.

If the data that go into the analysis are flawed, *the specific technical details of the analysis don't matter*. One can obtain stupid results from bad data without any statistical trickery. And this is often how bullshit arguments are created, deliberately or otherwise. To catch this sort of bullshit, you don't have to unpack the black box. All you have to do is think carefully about the data that went into the black box and the results that came out. Are the data unbiased, reasonable, and relevant to the problem at hand? Do the results pass basic plausibility checks? Do they support whatever conclusions are drawn?

Being able to spot bullshit based on data is a critical skill. Decades ago, fancy language and superfluous detail might have served a bull-shitter's needs. Today, we are accustomed to receiving information in quantitative form, but hesitant to question that information once we receive it. Quantitative evidence generally seems to carry more weight than qualitative arguments. This weight is largely undeserved—only modest skill is required to construct specious quantitative arguments. But we defer to such arguments nonetheless. Consequently, numbers offer the biggest bang for the bullshitting buck.

CRIMINAL MACHINE LEARNING

Let's take a moment to illustrate how we can call bullshit on a fancy algorithm without ever delving into the details of how it works, i.e., without opening the black box.

In late 2016, engineering researchers Xiaolin Wu and Xi Zhang submitted an article titled "Automated Inference on Criminality Using Face Images" to a widely used online repository of research papers known as the arXiv. In their article, Wu and Zhang explore the use of machine learning to detect features of the human face that are associated with "criminality." They claim that their algorithm can use simple headshots to distinguish criminals from noncriminals with high accuracy. If this strikes you as frighteningly close to Philip K. Dick's Precrime police in *Minority Report,* and to other dystopian science fiction, you're not alone. The media thought so too. A number of technology-focused press outlets picked up on the story and explored the algorithm's ethical implications. If an algorithm could really detect criminality from the structure of a person's face, we would face an enormous ethical challenge. How would we have to adjust our notions of innocence and guilt if we could identify people as criminals even before they committed a crime?

The notion that criminals are betrayed by their physiognomy is not a new one. In the nineteenth century, an Italian doctor named Cesare Lombroso studied the anatomy of hundreds of criminals. His aim was to develop a scientific theory of criminality. He proposed that people were born to be criminals or to be upstanding citizens. Born criminals, he postulated, exhibit different psychological drives and physical features. Lombroso saw these features as hearkening back to our subhuman evolutionary past. He was particularly interested in what could be learned from faces. In his view, the shape of the jaw, the slope of the forehead, the size of the eyes, and the structure of the ear all contained important clues about a man's moral composition. Below, a figure from Cesare Lombroso's 1876 book *Criminal Man*.

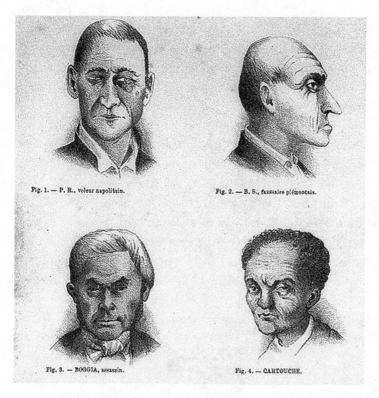

Fig. 1. — P. R., voleur napolitain.

Fig. 2. — B. S., faussaire piémontais.

Fig. 3. — BOGGIA, assassin.

Fig. 4. — CARTOUCHE.

Lombroso was wrong. None of his theories linking anatomy to moral character have a sound scientific basis. His ideas—many of which wrapped racist ideas of the time in a thin veneer of scientific language—were debunked in the first half of the twentieth century and disappeared from the field of criminology.

But in the 2016 arXiv paper, Wu and Zhang revisit Lombroso's program. Essentially, they aim to determine whether advanced computer vision can reveal subtle cues and patterns that Lombroso and his followers might have missed. To test this hypothesis, the authors use machine learning algorithms to determine what features of the human face are associated with "criminality." Wu and Zhang claim that based on a simple headshot, their programs can distinguish criminal from noncriminal faces with nearly 90 percent accuracy. Moreover, they argue that their computer algorithms are free from the myriad biases and prejudices that cloud human judgment:

Unlike a human examiner/judge, a computer vision algorithm or classifier has absolutely no subjective baggages [sic], having no emotions, no biases whatsoever due to past experience, race, religion, political doctrine, gender, age, etc., no mental fatigue, no preconditioning of a bad sleep or meal. The automated inference on criminality eliminates the variable of meta-accuracy (the competence of the human judge/examiner) all together.

Let's look at all of this in light of our black box schema. The machine learning algorithms compose the black box. Most readers will not have the expertise to dig into the fine workings of these algorithms. Even those who have the requisite background will be stymied by the limited description of the methods in the paper. Then there are the "training sets"—the images used to teach the algorithm how to distinguish a criminal from a noncriminal face. These are the data that are fed into the black box. And finally, there are the facial features that the algorithm predicts to be associated with criminality. These are the results that emerge from the black box.

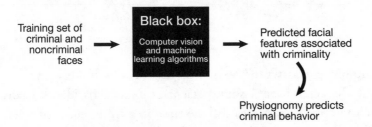

To understand the paper, we need to look at the training set. A machine learning algorithm can be only as good as the training data that it is provided. Wu and Zhang collected over 1,800 photos of Chinese men aged 18 to 55, with no distinguishing facial hair, scars, or tattoos. About 1,100 of these were noncriminals. Their photographs were taken from a variety of sources on the World Wide Web, including job-based social networking sites and staff listings from professional firms. Just over 700 of the subjects were convicted criminals. Their photos were provided by police departments and taken from official pieces of identification, not from mugshots.

We see two massive problems. The first is that the images of non-criminals were selected to cast the individuals in a positive light. By contrast, the images from the set of criminals are official ID photographs. While it is unclear exactly what this means, it's safe to guess that these have been selected neither by the person depicted, nor with the aim of casting him in a favorable light. Thank goodness no one judges our characters based upon our driver's license photos!

A second source of bias is that the authors are using photographs of *convicted* criminals. If there are facial differences between the two groups, we won't know whether these differences are associated with committing crimes or with being convicted. Indeed, appearance seems to matter for convictions. A recent study reports that in the US, unattractive individuals are more likely to be found guilty in jury trials than their attractive peers.[*] Thus while the authors claim that their algorithm is free of human biases, it could be picking up on *nothing but* these biases.

Having identified some potential problems with the data that go into the black box, we turn to the black box's output. As we mentioned, the authors find that their algorithm can classify criminal faces within their data set with 90 percent accuracy. What are the facial features that it uses to discriminate? The algorithm finds that criminals have shorter distances between the inner corners of the eyes, smaller angles θ between the nose and the corners of the mouth, and higher curvature ρ to the upper lip.

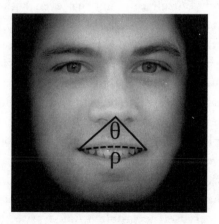

---

[*] While the Chinese criminal system is structured differently from that of the US and jury trials are rarer, the judges and occasional jurors in Chinese trials may suffer from similar biases.

Why would this possibly be?

There's a glaringly obvious explanation for the nose-mouth angle and the lip curvature. As one smiles, the corners of the mouth spread out and the upper lip straightens. Try it yourself in the mirror.

If you look at the original research paper, you can see six example images from the training set. The criminals are frowning or scowling. The noncriminals are faintly smiling. Now we have an alternative—and far more plausible—hypothesis for the authors' findings. There are not important differences in facial structure between criminals and noncriminals. Rather, noncriminals are smiling in their professional headshots, whereas criminals are not smiling in their government ID photographs. It appears that the authors have confused innate *facial features* with labile *facial expressions*. If so, their claims about detecting criminality are bullshit. They have not invented a criminality detector; they have invented a smile detector.

We can see further evidence of this in the output of their black box. To illustrate the purported facial differences between criminals and noncriminals, the authors produced composite images by aggregating features from each group. The criminal composites are frowning, whereas the noncriminal composites are smiling. This supports our hypothesis that the machine learning algorithm is picking up on situation-dependent facial expressions (whether a person is smiling or not) rather than underlying facial structure.

You might find yourself thinking that even without opening the black box, this type of analysis takes considerable time and focus. That's true. But fortunately, some claims should more readily trigger our bullshit detectors than others. In particular, *extraordinary claims require extraordinary evidence*. The authors of this paper make the extraordinary claim that facial structure reveals criminal tendencies. Here we see that their findings can be explained by a much more reasonable hypothesis: People are more likely to be smiling in professional headshots than in government ID photographs.

Notice that we established all of this without opening the black box. We didn't have to look at the details of the machine learning algorithms at all, because the problem didn't arise there. A machine learning algorithm is only as good as its training data, and these training data are fundamentally flawed. As is often the case, one does not need technical expertise in machine learning to call bullshit. A nonspecialist can do so by thinking carefully about what any generic learning system would conclude from the same data. The algorithm in this paper is not picking up some underlying physical structures associated with criminality. And it doesn't look like we have to worry about the ethical minefield of precrime just yet.

CHAPTER 4

Causality

I F WE COULD GO BACK IN TIME AND PROVIDE ONE PIECE OF ADVICE to our fifteen-year-old selves, it would be this: *Feeling insecure, clueless, unconfident, naïve? Fake it. That's all that anyone else is doing.* Expressing self-confidence and self-esteem go a long way in shaping how others view you, particularly at that age. Indeed, faking social confidence is an act so self-fulfilling that we scarcely consider it bullshit. The kids with abundant self-confidence seemed happy and popular. They had the largest number of friends. They started dating earlier. High school seemed easier for them. The rest of us admired, envied, and occasionally hated them for it.

A recent study titled "Never Been Kissed" appears to illustrate how effective this kind of positive thinking can be. Surveying seven hundred college students, the authors of the study identified the personality traits that go hand in hand with never having kissed a romantic partner before starting college.

The research report is charming in the way it assumes zero prior knowledge of the human experience. We are told that "kissing is generally a positively valanced behavior." We learn that "the first kiss is often considered a very positive experience." We are informed that "physical intimacy is important in romantic relationships, and kissing is a common aspect of that physical intimacy." Best of all we are told, with a phrase only an epidemiologist could turn, that kissing has "an average age of onset of about 15.5 [years]."

So what factors influence whether or not someone has been kissed by the start of college? Positive self-esteem is among the best predictors of having had a first kiss prior to college. What makes people popular on the high school dating scene isn't good looks, intellectual ability, or good taste in music—it's self-confidence.

It's a nice story, but even though the study found an association between self-esteem and kissing, it is not so obvious which way that association goes. It's possible that self-esteem leads to kissing. But it's also possible that kissing leads to self-esteem. Or maybe kissing neither causes nor is caused by self-esteem. Maybe both are caused by having great hair.

This objection introduces us to a pervasive source of bullshit. People take evidence about the association between two things, and try to sell you a story about how one *causes* the other. Circumcision is associated with autism. Constipation is associated with Parkinson's disease. The marriage rate is associated with the suicide rate. But this doesn't mean that circumcision causes autism, nor that constipation causes Parkinson's, nor that marriage causes suicide. It is human nature to infer that when two things are associated, one causes the other. After all, we have evolved to find patterns in the world. Doing so helps us avoid danger, obtain food, deal with social interactions, and so much more. But often we are too quick to leap to conclusions about what causes what. In this chapter, we will show you how to think rigorously about associations, correlations, and causes—and how to spot bullshit claims that confuse one for the other.

RED SKY AT NIGHT, SAILOR'S DELIGHT

"Red sky in the morning, sailors take warning. Red sky at night, sailor's delight." The rhyme reflects a pattern that people have known for over two thousand years. If you know what the sky looks like now, it tells you something about what the weather will be like later.

In wintertime in Seattle, an overcast sky usually means that it is relatively warm outside, because warm, wet air is sweeping overland from the ocean. When the sky is clear, it is usually colder outside because cold, dry air is blowing in from inland deserts. We don't need to step outside to know whether we need gloves and a hat; it's enough to simply look out the window. The cloud cover is *associated* with the overall temperature. We say that two measurements are associated when knowing something about the state of one tells you something about the state of the other. Similarly, people's heights and weights are associated. If I tell you my friend is six feet four inches tall, you can safely guess that he will weigh more than many of my other acquaintances. If I tell you another friend is five feet one inch tall, you can guess that she is probably lighter than average.

In common language, we sometimes refer to associations as correlations. Someone might say, "I heard that your personality is correlated with your astrological sign. Aries are bold, whereas Taurus seek security." (This would be bullshit, but never mind that.) When scientists and statisticians talk about a correlation, however, they are usually talking about a linear correlation.* Linear correlations are so central to the way that scientists think about the world that we want to take a minute to explain how they work.

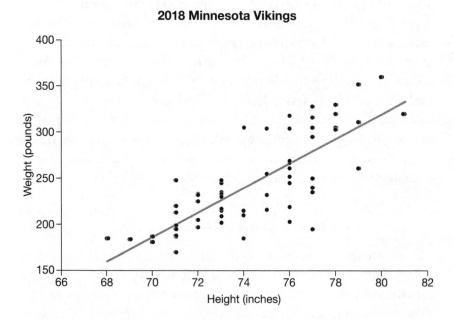

2018 Minnesota Vikings

---

* Linear correlations require variables with numerical values such as height and weight, whereas associations can occur between categorical values such as "favorite color" and "favorite ice cream flavor," or between numerical variables. Correlations are associations, but not all associations are correlations. Moreover, values can be highly predictable without being linearly correlated. For example, consider pairs of numbers $\{x, \sin(x)\}$. If we know x, we can predict exactly what $\sin(x)$ will be, but the correlation coefficient—a measure of linear correlation—between these numbers is zero across a full-cycle sine wave. There is no linear correlation between x and $\sin(x)$ because a best-fit line through $\{x, \sin(x)\}$ pairs has a slope of 0 and tells us nothing about the likely value of $\sin(x)$ for any given value of x.

The easiest way to understand linear correlations is to imagine a scatter plot relating two kinds of measurements, such as the heights and weights of football players. We call each type of measurement a variable. Loosely speaking, two variables are linearly correlated if we can draw a slanted line that gets close to most of the points.

In the plot on page 52, each dot corresponds to a single player on the 2018 Minnesota Vikings football team. The horizontal position of a dot indicates the player's height, and the vertical position indicates the player's weight. For the Vikings, there is a linear correlation between players' heights and weights. The points lie roughly along the trend line superimposed on the points. Of course, the players' heights and weights don't lie right on the line. Quarterbacks and kickers, for example, tend to be lighter than you would expect given their height, whereas running backs and linemen tend to be heavier.

The strength of a linear correlation is measured as a *correlation coefficient,* which is a number between 1 and −1. A correlation of 1 means that the two measurements form a perfect line on a scatter plot, such that when one increases, the other increases as well. For example, distance in meters and distance in kilometers have a correlation coefficient of 1, because the former is just one thousand times the latter. A correlation of −1 means that two measurements form another kind of perfect line on a scatter plot, such that when one increases, the other decreases. For example, the time elapsed and the time remaining in a hockey game add up to sixty minutes. As one increases, the other decreases by the same amount. These two quantities have a correlation of −1.

A correlation coefficient of 0 means that a best-fit line through the points doesn't tell you anything.* In other words, one measurement tells you nothing about the other.† For example, psychologists sometimes use the Eysenck Personality Inventory questionnaire as a way to summarize aspects of personality known as impulsivity, sociability, and neuroticism. Across individuals, impulsivity and neuroticism are essen-

---

* In the rare case where the data points form either a vertical or horizontal line, the correlation coefficient is undefined. In these cases, knowing one measurement also tells you nothing about the other measurement.

† Strictly speaking, this is true only if you are restricted to using a linear model to predict one variable as a function of the other. A nonlinear model may be informative even if the correlation coefficient is 0.

tially uncorrelated, with a correlation coefficient of −0.07. In other words, knowing something about a person's impulsivity tells you very little (if anything) about his neuroticism and vice versa. The plot below illustrates neuroticism and impulsivity scores for a number of people. Darker points indicate multiple individuals with the same score.

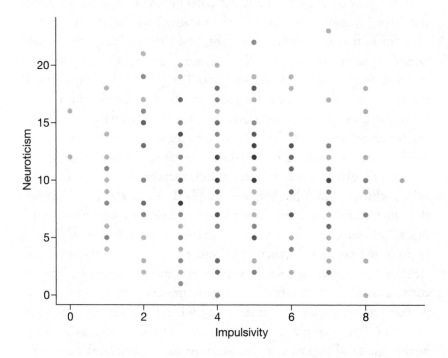

Most correlation coefficients lie somewhere in between 0 and 1, or they are smaller than 0 but bigger than −1. In either case, knowing one value tells us something, but not everything, about what the other value is likely to be.

To continue with sports examples, knowing the amount that a sports team spends tells you something about their likely win-loss record. Everyone knows that huge payrolls help the New York Yankees and FC Barcelona remain perpetual contenders in their respective leagues.

It is more surprising that this pattern holds even in US college sports, where the athletes are purportedly unpaid. If you look at the ranking by budget of college football programs and the ranking by competitive success, there is a strong relationship. On the following page are rankings for college football programs from 2006 to 2015.

The correlation coefficient between budget ranking and success ranking is 0.78. The powerhouse programs such as Alabama, Michigan, etc., are highly ranked, but they also spend the most money. Of course, the correlation is not perfect; outliers like Boise State have produced more wins than expected given their small budgets. It's not clear which way causality goes: Does money breed success, or does success generate more revenue from television, licensing, and donations? Most likely it goes both ways.

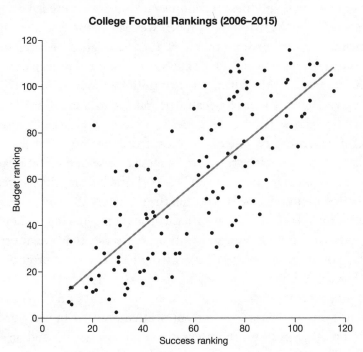

College Football Rankings (2006–2015)

CONTEMPLATING CAUSATION

Ask a philosopher what causation is, and you open an enormous can of worms. When a perfectly struck cue ball knocks the eight ball into the corner pocket, why do we say that the cue ball *causes* the eight ball to travel across the table and drop? The dirty secret is that although we all have an everyday sense of what it means for one thing to cause another, and despite endless debate in the fields of physics and metaphysics alike, there is little agreement on what causation *is*. Fortunately, we don't need to know in order to use the notion of causation. In practice, we are usually interested in causation for *instrumental* purposes. We want to know how to cause things. We want to know why things went wrong in the past, so that we can make them go right in the future.

But it is rarely straightforward to figure out what effects an action will have. A large fraction of the time all we have to work with is information about correlations. Scientists have a number of techniques for measuring correlations and drawing inferences about causality from these correlations. But doing so is a tricky and sometimes contentious business, and these techniques are not always used as carefully as they ought to be. Moreover, when we read about recent studies in medicine or policy or any other area, these subtleties are often lost. It is a truism that *correlation does not imply causation*. Do not leap carelessly from data showing the former to assumptions about the latter.*

This is difficult to avoid, because people use data to tell stories. The stories that draw us in show a clear connection between cause and effect. Unfortunately, one of the most frequent misuses of data, particularly in the popular press, is to suggest a cause-and-effect relationship based on correlation alone. This is classic bullshit, in the vein of our earlier definition, because often the reporters and editors responsible for such stories don't care what you end up believing. When they tell you that drinking wine prevents heart disease, they are not trying to lead you into alcoholism or away from behaviors that promote cardiac health. At best, they are trying to tell a good story. At worst, they are trying to compel you to buy a magazine or click on a link.

One team of researchers recently attempted to figure out how common this type of misrepresentation is in news stories and on social media. They identified the fifty research studies shared most often on Facebook and Twitter about how factors such as diet, pollution, exercise, and medical treatment were correlated with health or illness. Because it is very difficult to demonstrate causality in a medical study, only fifteen of the fifty studies did a decent job of demonstrating cause-and-effect relationships. Of these, only two met the highest standards for doing so. The rest identified only correlations. That's okay; identifying correlations can generate important hypotheses,

---

* This principle holds for associations of any sort, not just for linear correlations. Though not as catchy a phrase, it's worth remembering that *association does not imply causation* either. That said, it is worth noticing that although correlation does not imply causation, *causation does imply association*. Causation may not generate a linear correlation, but it will generate some sort of association.

among other things. The problem is how the results were described. In a third of the studies, the medical journal articles themselves suggested causation in the absence of adequate evidence. Matters got worse in the popular press. Nearly half of news articles describing the studies made unwarranted claims about causation. When reading articles about medical trials or any other studies that purport to demonstrate causality, you can't count on the story being presented correctly. You need to be able to see through the bullshit.

Let's return to the never-been-kissed study that started off the chapter. The study found a strong association between positive self-esteem and having been kissed. To illustrate this association, we would draw a diagram such as the following:

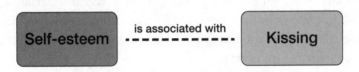

The dashed line indicates an association. If we are willing to accept the story that acting confidently leads to social and romantic success, this association would be causal. Having self-esteem would cause being kissed. We can indicate a causal relationship by replacing the dashed line with an arrow from cause to effect:

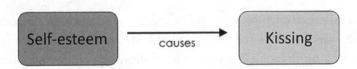

A causal arrow like this doesn't have to represent absolute certainty. Positive self-esteem doesn't have to *ensure* that one gets kissed. We just mean that the higher one's self-esteem, the more likely one is to engage in kissing. And while an abundance of self-esteem may lead some people to walk up and kiss strangers, that's a bit too much self-esteem for our taste. We might refine our diagram to include an intermediate step, for example:

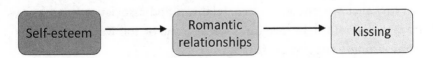

Alternatively, you might think that kissing is the cause, rather than the effect. Perhaps the wonder of a first kiss works miracles for one's self-esteem. It did for ours. In that case, the direction of causality would be reversed. In our diagram, we simply turn the causal arrow around.

Of course, it's probably a bit more complicated than that. Perhaps it's not the kissing itself that leads to positive self-esteem for adolescents—it's simply being engaged in a romantic relationship. And (as the research study takes pains to note) being involved in a romantic relationship is a strong predictor of kissing. So we might diagram causality as follows:

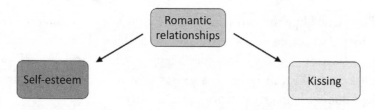

Causality can even flow in multiple directions and form a feedback loop. Having positive self-esteem may increase an adolescent's likelihood of being engaged in a romantic relationship, and being in such a relationship may in turn increase self-esteem. We would diagram that as follows, with the feedback loop illustrated by the dual arrows at left:

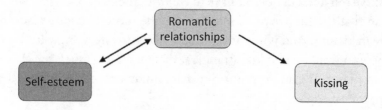

Now that we understand correlations and associations and know how to diagram them, we can look at some of the ways that correlations wrongly suggest causality.

CORRELATION DOESN'T SELL NEWSPAPERS

In the summer of 2018, the real estate website Zillow reported a negative correlation between changes in housing prices and changes in birth rates. Cities in which housing prices had increased the most from 2010 to 2016 exhibited greater declines in the fertility rate for women aged 25 to 29. The trend is illustrated below.

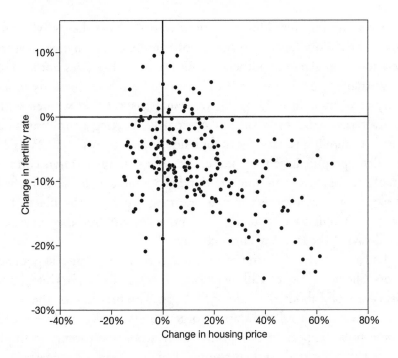

There is a striking and seductively simple story that one could tell here: Having children is expensive. By some estimates, the financial cost of raising a child to age eighteen is comparable to the median cost of a house. Many people report waiting to start a family until they have enough money. Perhaps couples are forced to choose between buying a house and having a child. But this is only one of many possible explanations. The Zillow report makes that clear and discusses some of the other possibilities:

> As a further caveat, the correlation observed here is by no means proof that home value growth *causes* fertility declines. One alternative explanation could be the possibility that there is

clustering into certain counties of people with careers that pay well enough for expensive homes but make it difficult to have children before 30; this could cause both trends observed in the chart above. There are many other confounding factors that could explain this relationship as well, such as the possibility that cultural values or the cost of child care varies across counties with some correlation to home values.

So far, no bullshit. This is the right way to report the study's findings. The Zillow article describes a correlation, and then uses this correlation to generate hypotheses about causation but does not leap to unwarranted conclusions about causality. Given that the study looks only at women aged 25 to 29, we might suspect that women with characteristics that make them likely to delay starting a family are also prone to moving to cities with high housing costs. After all, 25 to 29 is a demographic in which the frequency of childbirth differs considerably across socioeconomic strata and geographic regions. And when looking only at mothers in this age range, it is impossible to tell whether women are reducing the number of children they have, or are delaying the births of those children.

Unfortunately, this kind of distinction is often lost in the popular press. Shortly after the Zillow report was released, *MarketWatch* published a story about the Zillow findings. The first line of the story indicates a causal relationship: "Forget about a baby boom—rising home prices appear to be causing many would-be parents to think twice before expanding their family." Even the headline suggests causality: "Another Adverse Effect of High Home Prices: Fewer Babies." While this headline doesn't use the word "cause," it does use the word "effect"—another way of suggesting causal relationships. Correlation doesn't imply causation—but apparently it doesn't sell newspapers either.

If we have evidence of correlation but not causation, we shouldn't be making prescriptive claims. NPR reporter Scott Horsley posted a tweet announcing that "Washington Post poll finds NPR listeners are among the least likely to fall for politicians' false claims." Fair enough. But this poll demonstrated only correlation, not causation. Yet Horsley's tweet also recommended, "Inoculate yourself against B.S. Listen to NPR." The problem with this logic is easy to spot. It's indeed possible that listening to NPR inoculates people against believing bullshit. If so, Horsley's advice would be merited. But it's also possible that being skeptical of bullshit predisposes people to listen to NPR. In that case, listening to NPR will not have the protective effect that Horsley supposes. NPR listeners were quick to call bullshit on Horsley's error—but this reinforces evidence of the correlation; it still doesn't prove causation.

The NPR example is merely silly, but matters get more serious when people make prescriptive claims based on correlational data in medical journalism. A 2016 study published in the prestigious *Journal of the American Medical Association* reported that people who exercise less have increased rates of thirteen different cancers. This study does not tell us anything about causality. Perhaps exercising reduces cancer rates, or perhaps people who do not exercise have other characteristics that increase their cancer risk. While the researchers tried to control for obvious characteristics such as smoking or obesity, this does not mean that any remaining differences are causal. The press ignored this subtlety and suggested a causal connection anyway. "Exercise Can Lower Risk of Some Cancers by 20%," proclaimed *Time* magazine in their headline about the study. "Exercising Drives Down Risk for 13 Cancers, Research Shows," announced the *Los Angeles Times*. "Exercise Cuts Cancer Risk, Huge Study Finds," declared *U.S. News & World Report*.

What people really want to read about, especially where health news is concerned, is not just the fact of the matter—they want to know what they ought to be doing. It's a small step from the causal claim that exercise cuts cancer risk, to a recommendation such as "exercise thirty minutes a day to prevent cancer." Much of the prescriptive advice that we read in the popular press is based on associations with no underlying evidence of causality.

Original scientific articles can make this mistake as well. Nutritionists have debated the merits of whole milk versus reduced-fat milk in preventing obesity, and typically favor reduced-fat milk. However, a recent study of children in San Francisco revealed that children who consumed more milk fat were less likely to be severely obese. The authors of the study correctly cautioned that this is a correlation and does not demonstrate a causal relationship.

But the title of the article suggests otherwise: "Full Fat Milk Consumption *Protects* Against Severe Childhood Obesity in Latinos" (emphasis added). This is causal language. Evidence of correlation is being miscast as evidence of causation. Worse yet, the authors make a prescriptive suggestion: "These results call into question recommendations that promote consumption of lower fat milk." No! There's no evidence here that consuming milk fat causes a reduction in obesity, and no reason to question milk-drinking recommendations from previous studies. Whenever you see a prescriptive claim, ask yourself whether there is causal evidence to back it up.

Moving on, what if someone argued that smoking doesn't cause cancer—but rather that cancer causes smoking? Crazy as it sounds, this is precisely what Ronald A. Fisher, one of the greatest statisticians of all time, tried to argue. Fisher noted that chronic inflammation of the lungs is associated with cancerous or precancerous states. Perhaps, he conjectured, this inflammation creates a discomfort that can be soothed by the act of smoking. If so, people in the process of developing cancer might take to smoking as a way to alleviate their symptoms. Those not developing cancer would be less likely to take up the habit. Would it be a stretch, then, to say that cancer causes smoking? Fisher turned out to be wrong, of course, but he was making a point about the challenges of inferring causality—and probably justifying his beloved pipe-smoking habit at the same time. Fisher's suggestion about cancer and smoking never got much traction, but the tobacco industry found other ways to seed doubts about whether or not smoking caused disease. Their efforts delayed antismoking legislation for decades.

Other mistaken assumptions about causality have had a serious impact in debates about drugs and public health. In the 1980s, American university administrators and policy makers were concerned about the prevalence of binge drinking on university campuses. Psychologists, epidemiologists, public health experts, and others searched for ways to stem this epidemic of intemperance.

And why not? There are worse places to do fieldwork. In an influential 1986 paper titled "Naturalistic Observations of Beer Drinking among College Students," psychologist Scott Geller and colleagues looked at factors associated with greater consumption of beer at college pubs. What are "naturalistic observations"? They are the observations you make of a subject, in this case the college students, in their natural habitat, in this case the pub. We are amused by this detail from the methods section of the paper: "The observers attempted to remain as inconspicuous as possible by sitting at tables and *behaving as normal patrons*" (emphasis added). Does this mean drinking beer themselves? One must take pains to blend in, after all.

The researchers observed the number of beers that each student consumed and recorded whether each was purchased by the glass, the bottle, or the pitcher. They observed a strong correlation between the vessel in which beer was served and the amount consumed.

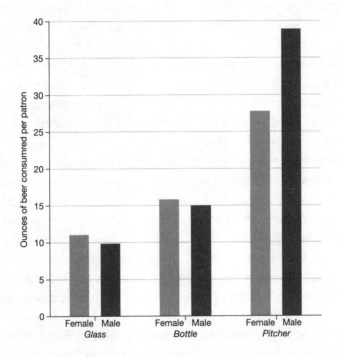

Students who drank beer from pitchers drank roughly two to four times as much beer as those who drank their beer by the glass or by the bottle. The original study was careful not to claim a causal relationship.* But the claim evolved as reports of the study filtered through the popular press and into the broader discussion about alcohol abuse on college campuses. "People drink more *when* beer is consumed in pitchers" was taken to mean "People drink more *because* beer is con-

* Geller and colleagues write: "It would be instructive to determine how much of the relationship between container type and drinking behavior was a cause-and-effect relationship versus a correlation attributable to a third variable (e.g., differential intentionality). For example, was greater beer consumption from pitchers due to drinkers feeling obligated to finish its contents, or did those who ordered a pitcher intend to drink more at the outset?"

sumed in pitchers." Based on this, people started making prescriptive claims: "We should ban pitchers so that students will drink less."

Perhaps you already see the problem with this inference. Students aren't necessarily drinking more beer because they ordered a pitcher. They are probably ordering pitchers because they intend to drink more beer. When we two authors go to a bar and want one beer each, we each order a glass. When we want two beers each, we order a pitcher and split it. And we are the kind of fellows who follow through on their intentions: When we intend to drink more beer, we usually do.

Geller's study doesn't necessarily show us that people drink more when served from pitchers. Instead, he may have discovered that people who want to drink lots of beer order more beer than people who want to drink a little bit of beer. Unfortunately, that doesn't make for very exciting headlines, so one can see why the newspapers tried to spin it in a different direction.

The two cases that we just treated are relatively clear-cut, at least with the advantage of hindsight. Smoking causes cancer; intending to drink more beer is associated both with ordering more beer and with drinking more beer. But in many cases we do not know which way causality flows. Studies have found an association between poor sleep and the buildup of beta-amyloid plaques that cause Alzheimer's disease. One hypothesis is that sleep provides a sort of downtime during which the brain can clean up these plaques. If so, a lack of sleep may be a cause of Alzheimer's. But from the available data, it is also possible that causality goes in the opposite direction. A buildup of beta-amyloid plaques may interfere with sleep, in which case it would be that Alzheimer's (or pre-Alzheimer's) causes poor sleep. As yet we simply don't know.

There are many ways to imply causality. Some are overt: "Smoking causes cancer," or "Red wine prevents heart disease." Some make prescriptions: "To avoid cancer, exercise three times a week." But others are less obvious. We can even imply causality with subtle grammatical shifts. We might express a correlation with a plain factual statement in the indicative mood: "If she *is* a Canadian, she *is* more likely to be bilingual." We express causation using a counterfactual statement in the subjunctive mood: "If she *were* a Canadian, she *would be* more likely to be bilingual." The former statement simply suggests an association. The latter statement suggests that being Canadian causes bilinguality. The former statement suggests that people are selected at random from a large group and their attributes compared: "If [the person we happen to pick] is a Canadian . . ." The second suggests that we pick someone and then change some of that person's characteristics: "If [the person we picked] were [turned into a] Canadian."

It is subtle, but the subjunctive mood sneaks in a suggestion of causality. "Where minimum wage is higher, poverty is lower" is not the same claim as "If minimum wage were to increase, poverty would decrease." The first reports a trend across cities: Those with higher minimum wage have lower poverty rates. The second suggests how one might go about reducing poverty in a particular city.

Data graphics can also suggest causality in subtle ways. Think back to the scatter plot of housing price changes versus fertility changes. In many graphs of this sort, the horizontal axis is used to illustrate the variable that causes—or at least influences—the variable shown on the vertical axis. In the Zillow graph, housing prices are shown on the horizontal axis and fertility rates are shown on the vertical axis. Without a word of causal language, this graph conveys a subtle suggestion that housing prices determine fertility rate. A graph like this can trick readers into presuming a causal relationship. When you see scatter plots and related forms of data visualization, ask yourself (and maybe the person who created the graph): Is the structure of the graph suggesting a causal relationship that isn't there?

DELAYED GRATIFICATION AND COMMON CAUSE

One of the hallmark discoveries of social psychology is the role that delayed gratification plays in a successful life. At the heart of delayed gratification theory is an experiment known as the marshmallow test. A four-year-old is presented with alternative rewards: one marshmallow or two marshmallows. He is told that he can have a single marshmallow anytime—but if he can wait for a while, he can have two marshmallows. The experimenter then leaves the room and measures the amount of time until the child says screw it, and takes the single marshmallow. (After fifteen minutes of open-ended waiting, a child who has not yet given up receives the two-marshmallow reward. But seriously—do you remember how long fifteen minutes seemed at that age?)

A number of studies have shown that children who can wait longer at age four have higher SAT scores in high school, and are rated by their parents as better-adjusted during adolescence. The authors of the original studies were careful to explain that their results demonstrated correlation: Delayed gratification is predictive of later academic success and emotional well-being. They did not demonstrate causation: The ability to delay gratification does not necessarily *cause* later success and well-being.* But as these results filtered through the popular press, the line between correlation and causation became blurred. The results of the marshmallow test and other related studies were reported as evidence that ability to delay gratification causes success later in life.

These assumptions about causation are often used as grounds to make a prescription: Improve your future by learning to delay gratification. In response to the marshmallow test, pop-psych and pop-business outlets promote training methods. *Lifehacker* exhorted us to "Build the Skill of Delayed Gratification." "If you can manage to turn delaying gratification into a regular habit," read the copy beneath a stock photo of marshmallows in *Fast Company,* "you may be able to take your own performance from just mediocre to top-notch." In an article titled "40-Year-Old Stanford Study Reveals the 1 Quality Your Children Need to Succeed In Life," *Inc.* magazine explains how to cultivate this ability in our children:

> In other words, actively establish a system for delayed gratification in your young one's brain by promising small rewards for any work done and then delivering on it. If you keep doing this, their brain will automatically gravitate toward doing hard work first; it's classical conditioning at work.

But here's the thing. These prescriptions are unwarranted, because we don't actually have strong evidence that the ability to delay gratification causes subsequent success. When a research team went back

---

* In a 1990 paper by a core group of researchers in the area, Shoda and colleagues, we are cautioned in the discussion that "stability in parent child-rearing practices and in the psychosocial environment in the family and the community may be a common factor underlying both preschool children's delay of gratification behavior and their cognitive and self-regulatory competence in adolescence. These commonalities may contribute to the observed long-term correlations." This turns out to be very close to the common cause explanation we will suggest.

and attempted to replicate the original marshmallow studies with a larger sample size and additional controls, they found only a fraction of the original effect. Moreover, there was a single factor that seemed responsible both for a child's ability to delay gratification and for success during adolescence: the parents' socioeconomic status.* Children from wealthy families were better able to wait for the second marshmallow. Why? Perhaps they felt a greater sense of overall stability, had greater trust in adults, recalled previous situations in which waiting had proven fruitful, and felt relative indifference—a marshmallow might not be such a special treat for these children. Parental wealth also is a major determinant of an adolescent's educational success. So both the ability to delay gratification and academic success are consequences of parental wealth. Neither effect causes the other. In a case like this, where parental wealth is a common cause of patience and success, we diagram it as follows.

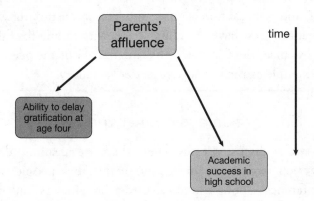

This causal diagram features an arrow to indicate the direction of time. Children are able to delay gratification (or not) at age four long before they are academically successful (or not) in adolescence. Causation flows only forward in time. If A happens before B does, we know that B doesn't cause A. That's useful. In this case, we can immediately rule out the possibility that academic success in high school causes the ability to delay gratification at age four.

But if one is not careful, looking at events chronologically can be

---

* Statisticians sometimes use the term *confounding* to refer to situations where a common cause influences two variables that you are measuring. In the present example, we would say that the ability to delay gratification, and adolescent academic success, are confounded by parent wealth.

misleading. Just because A happens before B does not mean that A causes B—even when A and B are associated. This mistake is so common and has been around for so long that it has a Latin name: *post hoc ergo propter hoc*. Translated, this means something like "after this, therefore because of it."

It's human to make these mistakes. We are excellent at seeing patterns, and this ability can help us generalize from one experience to another. We might learn that flying black insects don't sting, whereas flying yellow and black insects do. The observations we make now help us anticipate events in the future. We might notice that every time there is a heavy downpour, the river runs higher the next day and should be crossed with caution. We often apply rules of thumb, such as "if two things are associated, the one that happens first causes the one that happens second." Droughts and wildfires are associated; droughts happen first and are a cause of wildfires. But this pattern-seeking ability can also mislead us. If migrating geese arrive in early September every year and coho salmon begin to run later in the month, we might assume that the geese have something to do with calling the fish up the rivers. Of course, the fish don't give a damn about the geese. This is another example of the *post hoc ergo propter hoc* fallacy.

SPURIOUS CORRELATIONS

So far, we've discussed cases where there are meaningful correlations between two events or measurements, but people draw the wrong inferences about causality. Ordering pitchers and drinking more beer are legitimately associated, but it was a mistake to assume that ordering pitchers causes people to drink more beer. Some correlations do not rise even to this standard. They exist by chance, don't tell us anything meaningful about how the world works, and are unlikely to recur when tested with new data. Author Tyler Vigen has collected a delightful set of examples, and has a website where you can uncover these *spurious correlations* yourself. For example, did you know that the age of Miss America is tightly correlated to the number of people murdered with steam, hot vapors, and other hot objects?*

---

* In order to draw a smooth curve without jagged corners at each point, Vigen uses a technique called "splining." We have followed his lead in the subsequent figures.

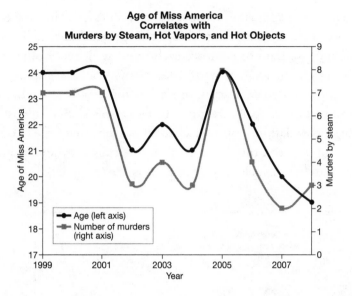

There is no way that this correlation captures something meaningful about how the world works. What possible causal connection could there be between these two things? Intuitively, we know this has to be a spurious correlation. It's just random chance that these measurements line up so well. Because it's just chance, we do not expect this trend to hold in the future. Indeed, it doesn't. If we continue the time series across the intervening years since Vigen published this figure, the correlation completely falls apart.

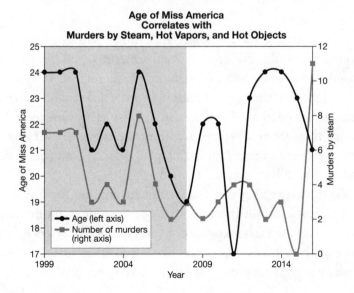

Vigen finds his spurious correlation examples by collecting a large number of data sets about how things change over time. Then he uses a computer program to compare each trend with every other trend. This is an extreme form of what data scientists call *data dredging*. With a mere one hundred data series, one can compare nearly ten thousand pairs. Some of these pairs are going to show very similar trends—and thus high correlations—just by chance. For example, check out the correlation between the numbers of deaths caused by anticoagulants and the number of sociology degrees awarded in the US:

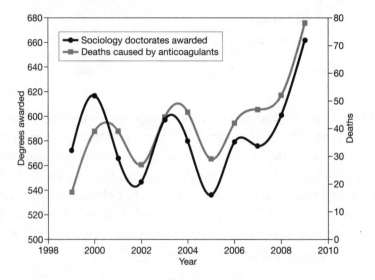

You look at these two trends and think, Wow—what are the chances they would line up that well? One in a hundred? One in a thousand? That must *mean* something. Well, sort of. It means that Vigen had to look through a hundred or even a thousand other comparisons before he found one that matched so well by chance. It doesn't mean that there is any meaningful connection between the two trends. It certainly doesn't mean that sociology grads are going around with rat poison and killing people.

In Vigen's case this is just funny. But his mining for silly correlations parallels a serious problem that can arise in scientific analyses. Particularly in the early exploratory stages, much of science involves a search for patterns in nature. As larger and larger data sets become available, with information about more and more variables, the search for patterns can start to look more and more like Vigen's humorous dragneting expedition.

Researchers have collected large survey data sets in which participants are asked dozens of questions about many aspects of their lives, values, personality traits, etc. When digging through these data sets to test hypotheses, researchers need to be careful that they aren't inadvertently doing what Vigen does on purpose: making so many different comparisons that they end up finding similarities that exist by chance rather than as a reflection of any real-world relationship.

One of the easiest ways to get a spurious correlation in trends over time is to look at very simple trends. There are millions of different things we could go out and measure. Many of them are increasing over time: the number of emails in Jevin's in-box, Amazon stock prices, a child's height, the cost of a new car, even the year on the Gregorian calendar. Many others are decreasing over time: the area of arctic sea ice on New Year's Day, cesium-137 levels in Chernobyl, rates of early-onset lung cancer, the cost of storing 1 gigabyte of data. If we compare any two of the increasing quantities, their values will be positively correlated in time. The same thing happens if we compare any two decreasing quantities. (If we compare an increasing quantity with a decreasing quantity, we will get a correlation as well—but it will be a negative correlation.) For the vast majority of pairs, there will be no causal connection at all. In a not-too-subtle jab at the natural health community, one user of the Reddit website posted the following graph.

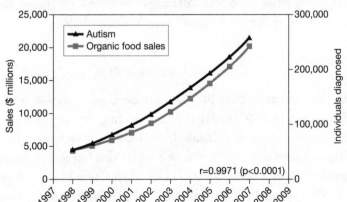

The Real Cause of Increasing Autism Prevalence?

Obviously there is no reason to assume any sort of causal relationship between organic food sales and autism, but that is the point of the joke. This erroneous attribution of causality is the same mistake that the natural health community makes in ascribing autism to vaccination.

In the late 1980s, a chemist used the same trick to publish a humorous graph in *Nature,* one of the top research journals in the world. The graph, titled "A New Parameter for Sex Education," serves as a cautionary tale against inferring too much from a correlation.

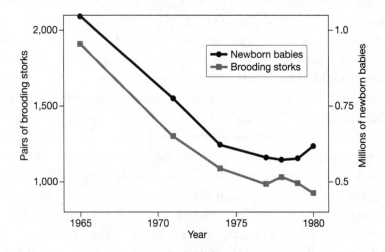

This graph compares two declining trends: pairs of brooding storks in West Germany and the number of newborn human babies. The winking implication is that one should consider a possible causal relationship here. Perhaps the old tall tale is right: Perhaps storks do bring babies after all. If the storks go away, no more babies.

SMOKING DOESN'T KILL?

In our discussions of causality, we have been talking about probabilities, not certainties. We say that drunk driving causes automobile accidents not because every drunk driver crashes or because every crash involves a drunk driver, but rather because driving drunk greatly increases the risk of a crash. There is a key distinction between a *probabilistic cause* (A increases the chance of B in a causal manner), a *sufficient cause* (if A happens, B always happens), and a *necessary cause* (unless A happens, B can't happen).

The distinction between necessary and sufficient causes is sometimes misused, particularly by those interested in denying causal relationships. For example, Mike Pence once made the following argument against government regulation of tobacco:

> Time for a quick reality check. Despite the hysteria from the political class and the media, smoking doesn't kill. In fact, 2 out of every three smokers does not die from a smoking related illness and 9 out of ten smokers do not contract lung cancer.

This is just plain bullshit, and bullshit of a higher grade than usually appears in print. In one sentence Pence says literally "Smoking doesn't kill," and in the very next he says that a third of smokers die of smoking-related illness.* Pence is conflating sufficient cause with probabilistic cause. Smoking is not sufficient to guarantee lung cancer or even smoking-related illness, but it does greatly increase the probability that someone will die of one or the other. A related argument might be that smoking doesn't cause lung cancer because some lung cancer victims—miners, for example—never smoked. This argument conflates necessary cause with probabilistic cause.

WHEN ALL ELSE FAILS, MANIPULATE

With all these traps and pitfalls, how can we ever be confident that one thing causes another? Scientists struggle with this problem all the time, and often use manipulative experiments to tease apart correlation and causation. Consider the biology of fever. We commonly think of fever as something that disease *does to us,* the way a cold gives us a sore throat, or measles covers the skin with pox. As such, physicians might aim to block or prevent fever, using drugs such as aspirin, Tylenol, or Advil. But fever seems to be different from a sore throat or an outbreak of pox. Multiple lines of evidence suggest that a moder-

---

* Pence's claim is a massive underestimate of the fraction killed by smoking-related illness. About two-thirds of smokers die from smoking-related illness, according to a recent large-scale study by Emily Banks and colleagues.

ate fever is one of the body's defenses against infection. For example, people who mount a fever are more likely to survive a bloodstream infection. But this is a correlation, not causation.

Does fever *cause* better outcomes, as diagrammed below?

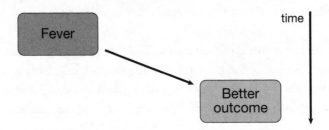

Or are patients who are in better condition (healthier overall, not malnourished, with less severe infections, or better off in any number of other ways) the ones who are able to mount a fever in the first place? Because these patients are in better condition to start with, we would expect these patients to have better outcomes, irrespective of the effects of fever.

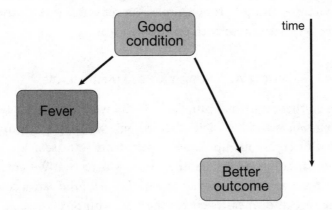

How do we distinguish between these two possibilities? How can we figure out whether fever actually causes better disease outcomes?

Experiments. With fever, there are "natural experiments" taking place all the time, in the sense that absent any experimenter, different patients are treated in different ways. In particular, when visiting the hospital or the general practitioner, some patients are given drugs to reduce fever, whereas others are not. Overall and across numerous studies, there is a strong trend: Patients who are given fever-reducing (antipyretic) drugs take longer to recover from viral infections.

Does this mean that fever is beneficial? Not necessarily, because fever-reducing drugs are not assigned randomly to patients. The group of patients who are given drugs may have properties different from the group of patients who do not receive drugs. What we are looking at here is a form of *selection bias*. In particular, it may be that people who are in poorer condition are more likely to receive drugs to reduce their fevers. If so, it might look like taking fever-reducing drugs caused negative outcomes. But in fact, it would be that people who were likely to experience worse outcomes were *selected* to receive fever-reducing drugs.

To get around this problem, we might explicitly *randomize* the treatments that patients receive. Then any differences in outcome would be due to the effects of the treatment, rather than differences in the conditions of the patients. While we cannot ethically randomize whether people get treated or not for life-threatening illnesses, we can—with consent from patients—do so for less severe diseases. Using this approach, researchers have found that drugs that block fever tend to slow the rate at which patients recover, and increase the chance that patients spread the illness to others. But we still don't know for certain that temperature is the main cause of these differences. It could be that the drugs themselves, not the changes in temperature that they induce, are responsible. Is it that fever-reducing drugs cause fever to drop, and that the reduction in fever causes worse disease outcomes? Or do fever-reducing drugs have their own negative consequences—independent of their effect on body temperature?

To rule out this possibility, scientists turned to experiments with laboratory animals. They physically cooled the animals. Doing so had the same effect on disease outcomes as did fever-reducing drugs. This suggests that the negative consequences of fever-reducing drugs arise through their effect on body temperature. With this piece in place, we now have a solid chain of evidence supporting the idea that fever is a beneficial defense against disease. Manipulative experiments offer some of the strongest evidence of causality because of the ability to isolate the purported cause and keep everything else constant. The problem is, such experiments are not always feasible, so we have to rely on other forms of evidence. That's all good and well, but when you do so don't be taken in by an unfounded leap from correlation to causation.

CHAPTER 5

Numbers and Nonsense

OUR WORLD IS THOROUGHLY QUANTIFIED. EVERYTHING IS COUNTED, measured, analyzed, and assessed. Internet companies track us around the Web and use algorithms to predict what we will buy. Smartphones count our steps, measure our calls, and trace our movements throughout the day. "Smart appliances" monitor how we use them and learn more about our daily routines than we might care to realize. Implanted medical devices collect a continuous stream of data from patients and watch for danger signs in real time. During service visits, our cars upload data about their performance and about our driving habits. Arrays of sensors and cameras laid out across our cities monitor everything from traffic to air quality to the identities of passersby.

Instead of collecting data about what people do through costly studies and surveys, companies let people come to them—and then record what those consumers do. Facebook knows whom we know; Google knows what we want to know. Uber knows where we want to go; Amazon knows what we want to buy. Match knows whom we want to marry; Tinder knows whom we want to be swiped by.

Data can help us understand the world based upon hard evidence, but hard numbers are a lot softer than one might think. It's like the old joke: A mathematician, an engineer, and an accountant are applying for a job. They are led to the interview room and given a math quiz. The first problem is a warm-up: What is 2 + 2? The mathematician rolls her eyes, writes the numeral 4, and moves on. The engineer pauses for a moment, then writes "Approximately 4." The accountant looks around nervously, then gets out of his chair and walks over to the fellow administering the test. "Before I put anything in writing," he says in a low whisper, "what do you want it to be?"

Numbers are ideal vehicles for promulgating bullshit. They feel objective, but are easily manipulated to tell whatever story one desires. Words are clearly constructs of human minds, but numbers? Numbers seem to come directly from Nature herself. We know words are subjective. We know they are used to bend and blur the truth. Words suggest intuition, feeling, and expressivity. But not numbers. Numbers suggest precision and imply a scientific approach. Numbers appear to have an existence separate from the humans reporting them.

People are so convinced of the primacy of numbers that skeptics claim they "just want to see the data," or demand to be shown "the raw numbers," or insist that we "let the measurements speak for themselves." We are told that "the data never lie." But this perspective can be dangerous. Even if a figure or measurement is correct, it can still be used to bullshit, as we'll demonstrate later in the chapter. For numbers to be transparent, they must be placed in an appropriate context. Numbers must presented in a way that allows for fair comparisons.

Let's start by thinking about where people find their numbers. Some numbers are obtained directly, through an exact tally or an immediate measurement. There are 50 states in the United States of America. There are 25 prime numbers less than 100. The Empire State Building has 102 floors. Baseball legend Tony Gwynn had 3,141 hits in 9,288 at-bats, for a lifetime Major League batting average of .338. In principle, exact counts should be fairly straightforward; there is a definitive answer and usually a definitive procedure for counting or measuring that we can use to find it. Not that this process is always trivial—one can miscount, mismeasure, or make mistakes about what one is counting. Take the number of planets in the solar system. From the time that Neptune was recognized as a planet in 1846 through to 1930 when Pluto was discovered, we believed there were eight planets in our solar system. Once Pluto was found, we said there were nine planets—until the unfortunate orb was demoted to a "dwarf planet" in 2006 and the tally within our solar system returned to eight.

More often, however, exact counts or exhaustive measurements are impossible. We cannot individually count every star in the measurable universe to arrive at the current estimate of about a trillion trillion.

Likewise we rely on estimates when we consider quantities such as the average height of adults by country. Men from the Netherlands are supposedly the tallest in the world, at an average height of 183 cm (six feet), but this was not determined by measuring every Dutch man and taking an average across the entire population. Rather, researchers took random samples of men from the country, measured the members of that sample, and extrapolated from there.

If one measured only a half dozen men and took their average height, it would be easy to get a misleading estimate simply by chance. Perhaps you sampled a few unusually tall guys. This is known as sampling error. Fortunately, with large samples things tend to average out, and sampling error will have a minimal effect on the outcome.

There can also be problems with measurement procedures. For example, researchers might ask subjects to report their own heights, but men commonly exaggerate their heights—and shorter men exaggerate more than taller men.

Other sources of error, such as bias in the way a sample is selected, are more pernicious. Suppose you decide to estimate people's heights by going to the local basketball court and measuring the players. Basketball players are probably taller than average, so your sample will not be representative of the population as a whole, and as a result your estimate of average height will be too high. Most mistakes of this sort aren't so obvious. We devote the rest of the chapter to considering the subtle ways in which a sample can turn out to be uncharacteristic of the population.

In these examples, we are observing a population with a range of values—a range of heights, for instance—and then summarizing that information with a single number that we call a *summary statistic*. For example, when describing the tall Dutch, we reported a mean height. Summary statistics can be a nice way to condense information, but if you choose an inappropriate summary statistic you can easily mislead your audience. Politicians use this trick when they propose a tax cut that will save the richest 1 percent of the population hundreds of thousands of dollars but offer no tax reduction whatsoever to the rest of us. Taking a mean of the tax cuts, they report that their tax plan will save families an average $4,000 per year. Maybe so, but the average family—if by that we mean one in the middle of the income range—will save nothing. The majority of us would be better off knowing the tax cut for a family with the *median* income. The median is the "middle" income: Half of US families earn more and half earn less. In this particular case, the median family would get no tax cut at all, because the tax cut benefits only the top 1 percent.

Sometimes one cannot directly observe the quantity one is trying to measure. Recently Carl blew through a speed trap on a straight flat highway in the Utah desert that was inexplicably encumbered with a 50 mph speed limit. He pulled over to the side of the road with the familiar red and blue lights glaring in the rearview mirror. "Do you know how fast you were going?" the state patrolman asked.

"No, I'm afraid not, Officer."

"Eighty-three miles per hour."

Eighty-three: a hard number with the potential to create serious problems. But where did this number come from? Some traffic cameras calculate speed by measuring distance you travel over a known interval of time, but that's not how the state patrol does it. The patrolman measured something different—the Doppler shift in radio waves emitted from his portable radar gun when they reflected off of Carl's speeding vehicle. The software built into his radar gun used a mathematical model grounded in wave mechanics to infer the car's speed from its measurements. Because the trooper was not directly measuring Carl's speed, his radar gun needed to be regularly calibrated. A standard method for getting out of a speeding ticket is to challenge the officer to produce timely calibration records. None of that in Carl's case, though. He knew he had been speeding and was grateful to face only a stiff fine for his haste.

Radar guns rely on highly regular principles of physics, but models used to infer other quantities can be more complicated and involve more guesswork. The International Whaling Commission publishes population estimates for several whale species. When they state that there are 2,300 blue whales left in the waters of the Southern Hemisphere, they have not arrived at this number by going through and counting each animal. Nor have they even sampled a patch of ocean exhaustively. Whales don't hold still, and most of the time you can't see them from the surface. So researchers need indirect ways to estimate population sizes. For example, they use sightings of unique individuals as identified by markings on the flukes and tail. To whatever degree these procedures are inaccurate, their estimate of population size may be off.

There are many ways for error to creep into facts and figures that seem entirely straightforward. Quantities can be miscounted. Small samples can fail to accurately reflect the properties of the whole population. Procedures used to infer quantities from other information can be faulty. And then, of course, numbers can be total bullshit, fabricated out of whole cloth in an effort to confer credibility on an otherwise flimsy argument. We need to keep all of these things in mind when we look at quantitative claims. They say the data never lie—but we need to remember that the data often mislead.

DISTILLING NUMBERS

Though unaged whiskey has become trendy of late,* freshly distilled whiskey can often be harsh and laden with undesirable by-products from the distillation process. A couple of years in a freshly charred oak barrel (for bourbon) or a longer period in a previously used barrel (for scotch) brings about a remarkable transformation. Flavors from the wood penetrate the liquor and some of the undesirable chemicals in the liquor are extracted through the wood.

This alchemy does not transpire for free. As the liquor ages in the barrel, a portion seeps out and evaporates into the air. A barrel that begins full will hold only a fraction of its initial volume by the time the aging process is complete. The portion of spirits lost to evaporation is known as the "angels' share." Romantic imagery aside, the angels' share represents a substantial cost in the production of bourbon and scotch.

How can we best describe this cost? We could start with the total loss: Approximately 440,000 barrels of whiskey are lost to evaporation in Scotland each year. Most people don't know how big a whiskey barrel is (about 66 gallons), so we might do better to say that in Scotland, about 29 million gallons are lost every year to the angels.

---

* At the risk of cynicism, we conjecture that this has everything to do with the proliferation of new microdistilleries that don't want to wait three or more years before bringing in revenue, and little to do with the flavor or other characteristics of unaged whiskey. If so, much of the advertising copy about the marvels of unaged whiskey is—you guessed it—bullshit.

We usually encounter whiskey in 750 ml bottles rather than gallons, so perhaps we would want to report this as a loss of 150 million bottles a year.

Aggregate totals are hard to grasp unless one knows the total amount of scotch being produced. We could break these numbers down and describe the amount of liquid lost by a single distillery during the process of barrel aging. Running at full capacity, the large Speyside distillery Macallan loses about 220,000 LPA—liters of pure alcohol—per year. (Notice yet another type of measurement; a distillery's capacity is often reported by tallying only the alcohol produced, not the total volume including water.) By contrast, the smaller Islay distillery Ardbeg loses about 26,000 LPA per year.

Because distilleries vary widely in size, perhaps we should report loss per barrel or, better yet, as a percentage of the starting volume. During the aging process for the legendary Pappy Van Winkle twenty-three-year-old bourbon, 58 percent of its initial volume is lost to evaporation. But instead of describing the loss as a percentage of the starting volume, I could describe it as a percentage of the final volume. For this bourbon, 1.38 liters are lost to evaporation for every liter bottled, so we could report the loss as 138 percent of the final volume. It is the exact same figure as the 58 percent of starting volume described above, but this way of presenting the data makes the loss appear larger.

Of course, different whiskies are aged for different amounts of time. Maybe instead of describing the total loss, it would make more sense to describe the annual loss. Scotch whiskies lose about 2 percent in volume per year of aging, or roughly 0.005 percent per day. Bourbons typically are aged under higher temperatures than scotch, and thus experience higher rates of evaporation; some may lose upward of 10 percent per year. Moreover, the rate of loss is not constant. The aforementioned Pappy Van Winkle loses about 10 percent of its volume over its first year in the barrel, but this drops to about 3 percent per year later in the aging process.

There are other decisions to make as well. For example, alcohol and water leave the barrel at different rates; we could report changes in alcohol volume, water volume, or the total. And then there is the issue of units: Metric or imperial? Liters or milliliters? Gallons or ounces?

To tell an honest story, it is not enough for numbers to be correct. They need to be placed in an appropriate context so that a reader or listener can properly interpret them. One thing that people often overlook is that presenting the numbers by themselves doesn't mean that the numbers have been separated from any context. The choices one makes about how to represent a numerical value *sets a context* for that value.

So what does it mean to tell an honest story? Numbers should be presented in ways that allow meaningful comparisons.

As one of us (Carl) is writing this chapter, the supply of malted milk ball candies in the box of Hershey's Whoppers on his desk is gradually dwindling—but there is no guilt, because a prominent splash of color on the box announces "25% Less Fat* Than the Average of the Leading Chocolate Candy Brands." The asterisk directs us to small print reading "5 grams of fat per 30 gram serving compared to 7 grams of fat in the average of the leading chocolate candy brands." Here's an example of a number provided without enough context to be meaningful. What brands are chosen as comparators? Is this an apples-to-apples comparison or are we comparing chocolate-covered malt balls to straight chocolate bars? How about sugar? Refined sugar may be a bigger health concern than fat; are Whoppers higher or lower in sugar? Are there other bad ingredients we should be concerned about? And so on, and so forth. The 25 percent figure sounds like an important nutritional metric, but it is really just *meaningless numerosity*.

PERNICIOUS PERCENTAGES

The twelfth chapter of Carl Sagan's 1996 book, *The Demon-Haunted World,* is called "The Fine Art of Baloney Detection." In that chapter, Sagan rips into the advertising world for bombarding us with dazzling but irrelevant facts and figures. Sagan highlights the same problem we address in this chapter: people are easily dazzled by numbers, and advertisers have known for decades how to use numbers to persuade. "You're not supposed to ask," Sagan writes. "Don't think. Buy."

Sagan focuses on the marketing tactics used in drug sales, a problem that expanded in scope a year after Sagan wrote his essay. In 1997, the

United States legalized direct-to-consumer marketing of prescription drugs. But rather than take on that troubling and complex issue, let's instead consider an amusing and largely harmless example.

Arriving in Washington, DC, late one evening, Carl was searching for something to drink before bed. He picked up a packet of instant hot cocoa in the hotel lobby. "99.9% caffeine-free," the packaging boasted. Given that he was already dealing with jet lag, a 99.9 percent caffeine-free drink seemed like a prudent alternative to a cup of coffee. But pause and think about it for a minute. Even though there's a lot of water in a cup of cocoa, caffeine is a remarkably powerful drug. So is a 99.9 percent caffeine-free drink really something you want to drink right before bed?

Let's figure it out. How much caffeine is in a cup of coffee? According to the Center for Science in the Public Interest, there are 415 milligrams of caffeine in a 20-ounce Starbucks coffee. That corresponds to about 21 mg of caffeine per ounce. A fluid ounce of water weighs about 28 grams. Thus, a Starbucks drip coffee is about 0.075 percent caffeine by weight. In other words, strong coffee is also 99.9 percent caffeine free!*

So while there's nothing inaccurate or dangerous about the 99.9 percent assertion, it's a pointless claim. Most regular coffees could be labeled in the exact same way. Nestlé has provided us with an excellent example of how something can be true and still bullshit of a sort. It is bullshit because it doesn't allow us to make meaningful comparisons the way a claim such as "only 1% as much caffeine as a cup of coffee" would.

A notorious *Breitbart* headline similarly denied readers the opportunity to make meaningful comparisons. This particular bit of scaremongering proclaimed that 2,139 of the DREAM Act recipients—undocumented adults who came to the United States as children—had been convicted or accused of crimes against Ameri-

---

* While we don't have an exact figure for this brand of cocoa, most cocoas have about 20 mg of caffeine in an 8-ounce cup; i.e., they're about 0.01 percent caffeine by weight. Thus we initially thought that perhaps the 99.9 percent figure referred to the powder, not the finished drink. But Nestlé's website makes it clear that they are referring to the prepared drink, not the powder: "With rich chocolate flavor and only 20 calories per single-serve packet, this cocoa makes a 99.9% caffeine-free, 8 fl oz serving." We also need to be careful about the difference between a fluid ounce, which is a measure of volume, and an ounce, which is a measure of weight. At room temperature at sea level, a fluid ounce of water weighs roughly 1.04 ounces. But we like our coffee hot, and as water approaches its boiling point its weight approaches 1.00 ounces per fluid ounce.

cans.* That sounds like a big number, a scary number. But of course, the DREAM Act pertains to a huge number of people—nearly 700,000 held DACA status concurrently and nearly 800,000 were granted DACA status at some point before the program was eliminated. This means that only about 0.3 percent of all DACA recipients—fewer than 1 in 300—have been accused of crimes against Americans. That sounds better, but how does this number compare to similar rates for American citizens? With 0.75 percent of Americans behind bars, US citizens are twice as likely to be presently incarcerated as DACA recipients are to have been accused of a crime. About 8.6 percent of American citizens have been convicted of a felony at some point in their lives, making the DACA population look better still.

Of course, DACA recipients are younger and had generally not been convicted of a crime prior to being awarded DACA status,† so they have had less time to commit crimes than your average American. But it turns out that 30 percent of Americans have been arrested for something other than a traffic violation by age twenty-three. Even assuming that *Breitbart*'s figures were correct, the news outlet presented them without the appropriate information a reader would need to put them into context.

Listing a raw total like this can make a small quantity, relatively speaking, appear to be large. We put this number into context by expressing it as a percentage. Indeed, percentages can be valuable tools for facilitating comparisons. But percentages can also obscure relevant comparisons in a number of ways. For starters, percentages can make large values look small.

In a blog post, Google VP of engineering Ben Gomes acknowledged the problem that their company faces from fake news, disinformation, and other inappropriate content:

> Our algorithms help identify reliable sources from the hundreds of billions of pages in our index. However, it's become very apparent that a small set of queries in our daily traffic

---

* Note that 2,139 is actually the number of DACA recipients who had lost DACA status at the publication date of the article due to felony or misdemeanor convictions, arrests, or suspected gang affiliation.

† To be eligible for DACA status, one must not have been convicted of a felony, a significant misdemeanor, or three misdemeanors of any kind.

(around 0.25 percent), have been returning offensive or clearly misleading content, which is not what people are looking for.

Two things are going on here. First, a large and largely irrelevant number is presented as if it helps set the context: "hundreds of billions of pages in our index." Juxtaposed against this vast number is a tiny one: "0.25 percent." But the hundreds-of-billions figure is largely irrelevant; it is the number of pages indexed, not anything about the number of search queries. It doesn't matter whether ten thousand or a hundred billion pages are indexed; if 0.25 percent of Google searches are misleading, you have a one-in-four-hundred chance of getting bullshit in your search results.*

We are not told how many search queries Google handles per day, but estimates place this figure at about 5.5 billion queries a day. So while 0.25 percent sounds small, it corresponds to well over thirteen million queries a day. These two ways of saying the same thing have very different connotations. If we tell you that Google is returning inappropriate search results only one time in four hundred, the system seems pretty sound. But if we tell you that more than thirteen million queries return inappropriate and inaccurate content every day, it sounds as though we are facing a serious crisis in information delivery.

Percentages can be particularly slippery when we use them to compare two quantities. We typically talk about percentage differences: "a 40 percent increase," "22 percent less fat," etc. But what is this a percentage *of*? The lower value? The higher value? This distinction matters. In the month of December 2017, the value of the bitcoin digital currency first surged to $19,211 per unit on the seventeenth of the month, and then plummeted to a low of $12,609 per unit thirteen days later. This is a decrease of $6,602 per unit. But what was the percentage change? Should we say it was 34 percent (because $6,602 is 34.3 percent of $19,221), or is it 52 percent (because $6,602 is 52.4 percent of $12,609)?

---

* The 0.25 percent figure is probably an underestimate when it comes to misinformation and disinformation in the news. We don't expect a lot of misinformation in response to queries such as "molecular weight of sodium" or "late night pizza delivery near me." Misinformation about health and politics and matters of that sort must occur more than 0.25 percent of the time in order to generate an overall average of 0.25 percent.

One can make a legitimate case for either number. In general, we advocate that a percentage change be reported with respect to the starting value. In this case the starting value was $19,211, so we say bitcoin lost 34 percent of its value over those thirteen days. This can be a subtle issue, however. One would say that bitcoin lost 34 percent of its value over this period, because when we talk about a loss in value, the starting value is the appropriate comparison. But we would also say that bitcoin was apparently overvalued by 52 percent at the start of December 2017, because when we talk about something being overvalued, the appropriate baseline for comparison is our current best estimate of value. Different ways of reporting give different impressions.

Instead of listing percentage changes, studies in health and medicine often report relative risks. New drivers aged sixteen and seventeen years have some of the highest accident rates on the road. But their accident rates depend on whether they are carrying passengers, and on whom those passengers are. Compared to teen drivers without passengers, the relative risk of a teen driver dying in a crash, per mile driven, is 1.44 for teens carrying a single passenger under the age of twenty-one. This relative risk value simply tells us how likely something is compared to an alternative. Here we see that teen drivers with a young passenger are 1.44 times as likely to be killed as teen drivers without a passenger. This is easily converted to a percentage value. A teen driver with a passenger has a 44 percent higher chance of being killed than a teen driver without a passenger. Carrying an older passenger has the opposite effect on the risk of fatal crashes. Compared to teen drivers without passengers, the relative risk of a teen driver dying in a crash while carrying a passenger over the age of thirty-five is 0.36. This means that the rate of fatal crashes is only 36 percent as high when carrying an older passenger as it is when driving alone.

Relative risks can help conceptualize the impact of various conditions, behaviors, or health treatments. But they sometimes fail to provide adequate context. A worldwide study of alcohol-related disease was reported with stark headlines such as "There's 'No Safe Level of Alcohol,' Major New Study Concludes." In particular, even very modest drinking—a single drink a day—was found to have negative health consequences. That sounds bad for those of us who enjoy a beer or glass of wine with dinner. But let's look more closely.

The press release from *The Lancet,* where the study was published, reports that:

They estimate that, for one year, in people aged 15–95 years, drinking one alcoholic drink a day increases the risk of developing one of the 23 alcohol-related health problems by 0.5%, compared with not drinking at all.

Scary stuff? To evaluate whether this is a substantial increase or not, we need to know how common are "alcohol-related health problems"—liver cirrhosis, various cancers, some forms of heart disease, self-harm, auto accidents, and other maladies—among nondrinkers. It turns out that these problems are rare among nondrinkers, occurring in less than 1 percent of the nondrinking population in a year. And while a drink per day increases this risk by 0.5 percent, that is 0.5 percent *of the very small baseline rate.* In other words, the relative risk of having one drink a day is 1.005. People who have a drink a day are 1.005 times as likely to suffer "alcohol-related disease" as those who do not drink.

The authors of the study calculated that having a single daily drink would lead to four additional cases of alcohol-related illness per 100,000 people. You would have to have 25,000 people consume one drink a day for a year in order to cause a single additional case of illness. Now the risk of low-level drinking doesn't sound as severe. To provide further perspective, David Spiegelhalter computed the amount of gin that those 25,000 people would drink over the course of the year: 400,000 bottles. Based on this number, he quipped that it would take 400,000 bottles of gin shared across 25,000 people to cause a single additional case of illness.

To be fair, this is the risk from drinking one drink a day; the risk rises substantially for those who consume larger amounts. People who drink two drinks a day have a relative risk of 1.07 (7 percent higher than nondrinkers) and those who drink five drinks a day have a relative risk of 1.37. The main point is that simply reporting a relative risk of a disease isn't enough to assess the effect unless we also know the baseline rate of the disease.

Percentages get even more slippery when we are comparing one percentage figure to another. We can look at the numerical difference between two percentages, but we can also create a new percentage, reflecting the percentage difference between our percentage values. Even professional scientists sometimes mix up a subtle issue in this regard: the difference between *percentages* and *percentage points*. An example is by far the easiest way to illustrate the difference. Suppose that on January 1, the sales tax increases from 4 percent to 6 percent of the purchase price. This is an increase of 2 percentage points: 6% − 4% = 2%. But it is also an increase of 50 percent: The 6 cents that I now pay on the dollar is 50 percent more than the 4 cents I paid previously.

So the same change can be expressed in very different ways that give substantially different impressions. If I want to make the tax increase sound small, I can say that there has been only a 2 percentage point increase. If I want to make it sound large, I can say that taxes have gone up 50 percent. Whether accomplished by accident or intent, we need to be wary of this distinction.

Another example: On her website, an MD questions the utility of the influenza vaccine. Quoting the abstract of a medical review article,* she writes:

> In the "relatively uncommon" case where the vaccine matched the annual flu variety, the rate of influenza was 4% for the unvaccinated and 1% for the vaccinated, so 3 less people out of every 100 would become ill. In the more common scenario of vaccine/flu mis-match the corresponding numbers were 2% sick among unvaccinated [and] 1% of the vaccinated, thus 1 less person per 100.

Her argument appears to be that when mismatched, the influenza vaccine is near to useless because it reduces influenza cases by a mere one person per hundred per year. The MD goes on to say that in lieu of vaccination, "I have a new 'health tonic' this year which I will try out if I feel some illness approaching and let you know [if] it works."

---

* In addition to our other arguments about the value of the influenza vaccine, the 2 percent influenza attack rate cited here is surprisingly low. The CDC estimates that since 2010, influenza attack rates in the US have ranged from about 3 percent to 11 percent. Part of this discrepancy is explained by the fact that this review paper looks only at studies of adults aged eighteen to sixty-four, whereas influenza rates are much higher in children, and part may be due to the international nature of the studies reviewed. Influenza rates in the US are commonly estimated to be several times higher than 2 percent even in adults.

Does that sound reasonable? If we think of the flu vaccine as helping only one person in a hundred, it may seem that some unspecified "health tonic" could perform as well. But the claim is misleading. First, notice that even in these years when the influenza vaccine is ineffective, it cuts the number of influenza cases among vaccinated individuals in half. Because influenza is relatively infrequent in the population, a 1 *percentage point* decrease in incidence corresponds to a 50 *percent* decrease.

Second, we can put these numbers into context with a well-chosen comparison. Like influenza vaccines in an ineffective year, the use of seatbelts drops the annual risk of injury from "only" about 2 percent to 1 percent.* Would you trust your health to an MD who advocated a "health tonic" in lieu of seatbelts?

Reporting numbers as percentages can obscure important changes in net values. For example, the US incarcerates African Americans at a shockingly high rate relative to members of other groups. African Americans are more than five times as likely as whites to be in jail or prison. In the year 2000, African Americans composed 12.9 percent of the US population but a staggering 41.3 percent of the inmates in US jails. Given that, it would seem to be good news that between the year 2000 and the year 2005, the fraction of the jail population that was African American declined from 41.3 percent to 38.9 percent.

But the real story isn't as encouraging as the percentage figures seem to indicate. Over this period, the number of African Americans in US jails actually *increased* by more than 13 percent. But this increase is obscured by the fact that over the same period, the number of Caucasians in US jails increased by an even larger fraction: 27 percent.

This is an example of a more general issue with comparisons that involve fractions or percentages: Changing denominators obscure changes in numerators. The numerator—the top part of the fraction, here the number of jailed African Americans—increased substantially from 2000 to 2005. But the denominator—the bottom part of the fraction, here the total number of jailed Americans—increased by an

---

* The National Safety Council estimates that in 2016, there were approximately 4.6 million injuries from automobile accidents that required medical consultation or treatment, corresponding to about 1.4 percent of the US population. The National Highway Traffic Safety Administration estimates that wearing a seatbelt reduces the risk of moderate to critical injury by 50 percent to passengers traveling in the front seat of a passenger car, and by even greater amounts to passengers traveling in light trucks.

even larger proportion over the same period. As a result, African Americans made up a smaller fraction of the incarcerated population in 2005 than they did in 2000. The fact that in 2005 more African Americans were locked up than ever before is obscured by this changing denominator.

Changing denominators wreak havoc on percentages. Consider the following. If the Dow Jones Industrial Average should rise by 10 percent today and then fall 10 percent tomorrow, you might think that it would end up right where it started—but it won't. Suppose the Dow is at 20,000. A 10 percent increase takes it up 2,000 points to 22,000. A subsequent 10 percent decrease, relative to its new higher value of 22,000, drops it 2,200 points to 19,800. It doesn't matter whether it rises and then drops or vice versa; you lose either way. If the Dow starts at 20,000 and loses 10 percent, it falls to 18,000. A 10 percent increase then takes it up to 19,800—the same place it ended up when it rose first and fell second. Be on the lookout for these kinds of perverse consequences of reporting data in terms of percentage changes.

Let's consider more of the strange ways that percentages can behave. In late April 2016, Uber was delivering about 161,000 rides per day in New York City while Lyft was delivering about 29,000 a day. A year later, Uber was delivering 291,000 rides per day and Lyft about 60,000 rides per day. This was an overall increase of 161,000 rides per day, from 190,000 rides per day to 351,000 rides per day. Of those 161,000 extra rides, Lyft contributed about 31,000 of them. Thus Lyft is responsible for about 16 percent of the increase, and Uber for the rest. So far so good.

Over the same period, the number of yellow taxi rides plummeted from 398,000 per day to 355,000. If we look at the total number of rides by yellow taxi, Uber, or Lyft, we see a net increase, from 588,000 to 696,000. That's a net increase of 108,000 rides per day. We already know that Lyft increased its rides by 31,000 per day over this period. So it looks like we could say that Lyft is responsible for 31,000 / 108,000 × 100 = 29% of the increase in overall rides.

But that is odd. We said Lyft is responsible for about 24 percent of the increase in rides that ride-hailing services provide, but now we're saying that Lyft responsible for about 34 percent of the increase in rides by ride-hailing *or* taxi. How could both things be true? Things get even weirder if we look at Uber's contribution to this increase in rides. Uber provided an extra 383,000 rides per day by the end of this period. We could say that the increase in Uber rides is responsible for 130,000 / 108,000 × 100 = 120% of the increase in total rides. What does that even mean? How could the Uber increase account for more than 100 percent of the total increase?

Percentage calculations can give strange answers when any of the numbers involved are negative. In general, if we can break the change down into different categories, and any of those categories decrease, we should not talk about percentage contributions to the total change. This is how Governor Scott Walker was able to claim in June 2011 that 50 percent of the nation's job growth had occurred in his home state of Wisconsin. What had actually happened was that a number of US states lost jobs overall, while others gained. These changes nearly balanced out, leaving a net change of only about 18,000 jobs. Wisconsin's net growth of 9,500 jobs was over half the size of the country's net growth, even though only a small fraction of the total jobs created in the country were created in Wisconsin.

GOODHART'S LAW

When scientists measure the molecular weights of the elements, the elements do not conspire to make themselves heavier and connive to sneak down the periodic table. But when administrators measure the productivity of their employees, they cannot expect these people to stand by idly: Employees want to look good. As a result, every time you quantify performance or rank individuals, you risk altering the behaviors you are trying to measure.

At the turn of the twentieth century, Vietnam was a part of the French colonies collectively known as French Indochina. Hanoi was developing into a prosperous modern city, and its sewer system provided European-style sanitation, mainly for the wealthy white neighborhoods around the city. Unfortunately, the sewer system also provided an ideal breeding ground for rats, which not only emerged from the sewers to terrorize the inhabitants but also spread diseases such as the bubonic plague. In an effort to rid the city of these pests, the colonial bureaucracy hired rat catchers to go into the sewers, and eventually offered a bounty on the creatures, paying a small reward for each rat tail delivered to the colonial offices. Many of the inhabitants of Hanoi were pleased to be a part of this enterprise, and rat tails started pouring in.

Before long, however, the inhabitants of Hanoi started to see tail-less rats skulking in the sewers. Apparently, the rat hunters preferred not to kill their prey. Better to slice off the tail for bounty and leave the rats to reproduce, guaranteeing a steady supply of tails in the future. Entrepreneurs imported rats from other cities, and even began raising rats in captivity to harvest their tails. The bounty program failed because people did what people always do at the prospect of a reward: They start gaming the system.

The same thing happens even when you aren't offering rewards directly. Take college rankings such as the one compiled by *U.S. News & World Report*. This survey accounts for numerous aspects of colleges, including the acceptance rates for applicants and the average SAT scores of the incoming classes. Once these college rankings began to influence the number of applicants, admissions departments started to play the angles. To lower their acceptance rates and thereby appear more selective, some schools aggressively recruited applications, even from students unlikely to be admitted. Many schools switched to the common application so that candidates could apply by simply checking a box. To get credit for teaching small classes, some universities capped many class sizes at eighteen or nineteen—just below the *U.S. News & World Report* class-size cutoff of twenty. To lift their average SAT scores, schools employed a range of stratagems: not requiring SAT for international applicants who typically have lower scores, bringing in lower-scoring students in the spring semester when their scores are not counted, or even paying admitted students to retake the SAT, with bonuses for substantive increases in score. These efforts to game the system undercut the value of the rankings. The rankings ended up being influenced as much by admissions departments' willingness to chase metrics as they did by the quality of schools' applicants.

This problem is canonized in a principle known as Goodhart's law. While Goodhart's original formulation is a bit opaque,* anthropologist Marilyn Strathern rephrased it clearly and concisely:

---

* Goodhart originally expressed his law as: "Any observed statistical regularity will tend to collapse once pressure is placed upon it for control purposes."

When a measure becomes a target, it ceases to be a good measure.

In other words, if sufficient rewards are attached to some measure, people will find ways to increase their scores one way or another, and in doing so will undercut the value of the measure for assessing what it was originally designed to assess.

We see this in any number of domains. In the sciences, the use of citation metrics to measure journal quality has led editors to game the system. Some pressure authors to include citations to papers in the same journal. Some publish an excess of articles in January, when they have the most time to be cited during the year. Others publish annual summary papers that cite many of the articles published within a year; yet others shift their focus to disciplines or types of articles that tend to attract more citations. All of these perverse behaviors undermine the mission of the journals and the effectiveness of citation measures as indicators of quality.

When the manager of an auto dealership provides bonuses to salespeople for hitting certain volume targets, the sales force will have incentives to offer larger discounts to their customers, in order to make the sale quickly. If salespeople were trying to maximize profits in making each sale, one might be able to use the number of cars sold to approximate how much money each salesperson brings in. But once the number of cars sold becomes a target, salespeople alter their sales strategies, more cars will be sold, and yet more cars sold will not necessarily correspond to higher profits as salespeople offer bigger discounts to make sales and make them quickly.

At around the same time that Goodhart proposed his law, psychologist Donald Campbell independently proposed an analogous principle:

The more any quantitative social indicator is used for social decision-making, the more subject it will be to corruption pressures and the more apt it will be to distort and corrupt the social processes it is intended to monitor.

Campbell illustrated his principle with the case of standardized testing in education:

Achievement tests may well be valuable indicators of general school achievement under conditions of normal teaching aimed at general competence. But when test scores become the goal of the teaching process, they both lose their value as indicators of educational status and distort the educational process in undesirable ways.

If no one knew that you were going to evaluate schools by looking at test scores of students, test scores might provide a reasonable way of measuring schools' effectiveness. But once teachers and administrators recognize that test scores will be used to evaluate their effectiveness, they have every incentive to find ways of raising their students' scores—even at the expense of the quality of their education. They may "teach to the test," for example, rather than teaching critical thinking. The consequences are twofold. Once this happens, test scores lose much of their value as a means of assessing a school's performance. The process of measurement may even actively undermine the quality of education, as time and effort are shifted away from valuable activity and toward the kind of memorization that improves test scores but is nearly useless from an educational perspective.

The same problem occurs in the sciences as well. A few years back, Jevin penned a commentary about the dangers of using quantitative metrics to measure the quality of scientific research. Getting the wrong answer is not the worst thing a metric can do. It's much worse to provide people with incentives to do bad science.

Campbell stresses the social element of this problem. As we mentioned at the start of this section, we don't have to worry about the laws of physics or chemistry gaming the metrics. Hydrogen doesn't care what you think its emission spectra are, or that its highest wavelength band is lower than that of helium. People do care about how they are measured. What can we do about this? If you are in the position to measure something, think about whether measuring it will change people's behaviors in ways that undermine the value of your results. If you are looking at quantitative indicators that others have compiled, ask yourself: Are these numbers measuring what they are intended to measure? Or are people gaming the system and rendering this measure useless?

MATHINESS

Online voters selected *truthiness* as the word of the year in a 2006 survey run by the publishers of the *Merriam-Webster* dictionary. The term, coined in 2005 by comedian Stephen Colbert, is defined as "the quality of seeming to be true according to one's intuition, opinion, or perception without regard to logic, factual evidence, or the like." In its disregard for actual logic and fact, this hews pretty closely to our definition of bullshit.

We propose an analogous expression, *mathiness*. Mathiness refers to formulas and expressions that may look and feel like math—even as they disregard the logical coherence and formal rigor of actual mathematics.

Let's begin with an example. The following formula, known as the VMMC Quality Equation, is apparently much discussed in the area of healthcare quality management.

$$Q = A \times \frac{O + S}{W}$$

Q: Quality
A: Appropriateness
O: Outcomes
S: Service
W: Waste

This looks like a rigorous mathematical way to consider patient care. But what does it actually mean? How would these quantities be measured, and in what units? Why does it take the form that it does? It is not clear whether any of these questions have satisfying answers.

We see mathiness as classic bullshit in the vein of our original definition. These equations make mathematical claims that cannot be supported by positing formal relationships—variables interacting multiplicatively or additively, for example—between ill-defined and impossible-to-measure quantities. In other words, mathiness, like truthiness and like bullshit, involves a disregard for logic or factual accuracy. Also, as in our definition of bullshit, mathiness is often produced for the purpose of impressing or persuading an audience, trading on the air of rigor conferred by mathematical equations, and throwing in a healthy dose of algebraic shock and awe for good measure. (We don't mean to attribute malice; some snake oil salesmen believe in the restorative powers of their tonics, and some peddlers of mathiness may think they are providing deep insights.)

Most examples of mathiness are not made up at random. Rather, they are designed to express basic truths about a given system. For example, the VMMC Quality Equation represents the idea that higher levels of Appropriateness, Outcomes, and Service all lead to higher Quality, whereas greater Waste decreases Quality.* This information could equally well be expressed in a simple table:

PARAMETER	EFFECT ON QUALITY
Appropriateness	+
Outcomes	+
Service	+
Waste	−

All of this is implied by the Quality Equation, but there are many other equations that have the same properties. The formula $Q = S \times \frac{O + A}{W}$ also reflects the qualitative relationship shown in this table, as does $Q = (A + O) \times S - W$. For that matter, so does $Q = {}^{W}\sqrt{A^O + S^O}$. If one is not able to explain why the VMMC Equation is $Q = A \times \frac{O + S}{W}$ and not any of these alternatives, the relationship should not be dignified with an equation in the first place.

The so-called Trust Equation, laid out in a 2005 book of the same title, provides us with another illustration of mathiness. According to the Trust Equation,

$$\text{Trust} = \frac{\text{Credibility} + \text{Reliability} + \text{Authenticity}}{\text{Perception of self-interest}}$$

As with the VMMC Equation, the general direction of the relationships seems right. Trust increases with credibility, reliability, and

---

* In more technical language, we suspect that equations with false mathiness are typically intended to express something about the signs of the partial derivatives of a function, to an audience not necessarily used to thinking about partial derivatives. For example, the main information in the VMMC Equation is probably that Quality can be represented as a function $Q = f(A, O, S, W)$ with $df/dA > 0$, $df/dO > 0$, $df/dS > 0$, and $df/dW < 0$. Beyond that, the functional form may be largely arbitrary.

authenticity, and decreases with perception of self-interest. So far, so good. But again there are any number of other equations that work this way as well. And the Trust Equation has some very specific implications for how trust works. Perhaps the strongest of these occurs because the sum of the other terms is *divided* by the perception of self-interest. This means that (provided the sum of the other terms is positive), the degree of trust becomes very large as the perception of self-interest gets very small. If one could eliminate the perception of self-interest entirely, trust should be infinitely strong! But the world doesn't work like that. Suppose I flip a coin to tell me what stock to buy. The coin is inarguably free from self-interest, so according to the equation I should trust it infinitely. In reality, why would I trust a random device rather than an expert predictor?

Second, notice that credibility, reliability, and authenticity are added together in the top part of the equation. That means that no matter how big or small credibility, reliability, and authenticity are, a one-unit increase in reliability has the same effect as a one-unit increase in authenticity. It also means that trust can be high even if one or two of these quantities is zero. If authenticity is high and perceived self-interest is low, the equation predicts that trust should be high even when the speaker has no credibility and is entirely unreliable. Again, this seems like an unintended consequence of expressing some general trends as a specific formula in order to create the perception of mathiness.

A somewhat more technical matter is the issue of units. Readers may remember learning dimensional analysis in high school. This is the process of tracking the units in a calculation to make sure that one's answer is in the right currency.

For example,* if a cyclist goes 45 miles in 3 hours, we don't just divide 45 by 3 and say that her speed is 15; we need to state the units of measurement. We treat the units much as we treat the numbers themselves, writing them out and simplifying, if necessary: 45 miles / 3 hours = 15 miles/hour.

We all know that the numerical values on each side of an equation

---

* A slightly more complicated example: In the Guinness Gastropod Championship, a snail covered a 13-inch course in 140 seconds. How fast was it going?

$$\frac{13 \text{ in.}}{140 \text{ sec.}} \times \frac{1 \text{ ft.}}{12 \text{ in.}} \times \frac{1 \text{ mile}}{5280 \text{ ft.}} \times \frac{60 \text{ sec.}}{1 \text{ min.}} \times \frac{60 \text{ min.}}{1 \text{ hr.}} = 0.0053 \text{ mile/hr.}$$

have to be the same. The key to dimensional analysis is that the units have to be the same as well. This provides a convenient way to keep careful track of units when making calculations in engineering and other quantitative disciplines, to make sure one is computing what one thinks one is computing.

When an equation exists only for the sake of mathiness, dimensional analysis often makes no sense. Let's look at an example. Every January, news outlets run or rerun a story about how scientists have found that "Blue Monday"—the third Monday of the month—is the saddest day of the year. This claim, advanced in various press releases, is based upon a formula proposed by a part-time tutor at Cardiff University named Cliff Arnall:

$$\frac{(W \,+\, D - d) * T^Q}{M * N_a}$$

The press release explains that W represents the weather, d debt, T time since Christmas, Q time since abandoning New Year's resolutions, M low levels of motivation, and N_a the need to take action. (It is unclear what D represents in the formula.)

By now you may be able to pick this example apart. For starters, it is unclear how "weather," "low levels of motivation," or "the need to take action" would be quantified. It gets worse. Any quantities that are added or subtracted have to be in the same units. We can't sensibly add miles and hours, for example, let alone mental exertion and Reuben sandwiches. But look at the Blue Monday equation. The first term, $(W + D - d)$, is presumably some sort of difference between weather and debt. What units could possibly apply to both quantities? Another rule is that when you raise a quantity to a power, that power has to be a dimensionless number. It makes sense to talk about time raised to the power of two, but not about time raised to the power of two milliseconds or two parakeets. But Q is not dimensionless; it is in units of time—and thus the expression T^Q makes no sense. Even if we could resolve these issues, we would run into any number of problems already discussed. We might think that sadness should increase with the need to take action and with low levels of motivation, but both quantities are in the denominator, meaning that sadness decreases with the need to take action and with low levels of motivation.

Martin Seligman, former president of the American Psychological Association, developed a famous formula for happiness: $H = S + C + V$, where S is a "set point" representing one's innate predisposition toward happiness, C is one's circumstances, and V is those aspects of life under voluntary control. Again, think about units. Even if set point, circumstances, and aspects under voluntary control were quantifiable, what could be the common unit in which all three are measured? And even if such a common unit exists, would this also be the appropriate unit to measure happiness, as implied by the equation? If Seligman had claimed that happiness *was a function* of S, C, and V, we might have been willing to go along. But to claim that it is the *mathematical sum* of these three quantities is an exercise in mathiness.

Perhaps we aren't supposed to take this equation-building approach literally. Why can't we use these equations as a metaphor or a mode of expression? Mathematical equations are useful precisely for their precision of expression—but all of these examples fail to deliver this precision. You make a false promise when you suggest that happiness is an arithmetic sum of three things, if all you mean is that it increases with each of them. It is like promising chia-seed-and-spelt waffles sweetened with wildflower honey; topped with blackberry compote, a lingonberry reduction, and house-whipped sweet cream—but delivering an Eggo with artificial maple syrup. You can claim your description wasn't meant to be taken literally, but why not say what you mean in the first place?

We do not know why so many writers are prone to invent equations that layer a veneer of mathiness atop their qualitative arguments. Obviously it impresses some of the people, some of the time, but why aren't these authors embarrassed to be caught out by the rest of us? Perhaps without a clear understanding of everything a mathematical equation entails, they fail to see the scale at which their faux equations underdeliver.

ZOMBIE STATISTICS

We close this chapter with a cautionary note. Look in sufficiently nerdy corners of the Internet, and you can find T-shirts, coffee mugs, mouse pads, and any number of other paraphernalia emblazoned with a slogan along the lines of "78.4% of statistics are made up on the spot." The precise number varies—53.2 percent, 72.9 percent, 78.4 percent, 84.3 percent—but the joke, of course, is that this particular statistic is among the made-up numbers it purports to describe.

Like most good jokes, this quip carries an element of truth. Without knowing the source and context, a particular statistic is worth little. Yet numbers and statistics appear rigorous and reliable simply by virtue of being quantitative, and have a tendency to spread. And as a result, there are a lot of *zombie statistics* out there. Zombie statistics are numbers that are cited badly out of context, are sorely outdated, or were entirely made up in the first place—but they are quoted so often that they simply won't die.

By way of example: We both spend a good deal of time studying the way that scientists make use of the scientific literature. Not a month goes by without someone repeating to us an old trope that 50 percent of scientific articles are never read by anyone. But where does this "50 percent" figure come from? No one seems to know.

Management professor Arthur Jago became curious about this number and set out to verify it. Jago first saw the claim, unsupported by any citation, in a *Chronicle of Higher Education* commentary. The author of that commentary pointed him to an article in *Smithsonian*. The citation given for this claim in *Smithsonian* was incorrect, but Jago was able to track it to a 2007 article in *Physics World*. The author of that article did not have a citation; the figure had been added by a journal editor late in the publication process. This editor, once reached, thought he perhaps got the material from a set of 2001 course notes. The instructor who wrote those course notes did not have a citation and provided only the unencouraging remark that "everything in those notes had a source, but whether I cross-checked them all before banging the notes out, I doubt."

Though this trail went dead, eventually Jago tracked the 50 percent statistic back to a pair of papers published in 1990 and 1991 in the journal *Science*. The original claim was that over 50 percent of papers go *uncited,* not unread. It's a big difference; a paper may be accessed in the library or downloaded from the Internet hundreds of times for every citation it receives.

Even with this correction, the 50 percent figure is inaccurate. First, this number represents the fraction of papers uncited after four years, not the fraction that will remain uncited forever. In some fields, such as mathematics, citations scarcely begin to accrue after four years. Second, this statistic is derived by looking at citation records in the Clarivate Web of Science. That database covers only a subset of journals, varies widely in how thoroughly it covers different fields, and does not index some of the most important types of publications—books in the humanities and conference proceedings in engineering. Third, to arrive at the 50 percent figure, the author considered citations to all types of articles published in scientific journals, including letters to the editor, news articles, opinion pieces, book reviews, even obituaries and errata. Saying that many book reviews and obituaries are uncited is very different from saying that many scientific articles are uncited.

Although numerous scholars challenged the 50 percent figure, they failed to stop its spread. Even Eugene Garfield—the father of citation analysis and founder of the Science Citation Index that was used to arrive at this number—also attempted to correct the record. The horse was out of the barn, however, and there was no getting it back. Garfield was resigned to this, and he responded to the error pessimistically, quoting Peggy Thomasson and Julian C. Stanley:

> The uncritical citation of disputed data by a writer, whether it be deliberate or not, is a serious matter. Of course, knowingly propagandizing unsubstantiated claims is particularly abhorrent, but just as many naïve students may be swayed by unfounded assertions presented by a writer who is unaware of the criticisms. Buried in scholarly journals, critical notes are increasingly likely to be overlooked with the passage of time, while the studies to which they pertain, having been reported more widely, are apt to be rediscovered.

This quotation refers to any sort of unsubstantiated claim, but simple figures and statistics are particularly prone to this type of spread. They leave context behind, and whatever halfhearted caveats were initially in place become lost as source after source repeats the basic number with none of the background.

In this chapter, we have seen that although numbers may seem to be pure facts that exist independently from any human judgment, they are heavily laden with context and shaped by decisions—from how they are calculated to the units in which they are expressed. In the next chapter we will look at some of the ways that *collections* of numbers are assembled and interpreted—and how such interpretations can be misleading. Without digging into any of the formal mathematics, we will explore the problems associated with picking a representative sample to study. We will look at how unrepresentative samples lead to unjustified conclusions, and can even be used by disingenuous authors to mislead their audiences.

CHAPTER 6

Selection Bias

W E ARE BOTH SKIERS, AND WE HAVE BOTH SPENT OUR SHARE of time in the Wasatch mountains outside of Salt Lake City, Utah, enjoying some of the best snow on the planet. The perfect Utah powder even factored into the choice that one of us made about what college to attend. A number of ski resorts are situated in the Wasatch mountains, and each resort has its own personality. Snowbird rises out of Little Cottonwood Canyon, splayed out in steel and glass and concrete, its gondola soaring over sheer cliffs to a cirque from which terrifyingly steep chutes drop away. Farther up the canyon, Alta has equally challenging terrain, even better snow, and feels lost in time. Its lodges are simple wooden structures and its lifts are bare-bones; it is one of three remaining resorts in the country that won't allow snowboarders. Start talking to a fellow skier at a party or on an airplane or in a city bar, and the odds are that she will mention one or both of these resorts as among the best in North America.

In nearby Big Cottonwood Canyon, the resorts Brighton and Solitude have a very different feel. They are beautiful and well suited for the family and great fun to ski. But few would describe them as epic, and they're hardly destination resorts. Yet if you take a day off from Alta or Snowbird to ski at Solitude, something interesting happens. Riding the lifts with other skiers, the conversation inevitably turns to the relative merits of the local resorts. But at Solitude, unlike Alta or Snowbird—or anywhere else, really—people often mention Solitude as the best place to ski in the world. They cite the great snow, the mellow family atmosphere, the moderate runs, the absence of lift lines, the beauty of the surrounding mountains, and numerous other factors.

When Carl skied Solitude for the first time, at fifteen, he was so taken by this tendency that he mentioned it to his father as they inhaled burgers at the base lodge before taking the bus back to the city.

"I think maybe I underestimated Solitude," Carl told him. "I had a pretty good day here. There is some good tree skiing, and if you like groomed cruising . . .

"And I bet I didn't even find the best runs," Carl continued. "There must be some amazing lines here. Probably two-thirds of the people I talked to today like this place even more than Alta or Snowbird! That's huge praise."

Carl's father chuckled. "Why do you think they're skiing at Solitude?" he asked.

This was Carl's first exposure to the logic of selection effects. *Of course* when you ask people at Solitude where they like to ski, they will answer "Solitude." If they didn't like to ski at Solitude, they would be at Alta or Snowbird or Brighton instead. The superlatives he'd heard in praise of Solitude that day were not randomly sampled from among the community of US skiers. Skiers at Solitude are not a representative sample of US skiers; they are skiers who could just as easily be at Alta or Snowbird and choose not to be. Obvious as that may be in this example, this basic principle is a major source of confusion and misunderstanding in the analysis of data.

In the third chapter of this book, we introduced the notion of statistical tests or data science algorithms as *black boxes* that can serve to conceal bullshit of various types. We argued that one can usually see this bullshit for what it is without having to delve into the fine details of how the black box itself works. In this chapter, the black boxes we will be considering are statistical analyses, and we will consider some of the common problems that can arise with the data that is fed into these black boxes.

Often we want to learn about the individuals in some group. We might want to know the incomes of families in Tucson, the strength of bolts from a particular factory in Detroit, or the health status of American high school teachers. As nice as it would be to be able to look at every single member of the group, doing so would be expensive if not outright infeasible. In statistical analysis, we deal with this problem by investigating small samples of a larger group and using that information to make broader inferences. If we want to know how many eggs are laid by nesting bluebirds, we don't have to look in every bluebird nest in the country. We can look at a few dozen nests and make a pretty good estimate from what we find. If we want to know how people are going to vote on an upcoming ballot measure, we don't need to ask every registered voter what they are thinking; we can survey a sample of voters and use that information to predict the outcome of the election.

The problem with this approach is that *what you see depends on where you look*. To draw valid conclusions, we have to be careful to ensure that the group we look at is a random sample of the population. People who shop at organic markets are more likely to have liberal political leanings; gun show attendees are more likely to be conservative. If we conduct a survey of voters at an organic grocery store—or at a gun show—we are likely to get a misleading impression of sentiments citywide.

We also need to think about whether the results we get are influenced by the act of sampling itself. Individuals being interviewed for a psychology study may give different answers depending on whether the interviewer is a man or a woman, for example. We run into this effect if we try to use the voluminous data from the Internet to understand aspects of social life. Facebook's autocomplete feature provides a quick, if informal, way to get a sense of what people are talking about on the social media platform. How healthy is the institution of marriage in 2019? Let's try a Facebook search query:

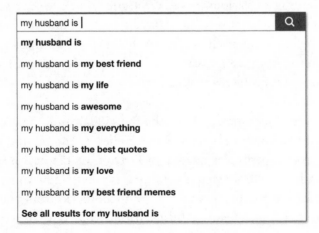

This paints a happy—if saccharine—picture. But on Facebook people generally try to portray their lives in the best possible light. The people who post about their husbands on Facebook may not be a random sample of married people; they may be the ones with happy marriages. And what people write on Facebook may not be a reliable indicator of their happiness. If we type the same query into Google and let Google's autocomplete feature tell us about contemporary matrimony, we see something very different:

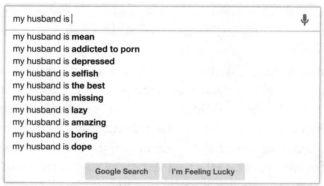

Yikes! At least "the best," "amazing," and "dope" (as opposed to "a dope") make the top ten. It seems that people turn to Google when looking for help, and turn to Facebook when boasting about their lives. What we find depends on where we look.

We should stress that a sample does not need to be completely random in order to be useful. It just needs to be random *with respect to whatever we are asking about.* Suppose we take an election poll based on only those voters whose names appear in the first ten pages of the phone book. This is a highly nonrandom sample of people. But unless having a name that begins with the letter *A* somehow correlates with political preference, our sample is random with respect to the question we are asking: How are you going to vote in the upcoming election?*

---

* Simply surveying people who are listed in the phone book can be a problem as well. Doing so excludes people who do not have landlines and people who have unlisted numbers. Moreover, those who take the time to answer a telephone survey may differ systematically from those who screen

Then there is the issue of how broadly we can expect a study's findings to apply. When can we extrapolate what we find from one population to other populations? One aim of social psychology is to uncover universals of human cognition, yet a vast majority of studies in social psychology are conducted on what Joe Henrich and colleagues have dubbed WEIRD populations: Western, Educated, Industrialized, Rich, and Democratic. Of these studies, most are conducted on the cheapest, most convenient population available: college students who have to serve as study subjects for course credit.

How far can we generalize based on the results of such studies? If we find that American college students are more likely to engage in violent behavior after listening to certain kinds of music, we need to be cautious about extrapolating this result to American retirees or German college students, let alone people in developing countries or members of traditional societies.

You might think that basic findings about something like visual perception should apply across demographic groups and cultures. Yet they do not. Members of different societies vary widely in their susceptibility to the famous Müller-Lyer illusion, in which the direction of arrowheads influences the apparent length of a line. The illusion has by far the strongest effect on American undergraduates.* Other groups see little or no difference in the apparent line length.

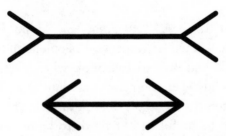

Again, where you look determines what you see.

their calls or hang up on the interviewer. As such, any form of sampling from a phone book may substantially undercount certain demographic groups including younger people and some minorities. This specific issue has become a major problem for telephone polling. Pollsters increasingly use cell phone interviews, but this approach comes with its own suite of problems.

* The reason that US undergraduates are most susceptible to the illusion is not well understood. One hypothesis notes that sharp, regular corners as in the arrowheads are relatively uncommon in nature. Perhaps the strength of the perceptual response to the arrowheads depends on the degree to which one has grown up in an environment with "carpentered corners." We are not sold, but we don't have a better explanation.

WHAT YOU SEE DEPENDS ON WHERE YOU LOOK

If you study one group and assume that your results apply to other groups, this is extrapolation. If you think you are studying one group, but do not manage to obtain a representative sample of that group, this is a different problem. It is a problem so important in statistics that it has a special name: *selection bias*. Selection bias arises when the individuals that you sample for your study differ systematically from the population of individuals eligible for your study.

For example, suppose we want to know how often students miss class sessions at the University of Washington. We survey the students in our Calling Bullshit class on a sunny Friday afternoon in May. The students' responses indicate that they miss, on average, two classes per semester. This seems implausibly low, given that our course is filled to capacity and yet only about two-thirds of the seats are occupied on any given day. So are our students lying to us? Not necessarily. The students who are answering our question are not a random sample of eligible individuals—all students in our class—*with respect to the question we are asking*. If they weren't particularly diligent in their attendance, the students in our sample wouldn't have been sitting there in the classroom while everyone else was outside soaking up the Friday afternoon sunshine.

Selection bias can create misleading impressions. Think about the ads you see for auto insurance. "New GEICO customers report average annual savings over $500" on car insurance. This sounds pretty impressive, and it would be easy to imagine that this means that *you* will save $500 per year by switching to GEICO.

But then if you look around, many other insurance agencies are running similar ads. Allstate advertisements proclaim that "drivers who switched to Allstate saved an average of $498 per year." Progressive claims that customers who switched to them saved over $500. Farmers claims that their insured who purchase multiple policies save an average of $502. Other insurance companies claim savings figures upward of $300. How can this be? How can all of the different agencies claim that switching to them saves a substantial amount of money? If some companies are cheaper than the competition, surely others must be more expensive.

The problem with thinking that you can save money by switching to GEICO (or Allstate, or Progressive, or Farmers) is that the people who switched to GEICO are nowhere near a random sample of customers in the market for automobile insurance. Think about it: What would it take to get you to go through the hassle of switching to GEICO (or any other agency)? You would have to save a substantial sum of money. People don't switch insurers in order to pay more!

Different insurance companies use different algorithms to determine your rates. Some weight your driving record more heavily; some put more emphasis on the number of miles you drive; some look at whether you store your car in a garage at night; others offer lower rates to students with good grades; some take into account the size of your engine; others offer a discount if you have antilock brakes and traction control. So when a driver shops around for insurance, she is looking for an insurer whose algorithms would lower her rates considerably. If she is already with the cheapest insurer for her personal situation, or if the other insurers are only a little cheaper, she is unlikely to switch. The only people who switch are those who will save big by doing so. And this is how all of the insurers can claim that those who switch to their policies save a substantial sum of money.

This is a classic example of selection bias. The people who switch to GEICO are not a random sample of insurance customers, but rather those who have the most to gain by switching. The ad copy could equivalently read, "Some people will see their insurance premiums go up if they switch to GEICO. Other people will see their premiums stay about the same. Yet others will see their premiums drop. Of these, a few people will see their premiums drop a lot. Of these who see a substantial drop, the average savings is $500." While accurate, you're unlikely to hear a talking reptile say something like this in a Super Bowl commercial.*

In all of these cases, the insurers presumably know that selection bias is responsible for the favorable numbers they are able to report. Smart consumers realize there is something misleading about the

---

* Your chances of finding a better deal on insurance appear not to be all that high. Only about one in three people shop for car insurance each year, and fewer than one-third of those shopping actually switch. Just because the average person who switches to Allstate saves $498, it doesn't mean that *you'll* save $498 by switching to Allstate. And just because almost every insurance company makes a similar claim, it doesn't mean that you'll save that kind of money if *you* switch. More likely, you'll end up being one of the majority of people who are unable to find a sufficiently compelling offer to justify a switch.

marketing, even if it isn't quite clear what that might be. But sometimes the insurance companies themselves can be caught unaware. An executive at a major insurance firm told us about one instance of selection bias that temporarily puzzled his team. Back in the 1990s, his employer was one of the first major agencies to sell insurance policies online. This seemed like a valuable market to enter early, but the firm's analytics team turned up a disturbing result about selling insurance to Internet-savvy customers. They discovered that individuals with email addresses were far more likely to have filed insurance claims than individuals without.

If the difference had been minor, it might have been tempting to assume it was a real pattern. One could even come up with any number of plausible *post hoc* explanations, e.g., that Internet users are more likely to be young males who drive more miles, more recklessly. But in this case, the difference in claim rates was huge. Our friend applied one of the most important rules for spotting bullshit: *If something seems too good or too bad to be true, it probably is.* He went back to the analytics team that found this pattern, told them it couldn't possibly be correct, and asked them to recheck their analysis. A week later, they reported back with a careful reanalysis that replicated the original result. Our friend still didn't believe it and sent them back to look yet again for an explanation.

This time they returned a bit sheepishly. The math was correct, they explained, but there was a problem with the data. The company did not solicit email addresses when initially selling a policy. The only time they asked for an email address was when someone was in the process of filing a claim. As a result, anyone who had an email address in the company's database had necessarily also filed a claim. People who used email were not more likely to file claims—but people who had filed claims were vastly more likely to have email addresses on file.

Selection effects appear everywhere, once you start looking for them. A psychiatrist friend of ours marveled at the asymmetry in how psychiatric disorders are manifested. "One in four Americans will suffer from excessive anxiety at some point," he explained, "but in my entire career I have only seen one patient who suffered from *too little* anxiety."

Of course! No one walks into their shrink's office and says "Doctor, you've got to help me. I lie awake night after night *not* worrying."

Most likely there are as many people with too little anxiety as there are with too much. It's just that they don't go in for treatment. Instead they end up in prison, or on Wall Street.

THE HIDDEN CAUSE OF MURPHY'S LAW

In Portugal, about 60 percent of families with children have only one child, but about 60 percent of children have siblings. This sounds impossible, but it's not. The picture below illustrates how this works. Out of twenty Portuguese families, we would expect to see about twelve with a single child, seven with two children, and one with three children. Thus most families are single-child, but because multi-child families each have multiple children, most children live in multi-child families.

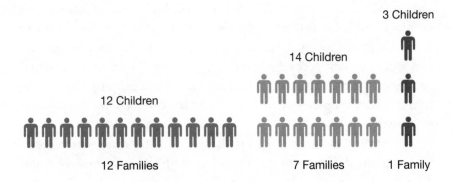

12 Children   14 Children   3 Children

12 Families   7 Families   1 Family

12/20 families have only one child
17/29 children have siblings

What does this have to do with bullshit? Universities boast about having small class sizes, but students often find these statistics hard to believe: "An average class size of 18? That's bullshit! In three years I've only had two classes with fewer than 50 students!"

Both the students and the university are right. How? This difference in perception arises because, just as multi-child families have a disproportionately large number of children, large classes serve a disproportionately large number of students. Suppose that in one semester, the biology department offers 20 classes with 20 students in each, and 4 classes with 200 students in each. Look at it from an administrator's perspective. Only 1 class in 6 is a large class. The mean class size is $[(20 \times 20) + (4 \times 200)] / 24 = 50$. So far so good.

But now notice that 800 students are taking 200-student classes and only 400 are taking 20-student classes. Five classes in six are small, but only one student in three is taking one of those classes. So if you ask a group of random students how big their classes are, the average of their responses will be approximately $[(800 \times 200) + (400 \times 20)] / 1{,}200 = 140$. We will call this the *experienced mean class size*,* because it reflects the class sizes that students actually experience.

Because larger classes contain more students, the average student is enrolled in a class that is larger than the average class. Institutions can exploit this distinction to promote their own agendas. A university recruiting pamphlet might proclaim, "The average biology class size is 50 students." The student government, lobbying for reduced class sizes, might report that "the average biology student is taking a class of 140." Neither is false, but they tell very different stories.

This principle explains why faculty are likely to have a different notion of class sizes than students do. If you wanted to know how big classes are, you might think you could ask either students or teachers and get the same answer. So long as everyone tells the truth, it shouldn't matter. But it does—a lot. Large or small, each class has one instructor. So if you sample instructors at random, you are likely to observe a large class or a small class in proportion to the frequency of such classes on campus. In our example above, there are more teachers teaching small classes. But large classes have many students and small classes have few, so if you sample students at random, students are more likely to be in large classes.†

Recall from chapter 5 Goodhart's law: "When a measure becomes

---

* Technically this is a weighted mean, albeit a curious one in which each value (class size) is weighed by that value itself.

† It is difficult to obtain exhaustive data on universities' course sizes, but Marquette University in Milwaukee provides a relatively fine-grained view, listing the number of courses of size 2–9, 10–19, 20–29, 30–39, 40–49, 50–99, and 100 or greater. We can use these data to estimate the gulf between average class size and experienced average class size at a midsize US institution. If we approximate the class sizes by the midpoints of the bins (and use 150 for the midpoint of the 100+ bin) we have the following class sizes (footnote continues on next page):

a target, it ceases to be a good measure." Class sizes provide an example. Every autumn, college and university administrators wait anxiously to learn their position in the *U.S. News & World Report* university rankings. A higher ranking improves the reputation of a school, which in turn draws applications from top students, increases alumni donations, and ultimately boosts revenue and reputation alike. It turns out that class size is a major ingredient in this ranking process, with a strong premium placed on small classes.

Schools receive the most credit in this index for their proportions of undergraduate classes with fewer than 20 students. Classes with 20 to 29 students score second highest, 30 to 39 students third highest and 40 to 49 students fourth highest. Classes that are 50 or more students receive no credit.

By summing up points across classes, the *U.S. News & World Report* ranking is rewarding schools that maximize the number of small classes they offer, rather than minimizing the experienced mean class size. Since the student experience is what matters, this may be a mistake. Consider the numerical example we provided earlier. The biology department in that example has 24 instructors and 1,200 students enrolled. Classes could be restructured so that each one has 50 students. In this case the experienced mean class size would plummet from 140 to 50, but the department would go from a good score to a bad score according to the *U.S. News & World Report* criterion.* To eliminate this perverse incentive for universities to pack most of their

Class size	5	15	25	35	45	75	150
Number of classes	101	318	197	59	66	28	22

Given this distribution of class sizes, the mean class size is about 26. But not from the students' perspective. Only 505 students are in 5-person classes, whereas 3,300 students are in 150-student classes. The experienced mean class size turns out to be approximately 51—nearly twice the mean class size.

* Or consider the data from Marquette University, as presented in the previous footnote. Marquette *could* improve its *U.S. News & World Report* ranking, without hiring additional instructors, by offering 726 "small" classes with 15 students each, and assigning the remaining students to 65 classes of 150 students each. In doing so it would go from its current impressive score of 61 percent small classes to an extraordinary 92 percent of small classes. Sounds good, right? But if Marquette chased the rankings in this way, they would substantially decrease the quality of the student experience, because a large number of students would be in 150-student classes and the experienced mean class size would climb from 51 to 73.

students into large classes, we suggest that the *U.S. News* ranking use experienced class size, rather than class size, in their calculations.

The same mathematical principles explain the curious fact that most likely, the majority of your friends have more friends than you do. This is not true merely because you are the kind of person who reads a book about bullshit for fun; it's true of anyone, and it's known as the friendship paradox. Understanding the friendship paradox is a bit more difficult than understanding the class size issue that we just treated, but a basic grasp of the problem should not be beyond reach. The sociologist Scott Feld, who first outlined this paradoxical result, explains it as follows. Suppose people have ten friends, on average. (We say ten rather than five hundred because Feld's paper was written in 1991, back when "friends" were people you actually had met in person—and often even liked.) Now suppose in your circle there is an introvert with five friends and a socialite with fifteen friends. Taken together they average ten friends each. But the socialite is friends with fifteen people and thus makes fifteen people feel insecure about how few friends they have, whereas the introvert is friends with only five and thus makes only five people feel better about themselves.

It's well and good to make intuitive arguments, but is the friendship paradox actually true in real life? Feld looked at a diagram of friendships among 146 adolescent girls, painstakingly collected three decades prior. He found while many of these girls had fewer friends than their friends, relatively few had more friends than their friends.

But this is just one sample of one group in one small town. We would like to address this question on a far broader scale, and in the social media age, researchers can do so. One team looked at 69 billion friendships among 720 million users on Facebook. They find, indeed, that most users have fewer friends than their friends. In fact, this is the case for 93 percent of Facebook users! Mind twisting, right? These researchers found that the Facebook users have, on average, 190 friends, but their friends have, on average, about 635 friends.

Subsequent studies have distinguished between a weak form and a strong form of the friendship paradox. The weak form pertains to the mean (average) number of friends that your friends have. The weak form is maybe not so surprising: Suppose you follow Rihanna and 499 other people on Twitter. Rihanna has over ninety million followers, so the 500 people you follow will average at the very least

90,000,000 / 500 = 180,000 followers—far more than you have. The strong form is more striking. It states that most people have fewer friends than their median friend has. In other words, order your friends by the number of friends they have. Pick the friend that is right in the middle. That friend likely has more friends than you do. This phenomenon can't be attributed to a single ultrapopular friend. The same research team found that the strong form holds on Facebook as well: 84 percent of Facebook users have fewer friends than the median friend count of their friends. Unless you are Kim Kardashian or someone of similar ilk, you are likely to be in the same situation.

You may find it disconcerting to realize that the same logic applies to your past sexual history. Chances are, the majority of your partners have slept with more people than you have.

Okay. Forget we mentioned that. Back to statistics. Selection effects like this one are sometimes known as *observation selection effects* because they are driven by an association between the very presence of the observer and the variable that the observer reports. In the class size example, if we ask *students* about the size of their classes, there is an association between the presence of the student observer and the class size. If instead we ask *teachers* about the sizes of their classes, there are no observation selection effects because each class has only one teacher—and therefore there is no association between the presence of a teacher in the classroom and the size of the class.

Observation selection effects explain some of what we typically attribute to bad luck. If you commute by bus on a regular basis, you have probably noticed that you often have to wait a surprisingly long time for the next bus to arrive. But what is considered a "long wait"? To answer this question, we need to compare your wait to the average waiting time. Suppose that buses leave a bus stop at regular ten minute intervals. If you arrive at an arbitrary time, how long do you expect to wait, on average? The answer: five minutes. Since you might arrive anywhere in the ten-minute window, a nine-minute wait is just as likely as a one-minute wait, an eight-minute wait is just as likely as a two-minute wait, and so on. Each pair averages out to five minutes. In general, when the buses run some number of minutes apart, your average waiting time will be half of that interval.

What happens if the city operates the same number of buses, so that buses leave every ten minutes *on average*—but traffic forces the buses to run somewhat irregularly? Sometimes the time between buses is quite short; other times it may extend for fifteen minutes or more. Now how long do you expect to wait? Five minutes might seem like a good guess again. After all, the same number of buses are running and the average time between buses is still ten minutes.

But the actual average time that you will wait is longer. If you were equally likely to arrive during any interval between buses, the differences in between-bus gaps would average out and your average waiting time would be five minutes, as before. But you are not equally likely to arrive during any interval. You are more likely to arrive during one of the long intervals than during one of the short intervals. As a result, you end up waiting longer than five minutes, on average.

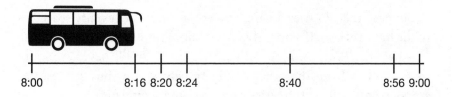

In the picture above, buses run every 10 minutes, on average, but they are clumped together so that some intervals are 16 minutes long and others are only 4 minutes long. You have an 80 percent chance of arriving during one of the long intervals, in which case you will wait 8 minutes on average. Only 20 percent of the time will you arrive during one of the short intervals and wait 2 minutes on average. Overall, your average wait time will be $(0.8 \times 8) + (0.2 \times 2) = 6.8$ minutes, substantially longer than the 5 minutes you would wait on average if the buses were evenly spaced.

So while it seems as though you tend to get unlucky with waiting times and wait longer than expected, it's not bad luck at all. It is just an observation selection effect. You are more likely to be present during a long between-bus interval, so you end up waiting and waiting.

Something similar happens at the airport when you are waiting for a hotel van, an airport parking bus, or a rental car shuttle. A few days after writing the section above, Carl and his daughter flew into Los

Angeles and waited to catch a rental car shuttle. They stood and watched as multiple shuttles from several other car rental companies drove past, but no sign of their shuttle. After a while, Carl's daughter complained about their bad luck—but it wasn't particularly bad luck. It was an observation selection effect. Here's the explanation he gave her on the LAX curb.

To keep things simple, let's just think about two rental car companies, yours and its main competitor.

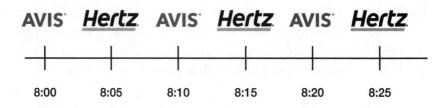

Suppose that shuttles for the two companies were evenly spaced as in the figure above. If you arrive at a random time, your bus will come first half the time, and second half the time. You'll never see more than one bus from the other company before your bus arrives. On average, you will see 0.5 buses from the other company.

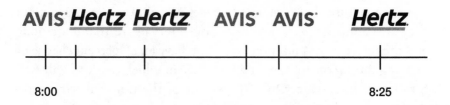

But now suppose that the buses are not spaced out regularly, and instead arrive at random times. Half the time your bus will arrive first, just as when the buses were staggered. But half the time, the other bus will arrive first. The key thing to notice is that if it does, you're back where you started right when you first arrived, with a one-half chance that your bus comes next and a one-half chance that *another* bus from the other company comes next. If the same number of buses are running but they arrive at completely random times, you will see an average of 1 bus from the other company instead of 0.5 buses. The same thing happens if there are many different rental car companies running shuttle buses. If *n* different companies run buses at the same rate, your bus will on average be the *n*th to arrive.* This feels like bad luck. "There are only eight rental car companies at this airport, and my bus was the eighth to arrive!" If your intuitions are based on the case where buses are spaced out evenly, this is twice as long a wait as you expect. As a result, you'll get the impression that your company runs only half as many buses as its competitors—no matter which company you choose.

Observation selection effects can also explain why, when driving on a congested four-lane highway, you so often seem to pick the slow lane. You might think that with two lanes to pick from, you ought to be able to pick the faster lane half of the time. Not so! On the highway, the faster cars are traveling, the greater the distance between them. If traffic is moving at different speeds in two adjacent lanes, the cars in the slower-moving lane are more tightly packed. When two lanes are going in the same direction but at different speeds, the majority of the cars on the road will be in the slower lane and the majority of drivers will be cursing their lane-picking luck.

---

* In slightly more technical language, we are referring to the case where buses for each company arrive according to the Poisson arrival process with the same arrival rate. The waiting time from when you arrive at the curb to when your bus comes is then exponentially distributed; the arrival times of the other companies' buses are also exponentially distributed with the same distribution of waiting times. The story about being right back where you started if the other bus arrives first can be expressed mathematically using *first-step analysis*. Suppose there are *n* different rental car companies, all running shuttles at the same frequency, and let *s* be the expected number of shuttles that pass before yours arrives. With probability $1/n$ your shuttle arrives first and then you see zero other shuttles. With probability $n-1 / n$ some other shuttle passes first, you've seen one shuttle so far, and then you are back right where you started. Therefore we can write $s = 0 \times (1/n) + (1+s) \times (n-1) / n$. Solving for *s*, we get $s = n-1$. If there are *n* shuttle companies, on average your bus will be the *n*th to arrive.

HOT GUYS AND TOP CODERS

Five years ago, engineers at Google applied machine learning techniques to their own hiring process, in an effort to identify the most productive employees. They found a surprising result: Job performance was negatively correlated with prior success in programming contests. This could be because people who are good at programming contests have other attributes that make them less than ideal as employees. Google research director Peter Norvig conjectured that perhaps contest winners are used to working quickly, whereas a slower pace is more effective on the job. But we should not rush to that conclusion. Instead, this negative correlation between programming contest results and job performance could have something to do with the fact that these employees are far from a random sample of the population at large. They have already been selected strongly for programming ability and other skills during Google's hiring process. But to understand how that could generate a negative correlation, we will first turn to a question of broader interest: Why are hot guys such jerks?

Mathematician Jordan Ellenberg has suggested that a phenomenon called Berkson's paradox can explain a common complaint. Our friends who are active on the dating scene sometimes complain that when they go out on a date with someone hot, the person turns out to be a jerk, whereas when they meet someone nice, the person is not particularly attractive. One common explanation for this disappointing observation is that attractive people can afford to be jerks because they're afforded high status and are highly sought as partners. But there is another possible explanation.

Ellenberg asks us to imagine placing potential partners on a two-dimensional plot, with how nice they are on the horizontal access and how attractive they are on the vertical axis. That might give you a plot of individuals that looks something like the next chart.

In this image, attractiveness and niceness are basically uncorrelated. Guys who are hot are no more or less likely to be jerks than guys who are not. So far, we have no reason to think that nice guys are unattractive and attractive guys are not nice.

But now let's look at what happens once you consider whom you'd

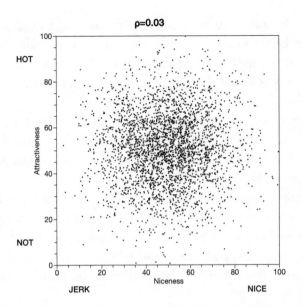

actually be willing to date. Certainly not anyone who is both unattractive and a jerk. Maybe you'd put up with some deficit in the looks department if a fellow was a really great person, or vice versa. So in the space of guys, the people you might date would be in the region above the diagonal:

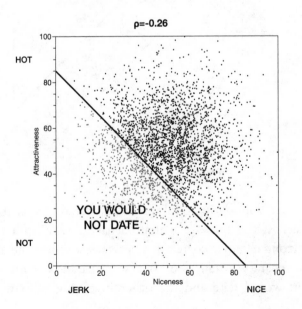

Among the guys you would date, there is now a modest negative correlation between attractiveness and niceness. A really hot guy is less likely to be nice than the average guy that you would date, and a really nice guy is less likely to be hot than the average guy you would date.

This is Berkson's paradox in operation. By selecting for both niceness and attractiveness, you have created a negative correlation between niceness and attractiveness among the people whom you would be willing to date.

An analogous process happens in the opposite direction. Not only do you pick whom you are willing to date, people pick whether they are willing to date you. We apologize for putting this bluntly, but unless you are John Legend, there will be some people who will have better options. So this rules out another set of possible people that you might date:

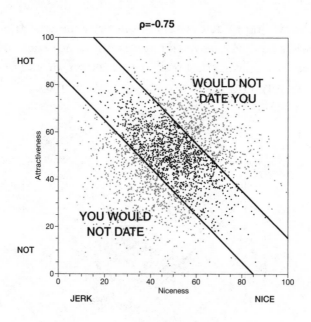

Who is left? Your dating pool is now restricted to a narrow diagonal band across the space of potential partners. Within this band, there is a strong negative correlation between niceness and attractiveness. Two separate instances of Berkson's paradox—one involving whom you would date and the other involving who would date you—have created this negative correlation among your potential partners, even though there is no negative trend in the population at large.

Let's return to the negative correlation between the ability to win programming contests and job performance at Google. In the population at large, we have every reason to expect a strong positive correlation between ability in programming contests and on-the-job ability at Google. The majority of US employees don't know how to program at all, but programming skill is a prerequisite for a job as a Google engineer. Google employees have been highly selected from the larger pool of potential employees, presumably for skills related to programming. Indeed, the assessments that hiring managers use during the hiring process may look a lot like the sorts of tasks or challenges that are posed in programming contests. Perhaps the hiring process puts a bit too much weight on programming contest ability at the expense of other qualities that make one effective at work. If this were the case, one could end up with a negative correlation between contest aptitude and job performance. The figure below illustrates:

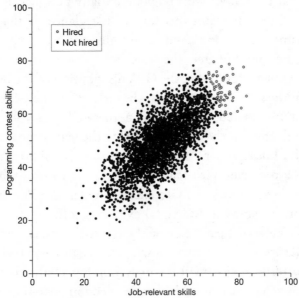

Correlation Among Entire Population: ρ=0.71
Correlation Among Hired: ρ=-0.21

Once you start thinking about Berkson's paradox, you'll see it all over the place. Why do the best fielders in Major League Baseball tend to be mediocre hitters, and the best hitters tend to be mediocre fielders? Answer: There are plenty of players who are mediocre both in the field and at the plate, but they never make it to The Show. If you play *Dungeons & Dragons,* why do your best fighters have such low charisma and why are your best sorcerers so weak? Answer: because you literally trade ability in one domain for ability in another when your character reaches a new level and you allocate bonus power points. Why are some of the best songwriters cursed with Dylanesque voices and some of the best singers incapable of writing their own songs? Answer: There are plenty of musicians who sing like Dylan and write lyrics fit for a hair metal band, but thankfully you'll never hear them on the radio.

Even when selection happens right out in the open, the statistical consequences can seem counterintuitive. Suppose that a school can nominate students for a national scholarship competition based upon their grade point averages (GPAs). After the nominations are announced, we look at the two hundred students who were nominated. We find that the nominated girls have a GPA of 3.84 whereas the nominated boys have a GPA of 3.72. There are so many students in the sample that the differences are not merely due to chance. Can we conclude that the school must be preferentially nominating boys despite lower GPAs? It seems this way at first glance. If the school is using the same nomination standards for girls and boys, why wouldn't their GPAs be approximately the same?

A likely explanation is that the GPA distribution of the boys is different from the GPA distribution of the girls. If so, the GPA distributions of the nominated boys and the nominated girls will still differ even after selecting the best students, using the very same nomination threshold for both genders. The figure on page 125 illustrates. In this figure, the top-scoring girls have extremely high scores whereas the top-scoring boys more narrowly exceed the cutoff. This drives the difference in averages for students above the cutoff.

This isn't Berkson's paradox exactly, but the point is that selection can have all sorts of interesting consequences, and when trying to understand patterns from data, it is worth thinking about whether there has been any selection bias or deliberate selection operating, and if so, how those factors affect the patterns you observe.

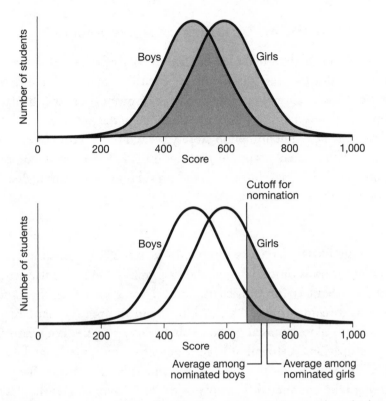

Finally, we want to note that Berkson's paradox provides a hitherto unrecognized explanation for William Butler Yeats's dark observation in his classic modernist poem "The Second Coming":

> The best lack all conviction, while the worst
> Are full of passionate intensity.

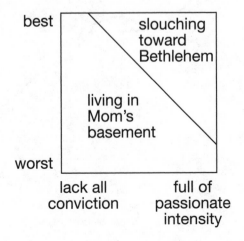

THE MORTAL DANGER OF MUSICIANSHIP

In a clinical trial designed to assess the severity of the side effects of a certain medication, the initial sample of patients may be random, but individuals who suffer side effects may be disproportionately likely to drop out of the trial and thus not be included in the final analysis. This is *data censoring,* a phenomenon closely related to selection bias. Censoring occurs when a sample may be initially selected at random, without selection bias, but a nonrandom subset of the sample doesn't figure into the final analysis.

LET'S DIVE RIGHT INTO an example. In March 2015, a striking graph made the rounds on social media. The graph, from a popular article about death rates for musicians, looked somewhat like the figure below and seems to reveal a shocking trend. It appears that being a musician in older musical genres—blues, jazz, gospel—is a relatively safe occupation. Performing in new genres—punk, metal, and especially rap and hip-hop—looks extraordinarily dangerous. The researcher who conducted the study told *The Washington Post* that "it's a cautionary tale to some degree. People who go into rap music or hip

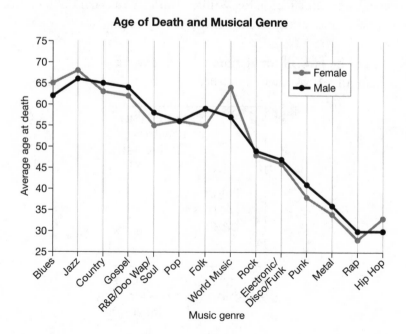

Age of Death and Musical Genre

hop or punk, they're in a much more occupational hazard [sic] profession compared to war. We don't lose half our army in a battle."

This graph became a meme, and spread widely on social media. Not only does it provide quantitative data about an interesting topic, but these data reinforce anecdotal impressions that many of us may already hold about the hard living that goes along with a life in the music business.

Looking at the graph for a moment, however, you can see something isn't right. Again, if something seems too good or too bad to be true, it probably is. This certainly seems too bad to be true. What aroused our suspicion about this graph was the implausibly large difference in ages at death. We wouldn't be particularly skeptical if the study found 5 to 10 percent declines for musicians in some genres. But look at the graph. Rap and hip-hop musicians purportedly die at about thirty years of age—half the age of performers in some other genres.

So what's going on? The data are misleading because they are *right-censored*—individuals who are still alive at the end of the study period are removed from the study.

Let's first look at an example of how right-censoring works, and then return to the musicians. Imagine that you are part of a conservation team studying the life cycle of a rare chameleon species on Madagascar. Chameleons are curiously short-lived; for them a full life is two to three years at most. In 2013, you begin banding every newly born individual in a patch of forest; you then track its survival until your funding runs out in 2017. The figure below illustrates the lon-

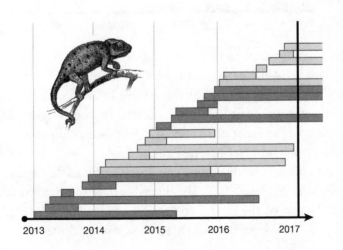

gevity of the individuals that you have banded. Each bar corresponds to one chameleon. At the bottom of the figure are the first individuals banded, back in 2013. Some die early, usually due to predation, but others live full chameleon lives. You record the date of death and indicate that in the graph. The same thing holds for the individuals born in 2014. But of the individuals born in 2015 and 2016, not all are deceased when the study ends in 2017. This is indicated by the bars that overrun the vertical line representing the end of the study.

So how do you record your data? If you were to simply count those individuals as dying at the study's end, you'd be introducing a strong bias to your data. They didn't really die; you just went home. So you decide that maybe the safest thing to do is to throw out those individuals from your data set entirely. In doing so, you are right-censoring your data: You are throwing out the data that run off the right side of the graph. The right-censored data are shown below.

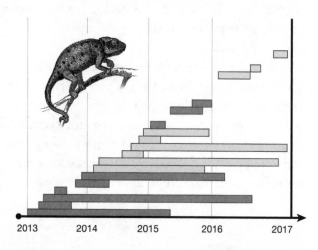

Look at what seems to be happening here. Some chameleons born in 2013 and 2014 die early, but others live two or three years. From these right-censored data, all of those born in 2015 and 2016 appear to die early. If you didn't know that the data had been right-censored, you might conclude that 2015 and 2016 were very dangerous years to be a chameleon and be concerned about the long-term health of this population. This is misleading. The distribution of life spans is unchanged from 2013 to 2017. By throwing out the individuals who live past the end of the study, you are looking at all individuals born in 2013 and 2014, but only the short-lived among those that are born in 2015 and 2016. By right-censoring the data, you've created a misleading impression of mortality patterns.

The right-censoring problem that we see here can be viewed as a form of selection bias. The individuals in our sample from 2015 and 2016 are not a random sample of chameleons born in those years. Rather, they are precisely those individuals with the shortest life spans.

The same problem arises in the graph of average age at death for musicians. Rap and hip-hop are new genres, maybe forty years old at the most, and popular musicians tend to launch their careers in their teens or twenties. As a consequence, most rap and hip-hop stars are still alive today, and thus omitted from the study. The only rap and hip-hop musicians who have died already are those who have died prematurely. Jazz, blues, country, and gospel, by comparison, have been around for a century or more. Many deceased performers of these styles lived into their eighties or longer. It's not that rap stars will likely die young; it's that the rap stars who have died must have died young, because rap hasn't been around long enough for it to be otherwise.

To be fair to the study's author, she acknowledges the right-censoring issue in her article. The problem is that readers may think that the striking differences shown in the graph are due to differing mortality rates by musical genre, whereas we suspect the majority of the pattern is a result of right-censoring. We don't like being presented with graphs in which some or even most of the pattern is due to statistical artifact, and then being told by the author, "But some of the pattern is real, trust me."

Another problem is that there is no caveat about the right-censoring issue in the data graphic itself. In a social media environment, we have to be prepared for data graphics—at least those from pieces directed to a popular audience—to be shared without the accompanying text. In our view, these data never should have been plotted in the way that they were. The graph here tells a story that is not consistent with the conclusions that a careful analysis would suggest.

DISARMING SELECTION BIAS

We have looked at a number of ways in which selection bias can arise. We conclude by considering ways to deal with the problem.

Selection biases often arise in clinical trials, because physicians, insurance companies, and the individual patients in the clinical trial have a say in what treatments are assigned to whom. As a consequence, the treatment group who receive the intervention may differ in important ways from the control group who do not receive the intervention. Randomizing which individuals receive a particular treatment provides a way to minimize selection biases.

A recent study of employer wellness programs shows us just how important this can be. If you work for a large company, you may be a participant in such a program already. The exact structures of corporate wellness programs vary, but the approach is grounded in preventative medicine. Wellness programs often involve disease screening, health education, fitness activities, nutritional advice, weight loss, and stress management. Many wellness programs track employees' activity and other aspects of their health. Some even require employees to wear fitness trackers that provide fine-scale detail on individual activity levels. A majority of them offer incentives for engaging in healthy behaviors. Some reward employees for participating in activities or reaching certain fitness milestones. Others penalize unhealthy behaviors, charging higher premiums to those who smoke, are overweight, and so forth.

Wellness programs raise ethical questions about employers having this level of control and ownership over employees' bodies. But there is also a fundamental question: Do they work? To answer that, we have to agree about what wellness programs are supposed to do. Employers say that they offer these programs because they care about their employees and want to improve their quality of life. That's mostly bullshit. A sand volleyball court on the company lawn may have some recruiting benefits. But the primary rationale for implementing a wellness program is that by improving the health of its employees, a company can lower insurance costs, decrease absenteeism, and perhaps even reduce the rate at which employees leave the company. All of these elements contribute to the company's bottom line.

Companies are getting on board. By 2017, the workplace wellness business had ballooned into an eight-billion-dollar industry in the US alone. One report suggests that half of firms with more than fifty employees offer wellness programs of some sort, with average costs running well over $500 per employee per year.

Meta-analyses—studies that aggregate the results of previous studies—seem encouraging. Such studies typically conclude that wellness programs reduce medical costs and absenteeism, generating considerable savings for employers. But the problem with almost all of these studies is that they allow selection biases to creep in. They compare employees within the same company who did take part in wellness activities with those who did not. Employers cannot force employees to participate, however, and the people who choose to participate may differ in important ways from the people who choose not to. In particular, those who opt in may already be healthier and leading healthier lifestyles than those who opt out.

Researchers found a way around this problem in a recent study. When the University of Illinois at Urbana-Champaign launched a workplace wellness program, they randomized employees into either a treatment group or a control group. Members of the treatment group had the option of participating but were not required to do so. Members of the control group were not even offered an opportunity to take part. This design provided the researchers with three categories: people who chose to participate, people who chose not to, and people who were not given the option to participate in the first place.* The authors obtained health data for all participants from the previous thirteen months, affording a baseline for comparing health before and after taking part in the study.

Unlike previous observational studies, this study found that offering a wellness program had no statistically significant effect on healthcare costs or absenteeism, nor did it increase gym visits and similar types of physical activity. (The one useful thing that the wellness program did was to increase the fraction of participants who underwent a health screening.) The figure on page 132 summarizes these results.

The randomized controlled trial found that being offered the wellness program had no effect on fitness activities, employee retention, or medical costs.

But why? Previous studies largely found beneficial effects. Was there something particularly ineffective about how the Illinois well-

---

* Those offered the option to participate in the workplace wellness program were actually divided into six groups that received different payments, etc., for participation, but to keep the story simple we will not go into those details here.

How the Illinois Wellness Program Affected...

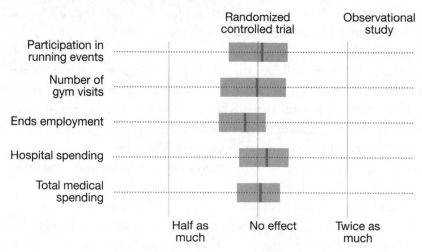

ness program was designed? Or did this point to selection effects in the previous studies? In order to find out, the investigators ran a second analysis in which they set aside their control group, and looked only at the employees who were offered the chance to participate in the wellness program. Comparing those who were active in that program with those who were not, they found strong disparities in activity, retention, and medical costs between those who opted to participate and those who opted not to. These differences remained even when the authors tried to control for differences between those who participated and those who declined, such as age, gender, weight, and other characteristics. If these authors had done an observational study like previous researchers, they would also have observed that employees in workplace wellness programs were healthier and less likely to leave the firm.

This is a classic example of a selection effect. People who are in good health are more likely to participate in wellness programs. It's not that wellness programs cause good health, it's that being in good health causes people to participate in wellness programs.[*]

---

[*] The authors note that if a workplace wellness program differentially recruits or retains individuals in the best health, it can confer financial benefits to the company by screening for the healthiest employees. Even though the program itself doesn't make anyone healthier, it does improve the average health of individuals who choose to join or to stay with the company.

How the Illinois Wellness Program Affected...

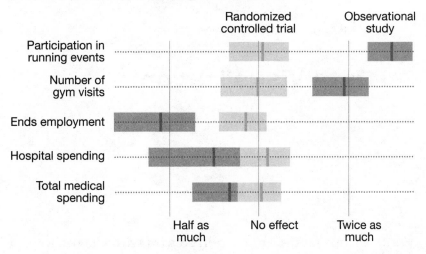

In this chapter, we looked at one of the most important ways that statistical analyses fail and mislead—namely, sampling nonrandomly. Another way to tell data stories is with visualizations and figures. Just like statistical analyses, visual presentations of data are subject to misuse as well. This will be our subject for the next chapter.

CHAPTER 7

Data Visualization

Throughout much of the United States, civilians have a legal right to kill an assailant when they are threatened—or even feel that they may be threatened—with serious bodily harm. According to "Stand Your Ground" laws, a person has no duty to retreat in the face of a violent threat. Rather, he or she is permitted to use whatever degree of force is necessary to defuse the situation, even if it means killing the assailant. Florida's statutes on the justifiable use of force, for example, mandate that the use of deadly force is permissible to deter a threat of death, great bodily harm, or even the commission of a forcible felony such as robbery or burglary.

Critics of Stand Your Ground laws point to racial disparities in application of these laws, and express concerns that they make it too easy for shooters to claim self-defense. Supporters counter that Stand Your Ground laws protect the rights of crime victims over those of criminals, and serve to deter violent crime more generally. But it is not clear that Stand Your Ground laws have this effect. Studies have looked at violent crime data within and across the states and return mixed results. Some find decreases in property crimes such as burglary after such laws are enacted, but others observe significant increases in homicides.

It was in the context of this debate that the news agency Reuters published a data visualization much like the one shown on the following page. The graph illustrates the number of homicides in the state of Florida over a period of twenty-two years.

At first glance, this graph conveys the impression that Florida's

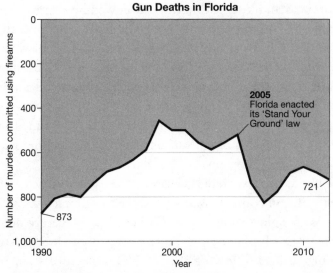

Source: Florida Department of Law Enforcement

2005 Stand Your Ground law worked wonders. Firearm murders appear to rise until the late 1990s, then plateau, and then drop precipitously once the Stand Your Ground law is adopted in 2005. But that's not what is happening. Look at the vertical axis on the graph above. It has been inverted! Zero is at the top of the graph, not the bottom. Points lower down correspond to higher numbers of murders. What seems to be a sharp drop in murders after 2005 is actually a rapid rise. Displayed in conventional form, the graph would look more like this:

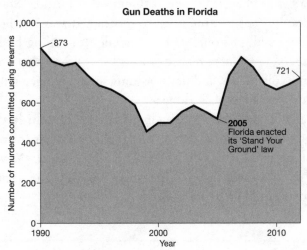

Source: Florida Department of Law Enforcement

In Florida, Stand Your Ground was followed by a large increase in the number of gun murders. (As we know from chapter 4, this does not mean that the law *caused* this increase.) With a bit of time, most readers might catch on and draw the right conclusions about the graph. But the point of data graphics is often to provide a quick and intuitive glimpse into a complex data set. All too often we simply glance at a figure like this one. Perhaps we don't have time to read it carefully as we scroll through our news feeds. We assume we know what it means, and move on.

In the United States, there is a heated debate between advocates and opponents of gun control. When we share this graph with US audiences, most people assume that this figure is deliberately deceptive. They take it for a duplicitous attempt by the pro-gun lobby to obscure the rise in murders following the 2005 Florida legislation. Not so. The graph has a more subtle and, in our view, more interesting backstory.

After critics decried the graph as misleading, the graphic designer explained her thought process in choosing an inverted vertical axis: "I prefer to show deaths in negative terms (inverted)."

Moreover, she added, her inspiration came from a forceful data graphic from the *South China Morning Post* that depicted casualties from the Iraq War. That graph also inverted the vertical axis, but it created the impression of dripping blood and was less prone to misinterpretation.

Contrary to what everyone assumes, the Florida Stand Your Ground graphic was not intended to mislead. It was just poorly designed. This highlights one of the principles for calling bullshit that we espouse. Never assume malice or mendacity when incompetence is a sufficient explanation, and never assume incompetence when a reasonable mistake can explain things.

How can you avoid being taken in by data on a graph? In this chapter, we look at the ways in the which graphs and other forms of data visualization can distract, confuse, and mislead readers. We will show you how to spot these forms of graphical bullshit, and explain how the same data could be better presented.

THE DAWN OF DATAVIZ

Computers are good at processing large quantitative data sets. Humans are not. We have a hard time understanding the pattern and structure of data when they are presented in raw form or even summarized in tables. We need to find ways to simplify information while highlighting important ideas. Data visualizations can help.

Researchers in the sciences have been using graphs to explore and communicate scientific and demographic data since the eighteenth century. During that period, the demographer William Playfair pioneered the forms of data visualization that Microsoft Excel now churns out by default: bar charts, line graphs, and pie charts. Around the same time, physical scientist Johann Heinrich Lambert published sophisticated scientific graphics of the sort we still use today. His

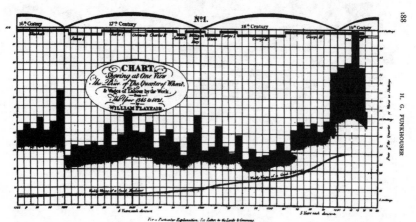

FIG. 5. An illustration of the mechanical perfection of PLAYFAIR's graphic work. From *A Letter on Our Agricultural Distresses*, 1821. (Size of original, 30,5 × 16 cm.).

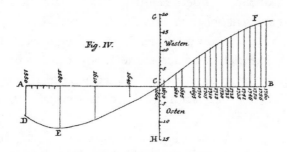

FIG. 2

Graph of magnetic variation. From J. H. Lambert, 'Theorie der Zuverlässigkeit der Beobachtungen und Versuche', *Beyträge zum Gebrauche der Mathematik und deren Anwendung* (Berlin, 1765), i. Plate 'Mathes. Adplicat: Tab. V'.

graphics plots are almost indistinguishable from the hand-drawn figures presented in scientific journals up through the 1980s.

Data visualizations saw limited use until the mid- to late nineteenth century. But by the turn of the twentieth century, natural and social scientists alike regularly employed such techniques to report their data and illustrate their theories. The popular press did not follow immediately. Throughout much of the twentieth century, newspapers and magazines would print the occasional map, pie chart, or bar chart, but even simple charts like these were uncommon.* Below is a map published in *The New York Times,* and on page 139 is a redrawing of a pie chart published in a 1920 *Cyclopedia of Fraternities.*

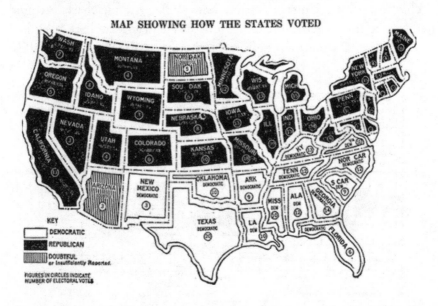

For much of the twentieth century, data visualizations in popular media either showed only a single variable, as in a pie chart, or showed how a variable changed over time. A graph might have shown how the price of wheat changed across the 1930s. But it would not have illustrated how the price of wheat changed as a function of rainfall in the Grain Belt. In 1982, statistician and data visualization guru Ed-

---

* The financial pages offered more sophisticated data visualizations, usually in the form of line charts. But these were not for popular consumption. Rather, they were specialized graphics for the use of professionals. We see them as having far more in common with the technical scientific literature.

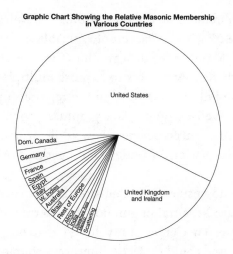

Graphic Chart Showing the Relative Masonic Membership
in Various Countries

ward Tufte tabulated the fraction of graphs that did show more complex relationships, for a range of news sources. One in every two hundred data visualizations published in *The New York Times* illustrated relationships among multiple variables (other than time). None of the data visualizations in *The Washington Post* or *The Wall Street Journal* did so.

In the 1980s, digital plotting software became readily available and newspapers started to publish more charts and data graphics than they had in the past.

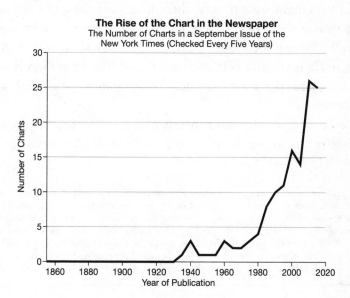

The Rise of the Chart in the Newspaper
The Number of Charts in a September Issue of the
New York Times (Checked Every Five Years)

As charts proliferated, so did their sophistication. Today, newspapers such as *The New York Times* employ sizable teams of data visualization experts. Many of the data graphics they create are interactive visualizations that allow readers to explore multiple facets of complex data sets and observe patterns in the relationships among multiple variables. Well-designed data graphics provide readers with deeper and more nuanced perspectives, while promoting the use of quantitative information in understanding the world and making decisions.

But there is a downside. Our educational system has not caught up. Readers may have little training in how to interpret data graphics. A recent Pew Research Center study found that only about half of Americans surveyed could correctly interpret a simple scatter plot.* In particular, individuals without a college degree were substantially less likely to be able to draw correct conclusions from the graph. This is a problem in a world where data graphics are commonplace.

Another problem is that while data visualizations may appear to be objective, the designer has a great deal of control over the message a graphic conveys. Even using accurate data, a designer can manipulate how those data make us *feel*. She can create the illusion of a correlation where none exists, or make a small difference between groups look big. Again, our educational system lags behind. Few people are taught how to spot these manipulations, or even taught to appreciate the power a designer has to shape the story that the data tell. We may be taught how to spot logical fallacies and how to verify claims from questionable sources. But we are rarely taught anything about the ways in which data graphics can be designed to mislead us.

One of our primary aims in this chapter is to provide you with these skills. Before we do that, we want to look at the way that good

---

* The Pew Research Center contended that 63 percent, not 50 percent, of those surveyed could read the chart. This was based on the fact that 63 percent chose the correct answer from four multiple-choice options. But notice that 25 percent would have been able to do it completely at random, even if no one could read the chart. A better model might assume that everyone who can interpret the chart gets the question right, and everyone else guesses randomly. To get to 63 percent correct, about half of those surveyed would be able to read the chart and would answer correctly; of the remaining half, roughly a fourth of them would guess correctly, bringing the total correct to 63 percent.

old-fashioned bullshit (rather than deliberate deception or misdirection) slips into data visualization.

DUCK!

If you drive along the main road through the small hamlet of Flanders, on New York's Long Island, you will come across a tall statue of a white duck with a huge yellow bill and eyes made from the taillights of a Model T Ford. If you stop and look more closely, you will see that the Big Duck, as it is known locally, is not actually a tall statue but rather a small building. A single door is recessed into the duck's breast and leads into a small and windowless room hollowed out from the duck's body.

The Big Duck was erected in 1931 by a duck farmer to serve as a storefront for selling his birds and their eggs. While ducks are no longer sold from within, the building has become a beloved symbol of Flanders and is one of the glorious roadside attractions that once delighted travelers on the pre-interstate highways of the United States.

The Big Duck is not particularly functional as a building, however. In architectural theory it has become an icon of what happens when form is put ahead of function, a metaphor for larger failings in the

modernist movement.* In architecture, the term "duck" refers to any building where ornament overwhelms purpose, though it is particularly common in reference to buildings that look like the products they sell. The headquarters of the Longaberger basket-making corporation looks like a giant picnic basket. A shaved ice stand that we visited in Santa Fe is shaped like the cylindrical blocks of ice from which their desserts are fashioned.

Edward Tufte pointed out that an analogous problem is common in data visualization. While aesthetics are important, data graphics should be about the data, not about eye-catching decoration. Graphs that violate this principle are called "ducks."

USA Today was among the pioneers of the dataviz duck. Its Daily Snapshots feature presents generally unimportant information in the form of simple graphs. Each Daily Snapshots graph is designed according to a loose connection to the topic at hand. Tubes of lipstick stand in as the bars of a chart about how much women spend on cosmetics. A ball of ice cream atop a cone becomes a pie chart in a graphic about popular ice cream brands. The line of sight from a man's face to a television screen zigs and zags to form a line graph of Olympic Games viewership over the years. It's hard to say any one example is

Days per week adults say they exercise 30 minutes or more

3 or more days — 52%
1–2 days — 19%
None — 30%

* "When modern architects righteously abandoned ornament on buildings they unconsciously designed buildings that *were* ornament. . . . It is all right to decorate construction, but never to construct decoration" (Robert Venturi et al. [1972], quoted in Edward Tufte [1983]).

dramatically worse than any other, but the image on the previous page is representative of the *USA Today* style.

USA Today has no monopoly on the form. In the graph below, modeled after one published by Mint.com, tines of two forks serve as the bars in a bar chart. What is so bad about this? Many things. The bars themselves—the information-carrying part of the graph— use only a small fraction of the total space occupied by the graphic. The slanted angle is challenging as well; we are not used to interpret- ing bar graphs angled in that way. Worse still, the way that the forks are arranged side by side results in a baseline on the left fork that sits well above the baseline of the right fork. That makes comparison be- tween the two forks even more difficult. Fortunately, the numerical values are written out. But if one has to rely on them to interpret the figure, the graphic elements are basically superfluous and the infor- mation could have been presented in a table.

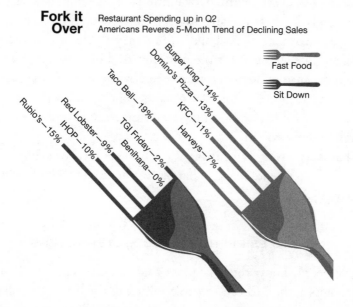

Ducks are usually a pathology of the popular press, but lately they have crept into the scientific literature. We have to give the authors of the figure below some points for creativity, but twisting a pie chart into a ram's horn only reduces the viewer's ability to make visual com- parisons among quantities.

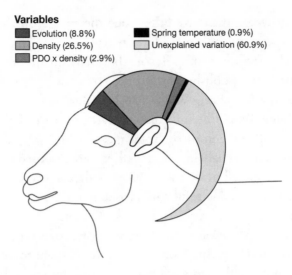

Variables

■ Evolution (8.8%)   ■ Spring temperature (0.9%)
□ Density (26.5%)   □ Unexplained variation (60.9%)
■ PDO x density (2.9%)

We have described bullshit as being intended to persuade or impress by distracting, overwhelming, or intimidating an audience with a blatant disregard for truth and logical coherence. Data visualization ducks may not be full-on bullshit, but they shade in that direction. Ducks are like clickbait for the mind; instead of generating a mouse click, they are trying to capture a few seconds of your attention. Whereas a bar graph or line chart may seem dry and perhaps complicated, a colorful illustration may seem fun enough and eye-catching enough to draw you in.

What is so wrong with that? What bothers us about ducks is that the attempt to be cute makes it harder for the reader to understand the underlying data.

GLASS SLIPPERS AND UGLY STEPSISTERS

Most people know the basic plot of Cinderella: A girl is adopted by an evil stepmother, forced to cook and clean for her stepmother and stepsisters, and doesn't get invited to the grand ball where the prince is seeking a bride. Her fairy godmother appears and turns her rags into a beautiful dress, her sandals into glass slippers, and a pumpkin into a glittering coach; she attends the ball and captures the prince's heart; knowing that the spell will wear off at midnight, she flees as the clock begins to strike twelve. The prince, aided by a glass slipper that Cinderella left behind in her flight, is determined to find this mystery woman who captured his heart. In a sort of reverse Cochran defense,* the slipper fits no one but Cinderella, the prince asks for her hand in marriage, and they live happily ever after. What may be less familiar is that in the original Grimm brothers' version of the tale, the evil stepsisters make desperate attempts to fit into the glass slipper. They slice off their toes and heels in an effort to fit their feet into the tiny and unyielding shoe.

If a data visualization duck shades toward bullshit, a class of visualizations that we call *glass slippers* is the real deal. Glass slippers take one type of data and shoehorn it into a visual form designed to display another. In doing so, they trade on the authority of good visualizations to appear authoritative themselves. They are to data visualization what mathiness is to mathematical equations.

The chemist Dmitri Mendeleev developed the periodic table in the second half of the nineteenth century. His efforts were a triumph of data visualization as a tool for organizing patterns and generating predictions in science. The periodic table is an arrangement of the chemical elements from lightest to heaviest. The left-to-right positions reflect what we now understand to be the fundamental atomic structure of each element, and predict the chemical interactions of those

1 H Hydrogen 1.008																	2 He Helium 4.003
3 Li Lithium 6.94	4 Be Beryllium 9.012											5 B Boron 10.81	6 C Carbon 12.011	7 N Nitrogen 14.007	8 O Oxygen 15.999	9 F Fluorine 18.998	10 Ne Neon 20.180
11 Na Sodium 22.990	12 Mg Magnesium 24.305											13 Al Aluminum 26.982	14 Si Silicon 28.085	15 P Phosphorus 30.974	16 S Sulfur 32.06	17 Cl Chlorine 35.45	18 Ar Argon 39.948
19 K Potassium 39.098	20 Ca Calcium 40.078	21 Sc Scandium 44.956	22 Ti Titanium 47.867	23 V Vanadium 50.942	24 Cr Chromium 51.996	25 Mn Manganese 54.938	26 Fe Iron 55.845	27 Co Cobalt 58.933	28 Ni Nickel 58.693	29 Cu Copper 63.546	30 Zn Zinc 65.38	31 Ga Gallium 69.723	32 Ge Germanium 72.630	33 As Arsenic 74.922	34 Se Selenium 78.97	35 Br Bromine 79.904	36 Kr Krypton 83.798
37 Rb Rubidium 85.468	38 Sr Strontium 87.62	39 Y Yttrium 88.906	40 Zr Zirconium 91.224	41 Nb Niobium 92.906	42 Mo Molybdenum 95.95	43 Tc Technetium [97]	44 Ru Ruthenium 101.07	45 Rh Rhodium 102.906	46 Pd Palladium 106.42	47 Ag Silver 107.868	48 Cd Cadmium 112.414	49 In Indium 114.818	50 Sn Tin 118.710	51 Sb Antimony 121.760	52 Te Tellurium 127.60	53 I Iodine 126.904	54 Xe Xenon 131.293
55 Cs Cesium 132.905	56 Ba Barium 137.327	* 57 - 70	71 Lu Lutetium 174.967	72 Hf Hafnium 178.49	73 Ta Tantalum 180.948	74 W Tungsten 183.84	75 Re Rhenium 186.207	76 Os Osmium 190.23	77 Ir Iridium 192.217	78 Pt Platinum 195.084	79 Au Gold 196.997	80 Hg Mercury 200.592	81 Tl Thallium 204.38	82 Pb Lead 207.2	83 Bi Bismuth 208.980	84 Po Polonium [209]	85 At Astatine [210]	86 Rn Radon [222]
87 Fr Francium [223]	88 Ra Radium [226]	** 89 - 102	103 Lr Lawrencium [262]	104 Rf Rutherfordium [267]	105 Db Dubnium [270]	106 Sg Seaborgium [269]	107 Bh Bohrium [270]	108 Hs Hassium [270]	109 Mt Meitnerium [278]	110 Ds Darmstadtium [281]	111 Rg Roentgenium [281]	112 Cn Copernicium [285]	113 Nh Nihonium [286]	114 Fl Flerovium [289]	115 Mc Moscovium [289]	116 Lv Livermorium [293]	117 Ts Tennessine [293]	118 Og Oganesson [294]

*Lanthanide series	57 La Lanthanum 138.905	58 Ce Cerium 140.116	59 Pr Praseodymium 140.908	60 Nd Neodymium 144.242	61 Pm Promethium [145]	62 Sm Samarium 150.36	63 Eu Europium 151.964	64 Gd Gadolinium 157.25	65 Tb Terbium 158.925	66 Dy Dysprosium 162.500	67 Ho Holmium 164.930	68 Er Erbium 167.259	69 Tm Thulium 168.934	70 Yb Ytterbium 173.045
**Actinide series	89 Ac Actinium [227]	90 Th Thorium 232.038	91 Pa Protactinium 231.036	92 U Uranium 238.029	93 Np Neptunium [237]	94 Pu Plutonium [244]	95 Am Americium [243]	96 Cm Curium [247]	97 Bk Berkelium [247]	98 Cf Californium [251]	99 Es Einsteinium [252]	100 Fm Fermium [257]	101 Md Mendelevium [258]	102 No Nobelium [259]

* In the high-profile 1995 murder trial of O. J. Simpson, defense attorney Johnnie Cochran had his client try on the bloody glove that the murderer had worn. Almost all Americans of our generation remember the dramatic moments as Simpson struggled to pull on the glove and Cochran deemed it too small to have possibly been his. Fewer of us remember that Cochran's famous instructions to the jury, "If it doesn't fit, you must acquit," referred not to the glove but to the prosecutor's story.

elements. The particular blocky structure of the periodic table reflects the way in which electrons fill the electron subshells around the atomic nucleus. By laying out the known elements in a way that captured the patterns among them, Mendeleev was able to predict the existence and properties of chemical elements that had not yet been discovered. In short, the periodic table is a highly specific form of data visualization, with a structure that reflects the logic of atomic chemistry.

Yet designers create periodic tables of everything under the sun. We've seen periodic tables of cloud computing, cybersecurity, typefaces, cryptocurrencies, data science, tech investing, Adobe Illustrator shortcuts, bibliometrics, and more. Some, such as the periodic table of swearing, the periodic table of elephants, and the periodic table of hot dogs, are almost certainly tongue in cheek. Others seem painfully serious: the periodic table of content marketing, the periodic table of digital marketing, the periodic table of commerce marketing, the periodic table of email marketing, the periodic table of online marketing, the periodic table of marketing attribution, the periodic table of marketing signals, the periodic table of marketing strategies, and let's not forget the periodic table of b2b digital marketing metrics. Don't even get us started on the dozens of periodic tables of SEO—search engine optimization. Having a hard time keeping track of all this? Fortunately, someone has created a periodic table of periodic tables.

These faux periodic tables adopt a structure that doesn't match the information being classified. Mendeleev's original periodic tables had a strong enough theoretical basis that he was able to include gaps for elements yet to be discovered. By contrast, entries in mock periodic tables are rarely exhaustive, and criteria for inclusion are often unclear. There are no gaps in the periodic table of data visualization reproduced above. Does anyone really believe we've discovered all the possible techniques for visualizing data? The majority of these other periodic tables take pains to retain the structure of Mendeleev's periodic table of elements. Typically, each entry is assigned a number in ascending order, but rarely if ever do these numbers have anything like the fundamental importance of the atomic numbers listed on Mendeleev's table. These copycat tables hope to convey the illusion of systematic classification, but they disregard logical coherence by aping the structure of Mendeleev's table instead of finding a more natural scheme for their members. All of them are bullshit.

In its ordinary use, the subway map is an exemplary form of visualization. Subway maps take a large amount of complex geographic information and compress it. They discard all irrelevant detail in order to highlight the information a commuter needs to navigate the subway system. The result is a simple map that is easy to read. The subway map has just a few elements: subway stops arrayed in two dimensions, subway lines linking these stops in linear (or circular) order, and transfer stations where two lines join.

Unfortunately, designers find the subway irresistible—even when displaying content that has none of the features of a subway system. We have seen subway maps of scientists, websites, national parks, moral philosophy, Shakespearean plays, the books of the Bible, the plot of James Joyce's *Ulysses,* the Agile development and management framework, data science skills, and more.

Some instantiations of the subway map metaphor do a better job than others. The Rock 'n' Roll Metro Map uses the subway lines to represent genres: heavy metal, punk, alternative, etc., where each station along the line is a band. The sequential structure of each "line" is meaningful in this map. Lines proceed from the earliest to the most recent bands. Transfer stations represent bands that span genres. But the physical positions of the bands on the page don't correspond to anything analogous to the positions of subway stations within a city.

The Underskin map of the human body uses different subway lines to represent different bodily systems: the nervous system, the digestive system, the skeletal system, the lymphatic system, etc. Each stop is an organ or structure. Transfer stations represent involvement in multiple systems. Physical position on the page corresponds to physical position within the body. Subway maps of river systems and the Milky Way galaxy make similarly appropriate use of two spatial dimensions. We concede that the components of a traditional subway map are put to meaningful use in these cases, but these maps still strike us as gimmicks. More appropriate visualization—anatomical diagrams, river charts, star maps—are already commonplace.

Subway maps are so misused that, like periodic tables, they have provoked meta-level commentary in the form of a Subway Map of Maps that Use Subway Maps as Metaphor.

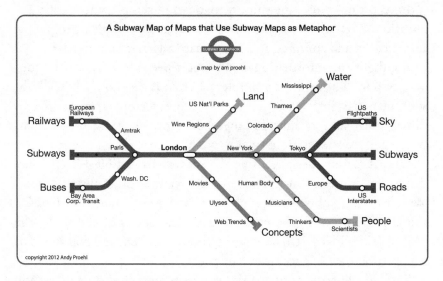

Some sort of prize for perversity should be awarded to the Underground Map of the Elements.*

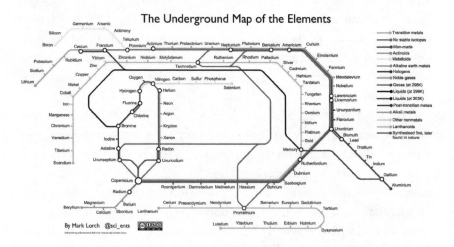

* If you search on the Internet you will find that the Underground Map of the Elements has an evil twin, the Periodic Table of the London Underground. We have no quarrel with these deliberately perverse examples. They are clever and self-aware. In the discussion accompanying the Underground Map of the Elements, author Mark Lorch explains why the periodic table is such a brilliant way to organize the chemical elements, and gets at some of the same reasons we have discussed for why periodic tables of other things are just silly.

Periodic tables and subway maps are highly specific forms of visualization. But even very general visualization methods can be glass slippers. Venn diagrams, the overlapping ovals used to represent group membership for items that may belong to multiple groups, are popular glass slippers.

The following diagram purports to illustrate the fraction of Canadians who have used marijuana.

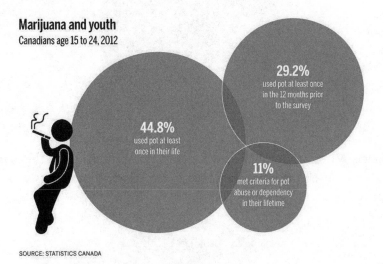

Marijuana and youth
Canadians age 15 to 24, 2012

29.2%
used pot at least once
in the 12 months prior
to the survey

44.8%
used pot at least
once in their life

11%
met criteria for pot
abuse or dependency
in their lifetime

SOURCE: STATISTICS CANADA

With its shaded overlapping circles, the image screams "Venn diagram." But think about it. The 44.8 percent and 11 percent circles barely overlap. If this were a Venn diagram, that would mean that most of the people who "met criteria for pot abuse or dependency in their lifetime" had not "used pot at least once in their lifetime." Instead, each circle simply indicates the size of the group in question. The overlaps do not convey any meaning.

Hillary Clinton posted a graph like the following to Twitter. Again, this looks like a Venn diagram, but the labeling doesn't make sense. Instead, each region seems to be nothing more than a slot in which to place some text. The figure is just a confusing way of saying the text enclosed: "90% of Americans, and 83% of gun owners, support background checks."

We see something similar in this figure from a scientific paper about the use of Twitter data for studying public engagement with scientific

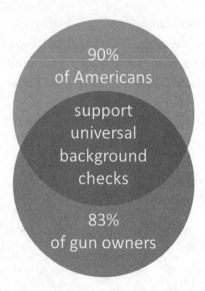

papers. While the figure below looks like a Venn diagram, the nested ovals are purely an ornamental backdrop for three numbers and five words.

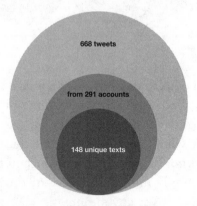

In addition to diagrams that look like Venn diagrams but are not, we often see Venn diagrams that mostly serve as a way to list various desired attributes. The example on the next page is emblematic of the genre. Product excellence, effective branding, and promotional focus all seem like good things. And at their intersection, another good thing: profit. But look at the other entries. Why is demand generation at the intersection of effective branding and promotional focus, to the exclusion of product excellence? Why does revenue growth exclude effective branding? Why does industry leadership exclude promotional focus? Nobody seems to have thought these things through. It seems more like a series of self-congratulatory phrases were dropped into the diagram at random in the hope that no one would think too carefully about their placement.

And then of course there is the risk of invoking the Venn diagram metaphor accidentally. One prominent informatics company produced posters that looked something like the following. While intended to be visually attractive fluff, the implication this makes to anyone who has seen a Venn diagram is that the company's values mostly exclude trust, partnership, innovation, and performance.

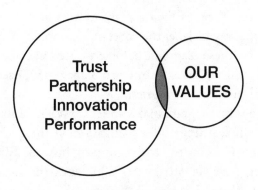

Another popular form of diagram, particularly in fields such as engineering and anatomy, is the labeled schematic. Below, examples of each.

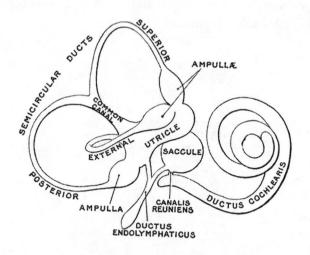

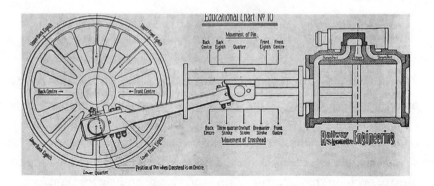

This is a classic form of data visualization, and such diagrams provide an efficient way to label the parts of a complex image. But more and more we see these diagrams being co-opted in some sort of loose metaphorical fashion. Take the unicorn on page 153, used to advertise a business analytics award program.

The labels on this diagram make no sense. What do forelegs have to do with machine learning and visualization? Is there any reason that R programming is associated with a hind leg instead? Why doesn't the right hind leg have an attribute? Why does the head "analytical thinker" refer to a kind of person, whereas the other body parts refer

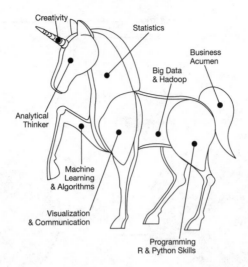

to skills? Why does "business acumen" correspond to the tail? (We don't think the designers meant to suggest that it's the closest of the categories to a horse's ass.) This is just a list of terms that the designer thinks are important, made to look like a labeled diagram.

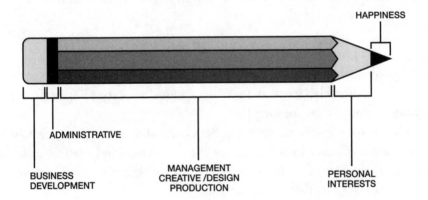

This pencil has the same problem. We are not sure how the parts of the pencil correspond to their labels, or even what information we are supposed to take away from this figure. Perhaps that business development erases the mark of happiness?

We conclude with an example of a metaphor taken so far over the top that it becomes self-parody.

The figure on the next page has something to do with learning and education, but we have no idea what.

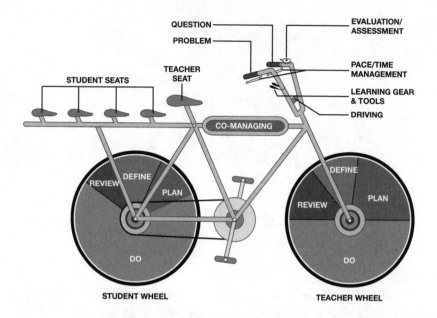

Ducks decorate or obscure the meaningful data in a graphic by aiming to be cute. Glass slippers create a false sense of rigor by shoehorning one type of data into a wholly unsuitable data visualization.

AN AXIS OF EVIL

Data visualizations can also mislead, either by intention or by accident. Fortunately, most of these deceptions are easy to spot if you know what you are looking for.

Many data graphics, including bar charts and scatter plots, display information along axes. These are the horizontal and vertical scales framing the plot of numeric values. Always look at the axes when you see a data graphic that includes them.

Designers have a number of tricks for manipulating the axes of a graph. In 2016, columnist and professor Andrew Potter created a furor with a commentary in the Canadian news magazine *Maclean's*. In that piece, he argued that many of Quebec's problems could be traced to the fact that "compared to the rest of the country, Quebec is an almost pathologically alienated and low-trust society, deficient in many of the most basic forms of social capital that other Canadians take for granted." In an effort to support Potter's argument, the magazine subsequently published the following data graphic.

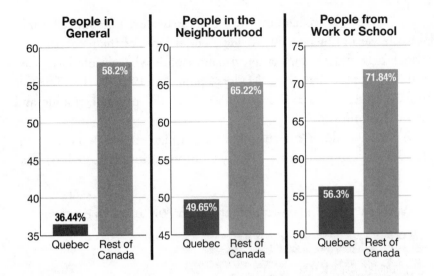

At a glance, this graph appears to provide Potter's premise with strong support. The bars for trust are far lower for Quebec than for the rest of Canada. But pause for a moment and look at the vertical (y) axes. These bars don't go down to zero. They go to 35, 45, and 50, respectively. By truncating the Quebec bars just below their tops, the designer has visually exaggerated the difference between Quebec and the rest of the country. If the bars were allowed to continue to zero, the graph would provide a different impression:

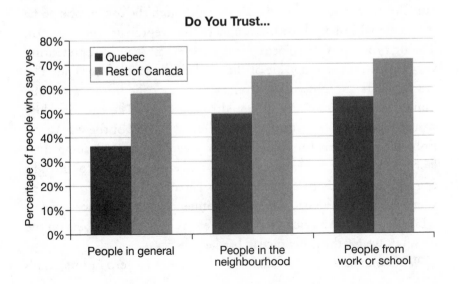

On this new visualization, we see that trust levels are indeed somewhat lower in Quebec, but we get a better sense of the magnitude by which trust differs. This latter visualization is what should have been published in the first place. *Maclean's* published it as a correction after readers spotted the axis manipulations in the original graphic and wrote to complain.

A bar chart doesn't need to have an explicit axis to be misleading. Here is an example that the Hillary Clinton campaign posted to Instagram.

Women's Earnings as a Percentage of White Men's Earnings

Hispanic or Latino	55%
American Indian & Alaskan Native	59%
African American	60%
Native Hawaiian & Other Pacific Islander	62%
White	75%
Asian American	84%

Here the bars run left to right instead of bottom to top. This is appropriate, because each bar represents a category without any natural ordering rather than a numerical value (e.g., a year, an age, an income range). What is not appropriate is that although the bars appear to be proportional in length to the numbers they represent, they are not. The first four bars are approximately correct in length, representing very close to the stated value of the full length from left to right. The last two bars are substantially longer than they should be, given the numerical values they are supposed to represent. The bar for white women is labeled 75 percent but stretches 78 percent of the way to the right edge. The bar for Asian women is even more misleading. It is labeled 84 percent but extends a full 90 percent of the way to the right edge. The effect is to exaggerate the perceived difference between wages paid to non–Asian American women of color and those paid to white and Asian American women. We may read the numbers on the bars, but we *feel* the difference in bar lengths.

While the bars in a bar chart should extend to zero, a line graph does not need to include zero on the dependent variable axis. The line graph below illustrates how in the state of California, the fraction of families with all parents working has increased since 1970. Like the original graph of trust in Quebec, this graph uses a vertical axis that does not go all the way to zero.

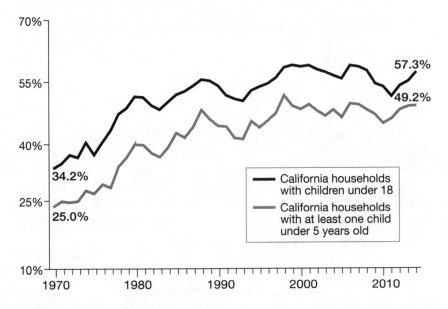

What is the difference? Why does a bar graph need to include zero on the vertical axis whereas a line graph need not do so? The two types of graphs are telling different stories. By its design, a bar graph emphasizes the absolute magnitude of values associated with each category, whereas a line graph emphasizes the change in the dependent variable (usually the y value) as the independent variable (usually the x value) changes.

In fact, line graphs can sometimes be misleading if their vertical axes do go to zero. One notorious example, titled "The Only Global Warming Chart You Need From Now On," was created by Steven Hayward for the *Powerline* blog and was shared further after it was posted to Twitter by the *National Review* in late 2015. Explaining his diagram, Hayward wrote:

> A little hard to get worked up about this, isn't it? In fact you can barely spot the warming.

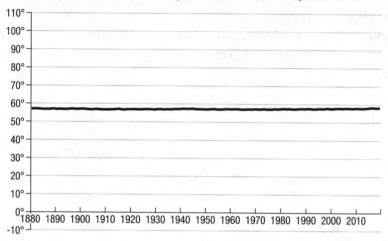

Average Annual Global Temperature in Fahrenheit, 1880–2019

This is silly. The absolute temperature is irrelevant. There is no point in zooming out so far that all pattern is obscured. If we want to draw conclusions about whether the climate is changing, we need a scale something like the one in the next graph.

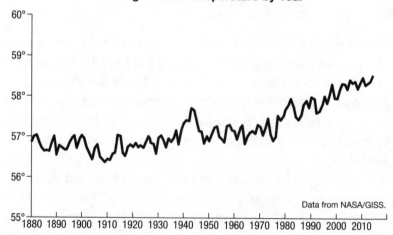

Average Global Temperature by Year

Data from NASA/GISS.

The disingenuous aspect of the *Powerline* graph is that Hayward *made graphical display choices that are inconsistent with the story he is telling.* Hayward claims to be writing about the change (or lack thereof) in temperatures on Earth, but instead of choosing a plot designed to reveal change, he chooses one designed to obscure changes in favor of information about absolute magnitudes.*

We have to be even more careful when a graph uses two different vertical axis scales. By selectively changing the scale of the axes relative to each other, designers can make the data tell almost any story they want. For example, a 2015 research paper in a lower-tier journal attempted to resurrect the long-debunked conspiracy theory relating autism to the measles-mumps-rubella (MMR) vaccine. A figure like the following was provided as evidence.

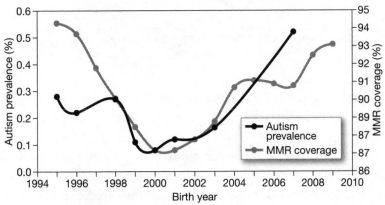

Even if we were willing to set aside major problems in the selection and analysis of the data, what should we make of the correspondence this graph suggests? At first glance, autism rates seem to track vaccination rates closely. But look at the axes. Autism prevalence is plotted from 0 to 0.6 percent. MMR coverage is plotted from 86 percent to 95 percent. What we see over this period is a large proportional change in autism—roughly a tenfold increase from 2000 to 2007—but a very small proportional change in MMR coverage. This becomes clear if

---

* Hayward's chart doesn't even do a good job of illustrating absolute magnitudes, because everyday temperatures are *interval variables* specified on scales with arbitrary zero points. Zero degrees Celsius corresponds rather to the happenstance of the freezing temperature of water. The zero point on the Fahrenheit scale is even more arbitrary; it corresponds to the coldest temperature that Daniel Fahrenheit could produce in his laboratory in the early eighteenth century. If one actually wanted to argue that a temperature axis should include zero, temperature would have to be measured as a *ratio variable,* i.e., on a scale with a meaningful zero point. For example, you could use the Kelvin scale, for which absolute zero has a natural physical meaning independent of human cultural conventions.

we rescale the graph. We don't have to show both trends on the same scale, but we do need to ensure that both axes include zero.

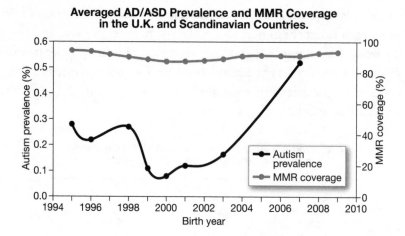

Viewed this way, it is clear that the small relative changes in MMR coverage are unlikely to be driving the large relative changes in autism rate.

Here is another example, redrawn from a research paper in an obscure scientific journal. This graph purports to illustrate a temporal correlation between thyroid cancer and the use of the pesticide glyphosate (Roundup):

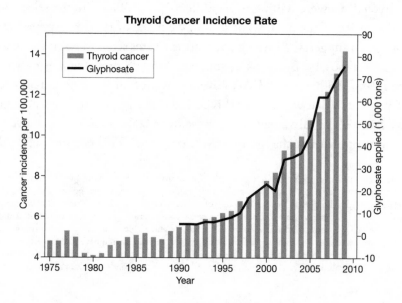

Now, exposure to Roundup may well have serious health consequences. But whatever they may be, this particular graph is not persuasive. First of all, correlation is not causation. One would find a similar correlation between cell phone usage and thyroid cancer, for example—or even between cell phone usage and Roundup usage! Below, we've added cell phone ownership to the plot.

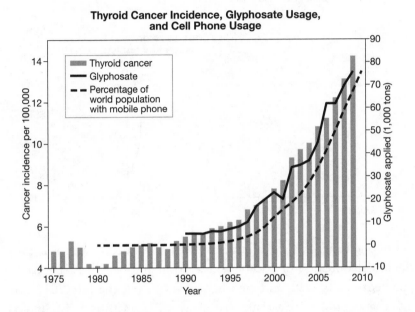

Thyroid Cancer Incidence, Glyphosate Usage, and Cell Phone Usage

If we are to believe the logic of the original argument, perhaps we should be worried that cell phones are causing thyroid cancer—or even that Roundup is causing cell phones.

Now look at the axes in this figure. The vertical axis at left, corresponding to the bar chart, doesn't go to zero. We've already noted why this is problematic. But it gets worse. Both the scale and the intercept of the vertical axis at right have been adjusted so that the curve for glyphosate traces the peaks of the bars for cancer incidence. Most remarkably, to make the curves do this, the axis has to go all the way to negative 10,000 tons glyphosate used. That just doesn't make any sense. We've noted that the vertical axis need not go to zero for a line graph, but if it goes to a negative value for a quantity that can take on only positive values, this should set off alarm bells.

While more often we may see monkey business with the vertical axis, horizontal axes can also be used to mislead. Perhaps the simplest way to do this is to pick data ranges that obscure part of the story. In July 2018, Facebook suffered a substantial drop in stock prices after it released a disappointing quarterly earnings report. The headline in *Business Insider* blared "Facebook's Earnings Disaster Erased $120 Billion in Market Value—The Biggest Wipeout in US Stock-Market History." Accompanying that headline was the a graph of Facebook share prices over a four-day period.

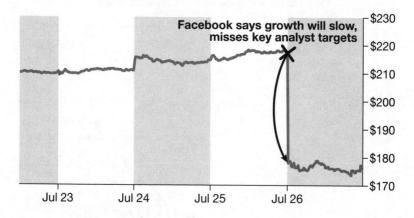

On one hand, this was a huge total loss in value, but this is because the initial valuation of Facebook was so high. Overall, Facebook has done extremely well, and we might want to put the July 2018 drop into that context with a graph that spans five years instead of four days:

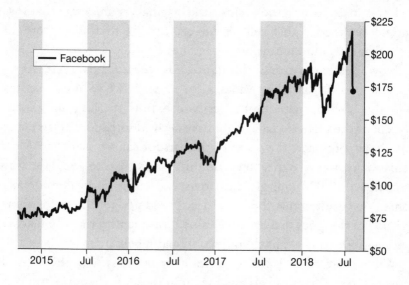

Shown this way, one sees a very different story about the Facebook stock crash. One also sees the rapid rebounds after previous crashes. We're less interested in whether the graph in *Business Insider* was or was not misleading than we are in pointing out how much spin relies on the range of time presented. Keep this in mind when looking at line charts and related forms of visualization. Make sure that the time frame depicted is appropriate for the point the graph is meant to illustrate.

Let's look at another way that the horizontal axis can be misleading. The graph below suggests that CO_2 emissions have reached a plateau. The description in the text reads: "Over the past few years, carbon dioxide emissions worldwide had stabilized relative to previous decades."

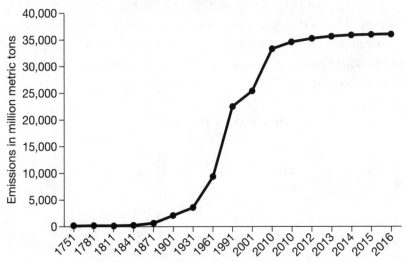

Carbon Dioxide Emissions from Global Fossil Fuel Combustion and Industrial Processes, 1751–2016

But look at what is going on with the horizontal axis. Each tick corresponds to a thirty-year interval until we reach 1991. The next step is a ten-year interval. The one after that is nine years. Thereafter, each interval represents only a single year. Redrawing this graph so that the x axis has a constant scale, we get a different picture:

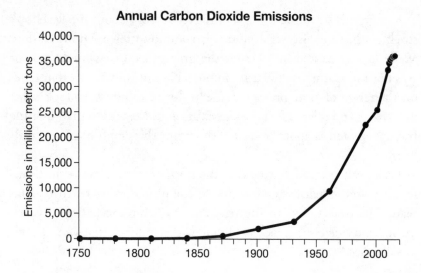

Carbon dioxide emissions may be increasing less rapidly, but they do not appear to be near a plateau as yet.

In general, we need to be on the lookout for uneven or varying scales on the x axis. Something similar can happen with bar charts, when data are "binned" together to form bars. Consider the following bar chart from an article in *The Wall Street Journal* about President Obama's tax plan.

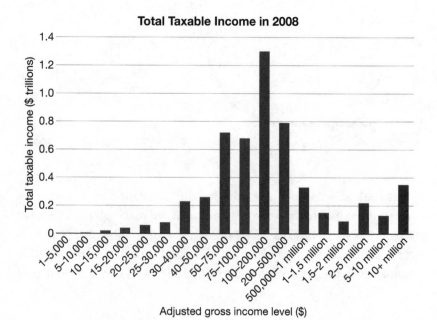

The graph purports to show the location of the bulk of the US tax base. Each bar represents taxpayers in a certain income range; this is what we mean by binning the data. These income ranges are displayed along the horizontal axis; along the vertical axis is the total income of all filers in a given range. Most of the taxable income, according to this figure, comes from the "middle class," the region from $50,000 to $200,000 where the bars extend the highest. (There is also a large block of taxable income in the range from $200,000 to $500,000, but even by *Wall Street Journal* standards this is hard to envision as middle class.)

The author makes the argument that the bulk of the burden from Obama's tax plans will inevitably fall on the middle class, not the rich.

> The rich aren't nearly rich enough to finance Mr. Obama's entitlement state ambitions—even before his health-care plan kicks in. So who else is there to tax? Well, in 2008, there was about $5.65 trillion in total taxable income from all individual taxpayers, and most of that came from middle income earners. The nearby chart shows the distribution, and the big hump in the center is where Democrats are inevitably headed for the same reason that Willie Sutton robbed banks.*

But take a careful look at this graph. The "bins" that constitute each bar on the graph vary wildly in size. The initial bins are in increments of five or ten thousand dollars. No wonder the bars are low: These are narrow bins! Then right as we get into the middle class—precisely where the author claims the tax base is largest—the bins expand dramatically in size. We get two bins that are twenty-five thousand dollars in width, and then a hundred-thousand-dollar bin. After that, the bins continue to expand. This choice of bin widths makes it look like the bulk of the taxable income is in the middle of the distribution.

Political scientist Ken Schultz wanted to highlight how a designer can tell completely different stories if allowed to choose variable bin widths. He took the same tax data but chose different sets of bins in order to tell three different stories.

---

* An apocryphal story relates that when asked "Why did you rob all those banks?" the legendary bank robber Willie Sutton replied, "Because that's where the money is."

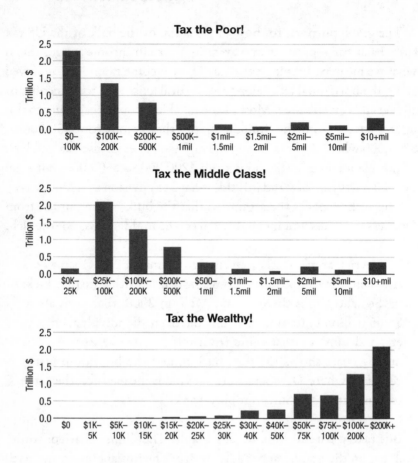

By changing the bin widths, Schultz was able to craft stories about how we need to tax the poor, the middle class (now defined as making less than $100,000 taxable income), and the very rich.

The Wall Street Journal may not have intended to mislead their readers. It turns out that the bins they depict are the same ones reported by the IRS. But, irrespective of the author's motives, you need to be on the lookout for all the ways the arrangement of data can influence a story.

Let's look at another example of how binned data can be deceptive. The data in the graph at the top of page 167 are intended to illustrate the degree to which genetics are predictive of educational achievement. The horizontal axis is an indicator of genetic composition, and the vertical axis is an average grade in high school classes. The trend looks extremely strong—at a glance, you would think that genes play a powerful role in determining educational outcomes.

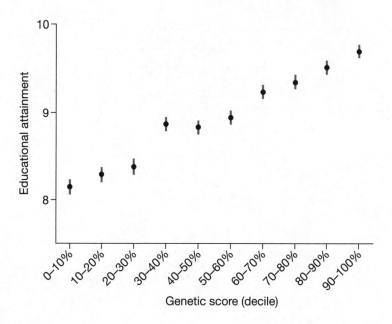

But when plotted this way, the data tell a misleading story. The problem is that they have been "binned." All of the points within each of ten intervals along the axis are collected together, and their average is plotted.* Taking averages like this conceals the huge variation in individual scores. The original data points, seen in the second graph on page 168, tell a different story. These are the very same data that were used to produce the earlier figure. Yet they look more like the aftermath of a shotgun blast than a strong linear trend! It turns out that the genetic score explains only 9 percent of the variation in educational attainment. If one is going to bin data, a so-called box-and-whisker plot does a much better job of representing the range of values within each bin.

Fortunately, the authors of this particular paper provide both views of the data so that we can see how misleading it can be to plot the means of binned data. But authors are not always so transparent. Sometimes only the binned means will appear in a scientific paper or

---

* Moreover, the error bars show the standard deviation of the mean, not the standard deviation of the observations. Thus they do not directly represent the dispersion of the points within the bin, but rather our uncertainty about a bin's mean value. This display choice exacerbates the misimpression that the data series forms a tight trend where genetic score is highly predictive of educational attainment.

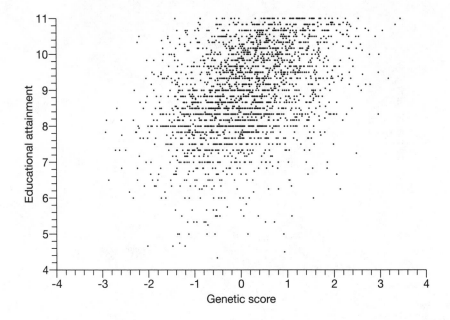

a news story about research results. Be on the lookout, lest you be duped into thinking that a trend is much stronger than it actually is.

THE PRINCIPLE OF PROPORTIONAL INK

ESPN summarized the results from a soccer match between West Bromwich and Arsenal with a data visualization like this:

Shots (on Goal)

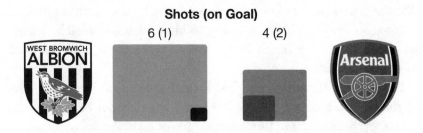

The graphic illustrates that West Bromwich had six shots, one of which was on goal, while Arsenal had four shots, two of which were on goal. But this is a misleading way to present those data. Consider the left panel. Because the shaded area representing shots on goal is so small compared to the lighter area representing all shots, one feels as if

West Bromwich was horribly inaccurate in shooting. But in fact, one-sixth of their shots were on target—which is not impressive, but not that bad either. The problem is that the dark region is one-sixth the width and one-sixth the height of the larger shaded area, giving it a mere one-thirty-sixth the area. The same problem arises in the right-hand panel. Half of Arsenal's shots were on goal, but the dark shaded region constitutes only a quarter of the larger shaded area.

The problem with this figure is that it uses shaded regions to represent numerical values, but the areas of these regions are not proportional to the values they represent. It violates what we term the principle of proportional ink:

> *When a shaded region is used to represent a numerical value, the size (i.e., area) of that shaded region should be directly proportional to the corresponding value.*

This rule derives from a more general principle that Edward Tufte set out in his classic book *The Visual Display of Quantitative Information.* There, Tufte states that "the representation of numbers, as physically measured on the surface of the graphic itself, should be directly proportional to the numerical quantities represented." The principle of proportional ink applies this rule to how shading is used on graphs. It sounds simple, but it is far-reaching. At the start of the previous section, we explained how a bar graph emphasizes magnitudes, whereas a line graph emphasizes the changes. As a result, a bar graph should always have a baseline at zero, whereas a line graph is better cropped tightly to best illustrate changing values. Why the apparent double standard?

The principle of proportional ink provides the answer. This principle is violated by a bar chart with axes that fail to reach zero. The bar chart from the Tennessee Department of Labor and Workforce Development, shown on the following page, illustrates the change over time in nonfarm jobs in that state.

In this chart the value for 2014 is approximately 1.08 times the value for 2010, but because the vertical axis has been truncated, the bar for 2014 uses approximately 2.7 times as much ink as the bar for 2010. This is not proportional ink.

Bar graphs can be misleading in the opposite direction as well, con-

Tennessee Total Nonfarm (Thousands)

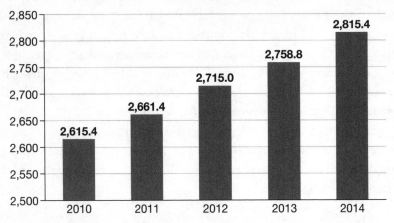

cealing differences instead of exaggerating them. The bar graph below, modeled on one published in *Business Insider,* purports to show the most read books in the world, though the fine print reveals that it actually shows the most sold books, a very different proposition. In any case, the graph is designed around the visual conceit of indicating

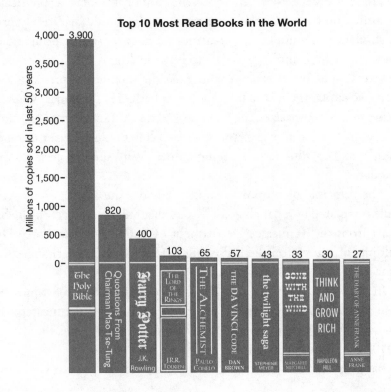

Top 10 Most Read Books in the World

the book's title by drawing the book as a part of the bar graph. The visual problem with this graph is that the portion of each bar used to display the title of each book is situated entirely below zero. As a result, the bars for *The Diary of Anne Frank* and for *The Da Vinci Code* differ in height by only a fraction of a percent, despite the fact that the latter has sold more than twice as many copies as the former.

As we discussed earlier in the chapter, line graphs need not include zero on the dependent variable axis. We noted that bar charts are designed to tell stories about magnitudes, whereas line graphs tell stories about changes. Note also that line graphs use *positions* rather than shaded areas to represent quantities. Because the amount of ink is not used to indicate the magnitude of a variable, the principle of proportional ink does not apply. Instead, a line graph should be scaled so as to make the position of each point maximally informative, usually by allowing the axis to span a region comparable in size to the range of the data values.

That said, a "filled" line chart, which does use shaded areas to represent values, should have an axis that goes to zero. In the example below, drawn after a figure published in *The Atlantic,* the vertical axis is cut off at 28 percent. This is misleading because it makes the decline in tax rates appear more substantial than it is. If the area below the curve were left unfilled, this would not be an issue.

Another violation of the principle of proportional ink arises in the

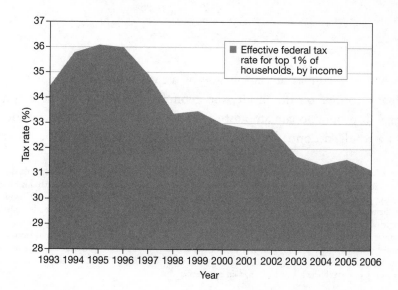

so-called donut bar chart. The donut is not yet common in data visualization work, but we are seeing it more often than we used to. Donut charts with multiple bars offer a particularly striking illustration of how a graph can exaggerate differences by violating the principle of proportional ink. The image below purports to illustrate differences in arable land per capita.

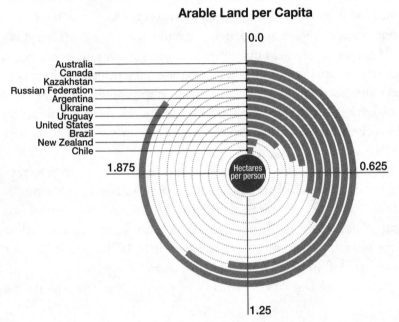

Source: CIA Factbook 2012 and FAO 2011

Just as a runner at the outside of a race track has farther to go than a runner on the inside, the geometry of the circles here confer a disproportionate amount of ink to bars farther on the outside.* As a result, a donut bar chart can exaggerate or conceal the differ-

---

* We can estimate the degree to which this graph deviates from the use of proportional ink. Take a curved band representing one value in the chart. If ϕ is the central angle associated with this band, r is the distance of between the center of the diagram and the center of the band, and w is the width of the band, the length of the band is ϕr and its area is approximately $\phi r w$. For example, the central angle of the band representing the US is approximately 75 degrees, and the central angle of the band representing Canada is approximately three times as large. The distance of the US band from the center of the diagram is approximately half the distance of the Canadian band. The widths of the two bands are the same. Thus while US value is one-third that of the Canadian value, the US band uses only one-sixth the ink of its Canadian counterpart.

ences between values, depending on how it is designed. When the bands are ordered from smallest in the center to largest at the periphery, as in the chart shown, the amount of ink used for each band exaggerates the differences in band sizes. If instead the bands were ordered from largest in the center to smallest at the periphery, the amount of ink used would play down the differences between values.

Another thing that can go wrong with data graphics involves comparisons of quantities with different denominators. If I tell you that one-quarter of car accidents involve drunk drivers, you don't conclude that drunk driving is safer than driving sober. You know that drunk driving is relatively rare, and that if one-quarter of accidents involve drunk drivers, there must be a huge increase in risk.

But we don't always carry these intuitions over into our analysis of data graphics. Consider the following bar chart about car accident rates by age:

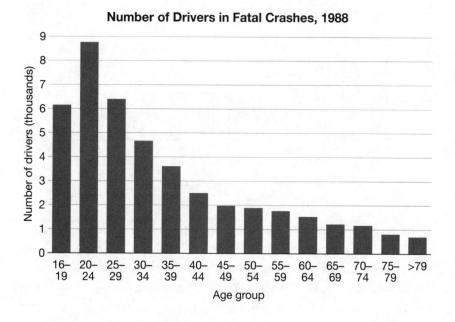

Number of Drivers in Fatal Crashes, 1988

Looking at this graph, two surprising things leap out. First, it appears that 16- to 19-year-olds may actually be better drivers than 20- to 24-year-olds. Second, it seems that people become better drivers as they age; we don't see the expected decline in driving ability among the elderly. But this graph is misleading because it reports the total number of fatal crashes, not the relative risk of a fatal crash. And critically, there are huge differences in the number of miles driven by people of different ages. The youngest and oldest drivers drive the fewest miles. When we look at the graph of fatal accidents per mile driven, we see a very different pattern. The youngest and oldest drivers are by the far the most dangerous.

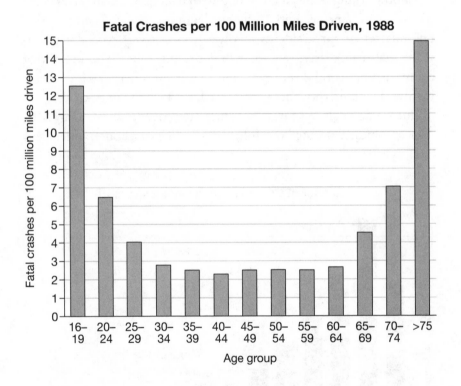

Fatal Crashes per 100 Million Miles Driven, 1988

In the late 1980s, a number of graphics software packages began to produce 3D bar charts. By the 1990s, the ability to create 3D bar charts was ubiquitous across data graphics packages, and these charts began to appear in venues ranging from corporate prospectuses to scientific papers to college recruiting brochures. 3D bar charts can serve a legitimate purpose when they are used to display values associated with a pair of independent variables, as in the 1996 example on the next page.

This is not a particularly attractive graph, and it suffers from a few issues that we'll discuss shortly, but it serves the purpose of organizing

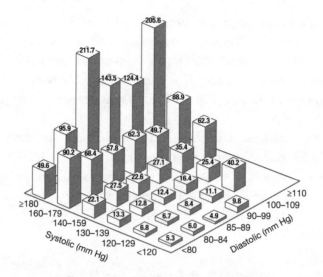

a two-dimensional matrix of values.* Where 3D data graphics move into straight-up bullshit territory is when they are used to represent data with only one independent variable. In these cases, a 2D line graph or bar graph would serve the purpose much better. The figure below illustrates the female birth rate in the US over the past eighty

Female Birth Rates by Age, U.S.A.

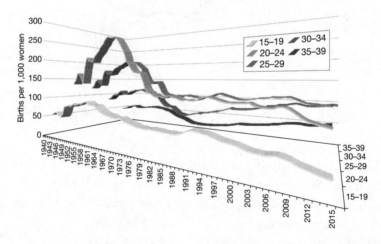

---

* The most common alternative to a 3D bar chart is a "heat map." This is a 2D grid with the same x and y axes as the 3D bar chart, but instead of using height to encode the third value, a heat map uses color. Heat maps look cleaner but are problematic because readers struggle to map variations in color to differences in numeric values. Moreover, difference between two regions may look big or small depending on the color palette. Finally, heat maps can be subject to the so-called checker shadow illusion, whereby the perceived shade of a region is influenced by that of its neighbors.

years. Look at the graph and ask yourself basic questions about the data. For example: Did the baby boom peak at the same time for women of all ages? When did the birth rate for women 35 to 39 surpass that for women 15 to 19? Is the birth rate for women 30 to 34 higher in 1940 or in 2010? It's difficult to answer any of the questions from this graph.

Below are the same data plotted as a standard 2D bar graph. Now it is straightforward to answer the types of questions we just asked. The baby boom *did* peak at about the same time for all age groups. The birth rate for women 35 to 39 exceeded that for women 15 to 19 around 2003. The birth rate for women 30 to 34 was higher in 2010 than in 1940.

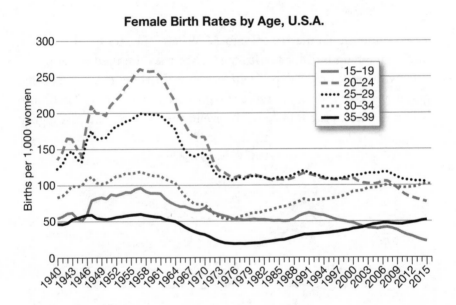

The only reason to use the third dimension seems to be to impress the viewer. Someone might have been impressed back in the early 1990s, when 3D rendering technology was new, but we have no idea why designers continue to use 3D line graphs today.

Another example: a bar chart of manure production in several US states. There are a few problems with the next graph. First, the endcaps extend the effective visual length of each bar; most of the ink that is used for Washington's bar goes to the endcap. Even though Washington produces only a fifth as much bullshit as California and

Annual Manure Production

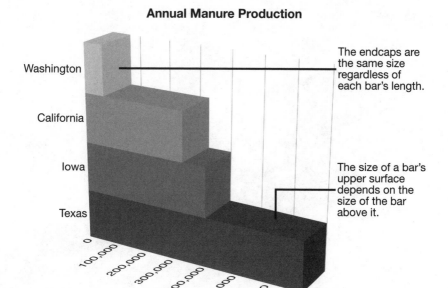

The endcaps are
the same size
regardless of
each bar's length.

The size of a bar's
upper surface
depends on the
size of the bar
above it.

only a tenth as much bullshit as Texas, all three endcaps are the same size. Second, the angle at which the graph is arrayed can make it difficult to assess the lengths of the bars. It would be much easier to see the exact values if the graph were shown squarely from the side. Third, because the bars are stacked atop one another, the tops of some bars are mostly visible and the tops of others are mostly obscured. In the graph above, the amount of ink used for the Texas bar depends not only on Texas's manure production but also on Iowa's. This is another violation of the principle of proportional ink.

Another serious deficit of 3D graphs is that the use of perspective makes it substantially harder for a viewer to assess the relative sizes of the chart elements. This effect is subtle in the manure production graph above but is highly conspicuous in the search engine market share graph at the top of page 178. In this graph, it is clear that the horizontal gridlines are not parallel but rather recede toward a vanishing point off the left side of the graph. As a result, bars toward the left are shorter, and use less ink, than equivalently valued bars toward the right. Again, this is pure visual bullshit: An element added to the graph to impress the viewer obscures its meaning without adding any additional information.

Search Engine Market Share

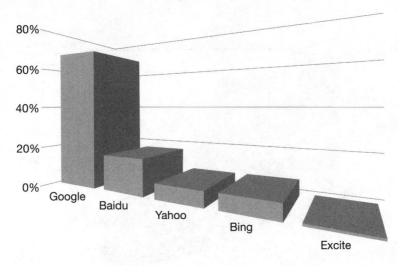

Three-dimensional pie charts, such as the Ontario polling chart below, are even worse.*

ONTARIO ELECTION POPULAR VOTE POLLING

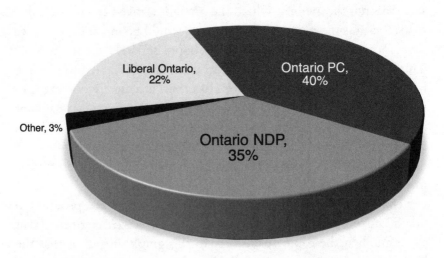

---

* We are not big fans of ordinary two-dimensional pie charts, for that matter. The main purpose of using a pie chart, rather than a bar graph, is to visually indicate that a set of values are fractions or percentages that add up to a whole. This message comes at a considerable cost: Comparing values is more difficult with a pie chart than with a bar chart because is harder for the viewer to compare the angles subtended by two arcs than to compare the height for two bars.

The main problem with 3D pie charts is that the frontmost wedges of the pie chart appear larger than the rear wedges. The Ontario NDP wedge represents 35 percent of the vote but takes up about 47 percent of the surface of the disk. By comparison, the Ontario PC wedge represents 40 percent of the vote but only 32 percent of the disk's surface. In this case, looking at the ink instead of the numbers flips the election in favor of the NDP. An additional problem is that the viewer sees the front edge but not the back edge of the pie chart, which violates the principle of proportional ink.

Data visualizations tell stories. Relatively subtle choices, such as the range of the axes in a bar chart or line graph, can have a big impact on the story that a figure tells. Ask yourself whether a graph has been designed to tell a story that accurately reflects the underlying data, or whether it has been designed to tell a story more closely aligned with what the designer would like you to believe.

CHAPTER 8

Calling Bullshit on Big Data

The Navy revealed the embryo of an electronic computer today that it expects will be able to walk, talk, see, write, reproduce itself and be conscious of its existence.

THUS BEGAN A JULY 8, 1958, ARTICLE IN *THE NEW YORK TIMES.* THE embryo was a simple building block called the *perceptron.*

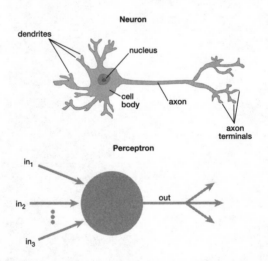

"Perceptron." The word sounds magical—Houdini's new act—but like any good conjuring trick, its real magic lies in its simplicity. A perceptron is a simple logical circuit designed to mimic a biological neuron. It takes a set of numerical values as inputs, and then spits out either a 0 or a 1. The numerical inputs might be the pixel values of a chest X-ray; the output, whether a patient has pneumonia.

Connect enough of these perceptrons together in the right ways, and you can build a chess-playing computer, a self-driving car, or an algorithm that translates speech in real time like Douglas Adams's Babel Fish. You don't hear the term "perceptron" often these days, but these circuits are the building blocks for the convolutional neural networks and deep learning technologies that appear in headlines daily. The same old magic is still selling tickets.

The inventor of the perceptron, Frank Rosenblatt, was a psychologist by training, with broad interests in astronomy and neurobiology. He also had a knack for selling big ideas. While working at the Cornell Aeronautical Laboratory, he used a two-million-dollar IBM 704 computer to simulate his first perceptron. He described his work in grandiose terms. His machine, he told *The New York Times,* would think the way that humans do and learn from experience. Someday, he predicted, his perceptrons would be able to recognize faces and translate speech in real time. Perceptrons would be able to assemble other perceptrons, and perhaps even attain consciousness. Someday they could become our eyes and ears in the universe, sent out beyond the bounds of Earth to explore the planets and stars on our behalf.

Imagine the buzz that this kind of talk would have generated in 1958. How many science fiction writers were inspired by Rosenblatt and the sensationalized reports that followed?

Let's fast-forward fifty-five years. On December 28, 2013, *The New York Times* published yet another article about neural networks and their brain-like capabilities—retelling the same 1958 story. Though the computer hardware is vastly more powerful, the basic approach remains close to what Rosenblatt described a half century earlier. The author of the 2013 article speculated that in a very short amount of time, these brain-like machines "will make possible a new generation of artificial intelligence [AI] systems that will perform some functions that humans do with ease: see, speak, listen, navigate, manipulate and control." It was as if the original writers outslept Rip Van Winkle, waking fifty-five years later to write the same article about the same technology using the same superlatives.

So, what has changed since Rosenblatt's early experiments with perceptrons? The hype certainly hasn't diminished. The newspapers are full of breathless articles gushing about the latest breakthrough that someone promises is just around the corner. AI jobs are paying superstar salaries. Tech firms are wooing away from campus professors with AI expertise. Venture capital firms are throwing money at anyone who can say "deep learning" with a straight face.

Here Rosenblatt deserves credit because many of his ambitious predictions have come true. The algorithms and basic architecture behind modern AI—machines that mimic human intelligence—are pretty much the same as he envisioned. Facial recognition technology, virtual assistants, machine translation systems, and stock-trading bots are all built upon perceptron-like algorithms. Most of the recent breakthroughs in machine learning—a subdiscipline of AI that studies algorithms designed to learn from data—can be ascribed to enormous leaps in the amount of data available and the processing power to deal with it, rather than to a fundamentally different approach.*

Indeed, machine learning and artificial intelligence live and die by the data they employ. With good data you can engineer remarkably effective algorithms for translating one language into another, for example. But there's no magical algorithm that can spin flax into gold. You can't compensate for bad data. If someone tells you otherwise, they are bullshitting.

How does machine learning work? It is a twist on the usual logic of computer programming. In a classical computer program, you write a program, give the computer data, and then the computer generates output:

In machine learning, you give the computer a set of *training data*. If you are teaching a computer to tell the difference between drawings of cats and dogs, these would be cat pictures and dog pictures. You

---

* Even though the term "big data" has already started to sound somewhat dated compared to fresher alternatives such as "machine intelligence" and "deep [anything]," we have titled this chapter around the phrase "big data" because it is data that is driving technology's current heyday. The algorithms are basically the same ones invented in the 1950s, and even computational power has started to level off over the past ten years.

also give the computer a set of *labels* for the training data that you know to be correct. In the cat and dog example, the computer would be told for each training image whether it was looking at a cat or a dog. The computer then uses a learning algorithm to produce a new program. For example, the learning algorithm might teach a neural network to distinguish cats from dogs. Then you can use the new program to label unfamiliar data, the *test data*. In the cat and dog example, you could then give the computer drawings it had never seen before, and it would tell you whether they are of cats or dogs.

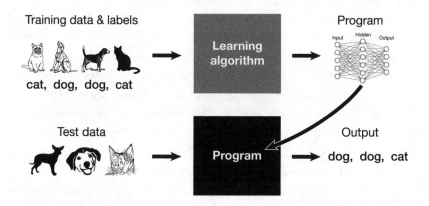

Because the data are central to these systems, one rarely needs professional training in computer science to spot unconvincing claims or problematic applications. Most of the time, we don't need to understand the learning algorithm in detail. Nor do we need to understand the workings of the program that the learning algorithm generates. (In so-called deep learning models, no one—including the creators of the algorithm—really understands the workings of the program that algorithm generates.) All you have to do to spot problems is to think about the training data and the labels that are fed into the algorithm. Begin with bad data and labels, and you'll get a bad program that makes bad predictions in return. This happens so often that there is an acronym for it in computer science: GIGO—garbage in, garbage out. We'd like to deflate the hype behind AI, with a focus on the data rather than the details of the algorithm inside the black box.

The promise of AI spurs economic activity and inspires exciting science fiction plots; but it also creates unreasonable expectations, drives irresponsible research in both industry and academia, threatens to extinguish any hope of personal privacy, and motivates misdirected policy. Researchers and technologists spend far too much time focusing on the sexy what-might-be, and far too little time on the important what-is. As Zachary Lipton, an AI researcher at Carnegie Mellon University, explains, "Policy makers [are] earnestly having meetings to discuss the rights of robots when they should be talking about discrimination in algorithmic decision making." Delving into the details of algorithmic auditing may be dull compared to drafting a Bill of Rights for robots, or devising ways to protect humanity against Terminator-like superintelligent machines. But to address the problems that AI is creating now, we need to understand the data and algorithms we are already using for more mundane purposes.

There is a vast gulf between AI alarmism in the popular press, and the reality of where AI research actually stands. Elon Musk, the founder of Tesla, SpaceX, and PayPal, warned US state governors at their national meeting in 2017 that AI posed a "fundamental risk to the existence of human civilization." Around the same time, *Fast Company* fueled those fears with an article headlined "AI Is Inventing Languages Humans Can't Understand. Should We Stop It?" Sounds scary, right? The story described a Facebook research project gone awry. While trying to build a chatbot that could carry on a convincing conversation, researchers tried having computer algorithms train one another to speak. But the speech that the algorithms developed was nothing like human language. *Fast Company* reported that the researchers quickly shut down the project. Skynet was officially on its way to self-awareness, but disaster had been averted—or so the story, and many others like it, suggested.

So what did this robot language look like? Let's take a look at some snippets of the chatbot conversation:

> BOB THE BOT: "I can can I I everything else."
> ALICE THE BOT: "Balls have zero to me to me to me to me to me to me to me to me to."
> BOB: "You I everything else."
> ALICE: "Balls have a ball to me to me to me to me to me to me to me to me."

It could be that AI will indeed evolve its own language and become self-aware. If it does, we hope it does so in peace and harmony with humans. But this Facebook chatbot was not headed down that particular road. The original blog post from the Facebook team simply described a research project where the chatbot language evolved the repetition of nonsensical sentences. The popular press distorted these into dramatic stories about shocked researchers scrambling to shut down the project and save the human race. But when asked by Snopes reporters about the story, the researchers commented that they had been unconcerned. It was the media response that surprised them. "There was no panic," one researcher said, "and the project hasn't been shut down." They weren't afraid for humankind. They simply observed that the chatbots were not heading toward the goal of human-like conversation, and went back to the drawing board.

We want to provide an antidote to this hype, but first, let's look at an instance in which machine learning delivers. It involves a boring, repetitive, everyday task that has received too little limelight rather than too much.

HOW MACHINES SEE

When you think about cutting-edge information technology, odds are you don't think about the US Postal Service. But in fact, few industries depend so critically upon advances in machine learning.

The US postal system processes half a billion pieces of mail every single day. It's a staggering number. If all seven billion people on the planet sent a letter or package, the postal service could process them all in a fortnight. This, even though the address on each piece of mail has to be read and interpreted. For typewritten addresses, this task is reasonably easy to delegate to machines. Handwriting is harder, but the US postal service has developed a remarkable handwriting recognition system that correctly interprets handwritten addresses 98 percent of the time. Those include your doctor's handwritten holiday cards, your grandma's letter to her local congresswoman, and your six-year-old's letter to the zoo pleading for a live video feed of the new baby giraffe.

What about the 2 percent of letters that can't be read by the machine? Those letters go to a massive postal complex in Salt Lake City. There, address experts decipher illegible addresses twenty-four hours a day, seven days a week, in thirty-three different shifts. The fastest of all the employees can process more than 1,800 addresses per hour, or one every two seconds! Santa's elves would have a hard time keeping up.

When it comes to open-ended tasks involving judgment and discretion, there is still no substitute for human intervention. Identifying fake news, detecting sarcasm, creating humor—for now, these are areas in which machines fall short of their human creators. However, reading addresses is relatively simple for a computer. The digit classification problem—figuring out whether a printed digit is a one, a two, a three, etc.—is a classic application of machine learning.

How does a computer do this? Much as we described in the cat and dog example. First we assemble a set of training data. We assemble a large collection of handwritten numbers—thousands of images— that humans have labeled as 0, 1, 2, . . . 9. Much of the time, the only limit to the computer's learning capacity is the availability of high-quality labels with which to train the machine. Fortunately for the postal service, an appropriate set of labeled, handwritten digits was created many years ago. It is called MNIST, the Modified National Institute of Standards and Technology database for handwritten digits, and it includes seventy thousand labeled images of handwritten digits, similar to those drawn below.

So how does the algorithm "see" images? If you don't have a background in computer vision, this may seem miraculous. Let's take a brief digression to consider how it works.

A computer stores an image as a matrix. A matrix can be thought of as a table of rows and columns. Each cell in this table contains a number. For simplicity, let's assume that our image is black and white. If a cell is black, the value is 0; otherwise, it is 1.*

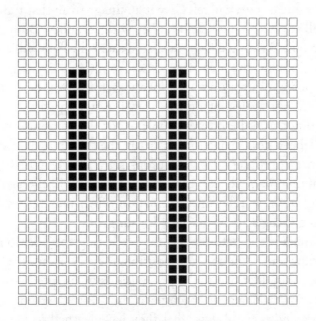

The 28-row-by-28-column image above indicates the numeral 4. There are 784 squares, and each square is filled with a 0 or 1. Computers "see" images through these matrices. Seeing the digit 4 means identifying the unique properties of matrices that correspond to a handwritten 4 and then comparing matrices of similar images.

The known images with "4" are the training data on which machines learn.† Given enough training data and quantitative methods

---

* Grayscale images provide more options. Instead of just 1 or 0, the cell values can be numbers between 0 and 255, with smaller numbers corresponding to darker shades of gray. For color images, each cell has a value for red, green, and blue, separately.

† When training data with known labels is available, we call this a supervised machine learning problem. When labels with right or wrong answers are not available, we generally call it an unsupervised machine learning problem. As an example of an unsupervised learning problem, we might aim to find groups of customers with similar purchasing patterns. In this chapter, we focus on supervised machine learning problems.

for penalizing mistakes, we can teach the machine to consistently classify a handwritten "4." To evaluate how well the machine is learning, we provide it with test data: data it has never seen before. It is in dealing with test data that the rubber hits the road.

Often algorithms will perfectly classify all the training data, by essentially memorizing every data point and all its attributes. For the handwritten numerals, the machine might memorize the exact position and value of every pixel. Give it an image from that training set, and it will correctly guess the number with certainty. But that is not good enough. Training data drawn from the real world will invariably be messy. Some of the messiness comes from the idiosyncrasies of individual penmanship; some from badly scanned images; some when an image is mislabeled or drawn from the wrong data set entirely. Memorizing this noise creates problems for the computer when it is asked to label a new image that wasn't in the training set. If the accuracy of the computer's labeling drops significantly when it moves from training data to test data, the model is likely *overfitting*— classifying noise as relevant information when making predictions. Overfitting is the bane of machine learning.*

When scientists create models for predicting the positions of the planets, they don't catalog every position of every planet at every possible time; they identify the key physical laws for predicting future positions. The challenge in machine learning is to develop algorithms that can *generalize,* applying what they have learned to identify patterns they haven't seen before.

To get a better sense of how machines identify patterns and make predictions, let's walk through an example with nothing more than open and filled circles. But you could think of this as a data set of patients with and without diabetes based on various health indicators. Suppose we want to come up with a rule to predict whether a new point, not among this set, will be light or dark. The hundred points we already have are our training data. The dark circles are mostly at the top and the light circles are mostly at the bottom, so we might try to come up with a boundary that separates the light circles from the dark ones.

---

* When a model ignores both the noise and relevant patterns in the data, we call this underfitting, and it too can be a problem. In this case, the algorithm may perform about as well on the test data as on the training data—but performance on both data sets will be poor.

Miscategorized: 0 Dark, 0 Light

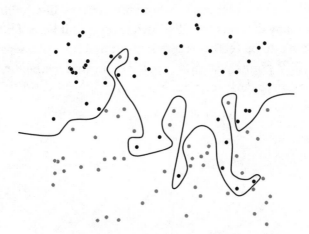

This boundary shown above—our model—does a beautiful job and gets every point of the training data correct. Every point above the boundary is dark, every point below is light. However, when given an additional hundred points (below), eleven filled points fall below the boundary and nine light points end up above it. What happened is that the boundary we picked from the training data weaved and wound its way between the light and dark points, and in doing so treated random noise in the data as if it were a meaningful pattern. Our model overfit the data.

Miscategorized: 11 Dark, 9 Light

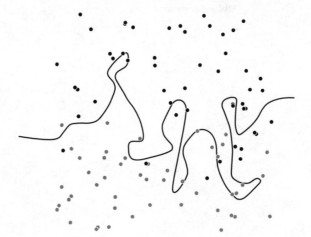

To avoid overfitting, we could try using a simpler model. Let's try a straight line for a boundary. Though a straight line might be too simple for many data sets, it will illustrate our point here. This simpler model doesn't do perfectly—there is no straight line that separates the light and dark points perfectly—but we can find a straight line that misclassifies seven dark and ten light points.

Miscategorized: 7 Dark, 10 Light

This simpler model doesn't go twisting and winding all over the place to get every single point in the right place; it hasn't overfit the training data. Thus it performs about as well on the test data as it did on the training data. On the test data, this model misclassifies six dark points and five light points.

Miscategorized: 6 Dark, 5 Light

This is just a toy example, but the same issues arise in most machine learning applications. Complicated models do a great job of fitting the training data, but simpler models often perform better on the test data than more complicated models. The trick is figuring out just how simple of a model to use. If the model you pick is too simple, you end up leaving useful information on the table.

GARBAGE IN, GARBAGE OUT

Why is it so important to understand the role of training data in machine learning? Because it is here where the most catastrophic mistakes are made—and it is here where an educated eye can call bullshit on machine learning applications. In chapter 3, we told a story about a machine learning algorithm that was supposed to detect who was a criminal, but instead learned to detect who was smiling. The problem was with the training data. The criminal faces used to train the algorithm were seldom smiling, whereas the noncriminal faces were usually smiling. In the real world, smiling is not a good indicator of whether someone is a criminal or not, but the machine didn't know it was supposed to be finding signs of criminality. It was just trying to discriminate between two different sets of faces in the training set. The presence or absence of a smile turned out to be a useful signal, because of the way the training images were chosen.

No algorithm, no matter how logically sound, can overcome flawed training data. Early computing pioneer Charles Babbage commented on this in the nineteenth century: "On two occasions I have been asked, 'Pray, Mr. Babbage, if you put into the machine wrong figures, will the right answers come out?' . . . I am not able rightly to apprehend the kind of confusion of ideas that could provoke such a question."

As we noted earlier, good training data are often difficult and expensive to obtain. In addition, training data typically come from the real world—but the real world is full of human biases and their consequences. For various reasons, the glamorous side of machine learning research involves developing new algorithms or tweaking old ones. But what is more sorely needed is research on how to select appropriate, representative data. Advances in that domain would pay rich dividends.

Let's now return to the post office. In this case, the data used to train the algorithm are actually quite good. The MNIST collection of handwritten letters and numbers is comprehensive. The correct label for each image is straightforward to determine. There isn't much bullshit to call. The methods work well, sorting mail quickly and efficiently, while saving shippers and taxpayers millions of dollars.

Even relatively straightforward problems reading handwritten addresses run into issues of sampling bias, however. If our training data included only numbers written by United States residents, the algorithm might misclassify many 1s as 7s, because elsewhere in the world, a 1 is sometimes written with a hook at the top (and a 7 is written with a crosshatch to distinguish it).

We need to be sure that the training data cover the same range of variation that our algorithm will encounter in the real world. Fortunately, even when we account for international variation in writing styles, numerals afford a relatively constrained set of possibilities compared to most other data sets. Compare the challenge of teaching an algorithm to classify news stories as true or fake. This is much harder than deciding whether a handwritten numeral is a six. You don't necessarily know the answer just by looking at it; you may have to do some research. It's not clear where to do that research, or what sources count as authoritative. Once you find an answer, reasonable people still might not agree whether you are looking at fake news, hyperpartisan news, satire, or some other type of misinformation. And because fake news is continually evolving, a training set of fake news stories from 2020 might be out of date by 2021.

To call bullshit on the newest AI startup, it is often sufficient to ask for details about the training data. Where did it come from? Who labeled it? How representative is the data? Remember our black box diagram:

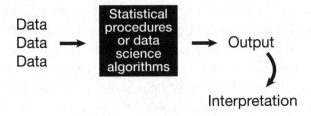

If the data going into the black box pass your initial interrogation, skip the algorithm and focus instead on the other end of the chain: what comes out of the black box and how it's interpreted.

GAYDAR MACHINES AND BULLSHIT CONCLUSIONS

In early September 2017, *The Economist* and *The Guardian* released a pair of oddly credulous news stories claiming that researchers at Stanford had developed AI capable of detecting a person's sexual orientation. The AI didn't need to observe a subject's behavior, examine his or her medical history (thank goodness), or ask anyone any questions. All it needed was a picture of a subject's face. The researchers announced that their AI could infer a person's sexual orientation from tiny differences in facial structure, differences too subtle for human observers to pick up at all.

This work attracted considerable attention from traditional and social media alike. Commentators mostly questioned the ethical implications of conducting such a study, given that homosexuality is often stigmatized, outlawed in a number of countries, and in some places even punishable by death. Should this sort of software have been developed at all? What were the implications of releasing it? What would this research mean for the LBGTQ community? These are all valid questions, but the first question should have been whether the study itself was any good.[*]

The *Economist* and *Guardian* stories described a research paper in which Stanford University researchers Yilun Wang and Michal Ko-

---

[*] We will assume that the authors reported their experiment accurately and that their algorithm performed as well as described. Indeed, their basic finding—that an algorithm can guess sexual orientation at a rate better than chance—was replicated using different training and test data in an unpublished master's thesis by John Leuner, though the algorithm had somewhat lower accuracy in that study.

sinski trained a deep neural network to predict whether someone was straight or gay by looking at their photograph. Wang and Kosinski collected a set of training images from an Internet dating website, photos of nearly eight thousand men and nearly seven thousand women, evenly split between straight and gay. The researchers used standard computer vision techniques for processing the facial images. When given pictures of two people, one straight and the other gay, the algorithm did better than chance at guessing which was which. It also did better than humans charged with the same task.

There are so many questions one could ask about the training data. What are the consequences of using training data that treats sexual preference as binary (gay or straight) instead of as a continuum? Do the photographs include a representative population? How were the photographs collected? Are the labels (straight or gay) accurate? What kinds of biases arise in the sample? These are all good questions, but here we want to look at what comes out of the black box instead of what goes in. We will ask whether the authors' two main inferences are justified based on their results.

Inference 1: The computer can detect subtle facial features that humans cannot.

The authors argue that the neural net is picking up on features that humans are unable to detect: "We show that faces contain much more information about sexual orientation than can be perceived and interpreted by the human brain." While the results are consistent with this claim, they do not come anywhere near demonstrating it. Indeed, there is a simpler explanation for why the computer does better than human subjects: The contest between the human and machine is not fair. For one thing, untrained human judges are pitted against a highly trained algorithm. The machine had thousands of images to learn from. The human players had no chance to practice, aside from exposure to a small number of images to make sure they understood the rules of the game.*

---

* Another concern is that the human judges were recruited through Amazon's Mechanical Turk crowdsourcing system. As such, they could have been working from anywhere in the world and may have not have been familiar with US cultural norms around how self-presentation varies with sexual orientation.

But there is a bigger problem. Humans are not good at aggregating information to make decisions, whereas computational learning algorithms do this sort of thing very well. Imagine the following: We provide a machine learning algorithm with a camera feed that shows a blackjack table. The machine then watches millions of blackjack games and learns to play. Blackjack is a simple game, and a standard learning algorithm could quickly infer good rules of thumb for playing. Once we have trained our algorithm, we compare the performance of the computer to the performance of nonexpert humans. The computer player would substantially outperform the average human player. So, what should we conclude?

One might conjecture that the machine can see some facet of the undealt cards that people cannot. Perhaps it is picking up information from the back of the facedown card atop the dealer's deck, for example. But notice that we are asking the computer and the humans to do two separate things: (1) detect cues on the game table, and (2) make good decisions about what to do given these cues. With our excellent visual systems and pattern detection abilities, humans are very good at the former task. How do we prove to websites that we are humans and not bots? By solving "CAPTCHA" visual processing challenges. But we are terrible at making probabilistic decisions based on partial information. It would be silly to conclude that the cards are somehow marked in a way visible to machines but hidden to humans. The simpler and more reasonable interpretation is that untrained humans are making stupid bets.

A parallel situation arises when we ask a computer or a human to determine, from photographs, which of two people is more likely to be gay. A human viewer gets all sorts of information from a photograph. Rather than trying to decide whether to hit or stand with a jack and a four while the dealer is showing a six,* you might see that one person has a baseball cap while the other has full sideburns. One has an eyebrow piercing, the other a tattoo. Each of these facts shifts your probability estimate of the subjects' sexual orientations. But by how much? How do these facts interact? Even trained humans are poor at making this kind of decision, and humans in this study are untrained. Of course they're no match for AI.

---

* Stand.

Inference 2: The differences the computer picks up
are due to prenatal hormone exposure.

After concluding that the computer was picking up cues that go undetected by humans, Wang and Kosinski set out to explore what these cues might be. They observed that the faces of people with homosexual and heterosexual orientation had, on average, slightly different contours. From this finding the authors made a bizarre inferential leap to something known as the prenatal hormone theory (PHT) of sexual orientation. This theory proposes that differences in sexual orientation arise due to differences in hormone exposure prior to birth. The authors explain:

> According to the PHT, same-gender sexual orientation stems from the underexposure of male fetuses or overexposure of female fetuses to androgens [hormones associated with development of male characteristics] that are responsible for sexual differentiation. . . . As the same androgens are responsible for the sexual dimorphism of the face, the PHT predicts that gay people will tend to have gender-atypical facial morphology. . . . According to the PHT, gay men should tend to have more feminine facial features than heterosexual men, while lesbians should tend to have more masculine features than heterosexual women. Thus, gay men are predicted to have smaller jaws and chins, slimmer eyebrows, longer noses, and larger foreheads; the opposite should be true for lesbians.

Wang and Kosinski conclude that their findings "provide strong support for the PHT."

But extraordinary claims require extraordinary evidence. The idea that homosexual and heterosexual people have differently shaped faces due to prenatal hormone exposure is an extraordinary claim. Instead of extraordinary evidence, however, we get almost no evidence at all. Instead, the authors present us with the observation that the facial contours inferred by the deep neural net look a bit different. The gold standard for demonstrating differences in facial shapes requires 3D facial measurements under controlled laboratory conditions; Wang and Kosinski use machine learning on self-selected 2D photographs from a dating site.

But all we really know is that a deep neural net can draw a distinction between self-selected photos of these two groups for reasons that we don't really understand. Any number of factors could be involved in the variation of these facial shapes, ranging from grooming to attire to photo choice to lighting. At the very least, the authors would need to show a statistically significant difference between face shapes. They fail to do even this.*

Suppose we were actually convinced that this study shows real structural, physiognomic differences (as opposed to differences in self-presentation) according to sexual orientation. Would these provide strong evidence for the PHT? Such results would be consistent with PHT, but, again, they don't offer strong evidence. What is the standard for strong evidence? To provide strong evidence for a hypothesis, a test has to put the hypothesis on the line—it has to have the potential to reject the hypothesis if the results come out a certain way. If this experiment had found no facial differences according to sexual preference, PHT proponents might explain that away either by pointing to the same kinds of limitations in study design that we have discussed above, or by positing that the primary effects of prenatal hormone exposure are behavioral rather than physiognomic.

On the other hand, if there are statistically significant actual physical differences in facial structure according to sexual orientation, they could arise from any of a number of mechanisms. The correlation between facial structure and sexual preference could be genetic. It could be due to some aspect of the environment other than hormone exposure. It could be due to hormone exposure outside the womb. It could be that people with different facial structures are treated differently, leading to differences in sexual orientation. Or it could be that differences in sexual orientation lead to differences in facial structure.

---

* The authors do find a statistically significant correlation between a measure that they call "facial femininity" and the probability of having a homosexual orientation. Moreover, the algorithm can make better-than-chance guesses based upon facial outline and nose shape. So the algorithm seems to be picking up something, but we suspect that facial contours and "facial femininity" are readily influenced by aspects of self-presentation including makeup, lighting, hairstyle, angle, photo choice, and so forth.

(This is not as silly as it sounds; facial width may be influenced by diet and exercise, which may be associated with sexual orientation.) We could go on and on. Our point is simply that the present study, even if taken at face value, does not support PHT over other possible explanations for homosexuality.

The results of the Wang and Kosinski paper are *consistent* with conclusions that the authors draw: that the possibility exists that computers can detect facial features that humans cannot, and that facial differences associated with sexual orientation arise through differences in prenatal hormone exposure. But the experiment fails to rule out numerous explanations that we consider more likely. We suspect the most likely explanation for their findings is that untrained humans are poor at integrating multiple cues to make good probabilistic estimates, and that sexual orientation influences grooming and self-presentation. Both of these are well-known facts; the former can explain why the neural network outperforms humans and the latter can explain why the neural network performs substantially better than chance. With those explanations in hand, there is no need to invoke mysterious features below the threshold of human perception, or effects of prenatal hormone exposure on facial structure. Wang and Kosinski overstepped in drawing strong conclusions from their weak results.

In the original paper and in conversations on Twitter, Wang and Kosinski expressed a wish that, for the sake of human rights, their results turn out to be wrong. We hope this analysis will help them rest easy.

HOW MACHINES THINK

It is not difficult to question the training data, as we did for the criminal faces paper in chapter 3, or the interpretation of the results, as we did for the gaydar paper in this chapter. And you can do both without opening the black box; in neither case did we have to discuss how a neural network operates.

Understanding the intricate details of how a specific algorithm makes decisions is a different story. It is extremely difficult to understand how even the most straightforward of artificial intelligence systems make decisions. Trying to explain how deep learning algorithms or convolutional neural networks do so is more difficult still. If you don't believe us, ask a computer scientist to explain how her neural network actually arrives at its results.

This opacity is a major challenge for the field of machine learning. The core purpose of the technology is to save people having to tell the computer what to learn in order to achieve its objective. Instead, the machines create their own rules to make decisions—and these rules often make little sense to humans.*

To better understand the decision-making process, researchers are finding new ways to peer into what the machines are "seeing" when they make decisions. Computer scientist Carlos Guestrin and his colleagues developed a straightforward, automated method for distinguishing photographs of huskies from photographs of wolves. In their paper they described the classification task, the methods they used, and how well their algorithm performed. Then they went one step further and looked at what information the algorithm was using in each image to draw the distinction.

Most studies don't take this extra step. It's difficult and the end users of these methods often don't care. "The method can distinguish huskies from wolves 70 percent of the time. Let's build an app." But we should care. This kind of examination allows us to better understand the limitations of AI and helps us interpret decisions that go awry in more serious applications.

Guestrin and his co-authors found that the algorithm was not paying much attention to snouts, eyes, fur, or any of the morphological features a person would use to distinguish a husky from a wolf. Instead, it was picking up on something external, a correlate of being a wolf that was present in the images. The machine learned that the wolf images but not the husky images tended to be shot in the snow, and exploited this difference in making its decisions.

---

* The AlphaGo program, which beat one of the best human Go players in the world, provides a good example. AlphaGo didn't start with any axioms, scoring systems, lists of opening moves, or anything of the sort. It taught itself how to play the game, and made probabilistic decisions based on the given board configuration. This is pretty amazing given the 10^{350} possible moves that Go affords. By comparison, chess has "only" about 10^{123}. Go masters have learned some new tricks from the play of AlphaGo, but good luck trying to understand what the machine is doing at any broad and general level.

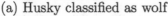

(a) Husky classified as wolf   (b) Explanation

When machine learning algorithms key in on auxiliary features of this sort, they may do well at analyzing images exactly like the ones they were trained on, but they will not be able to generalize effectively to other contexts. John Zech and colleagues at California Pacific Medical Center wanted to investigate how well neural networks could detect pathologies such as pneumonia and cardiomegaly—enlarged heart—using X-ray images. The team found that their algorithms performed relatively well in hospitals where they were trained, but poorly elsewhere.

It turned out that the machine was cueing on parts of the images that had nothing to do with the heart or lungs. For example, X-ray images produced by a portable imaging device had the word PORTABLE printed in the upper right corner—and the algorithm learned that this is a good indicator that a patient has pneumonia. Why? Because portable X-ray machines are used for the most severely ill patients, who cannot easily go to the radiology department of the hospital. Using this cue improved prediction in the original hospital. But it was of little practical value. It had little to do with identifying pneumonia, didn't cue in on anything doctors didn't already know, and wouldn't work in a different hospital that used a different type of portable X-ray machine.

Machines are not free of human biases; they perpetuate them, depending on the data they're fed. In the case of criminal sentencing, *ProPublica* and others have shown that algorithms currently in use are identifying black defendants as "future" criminals at nearly twice the rate as white defendants, which leads to differences in pretrial release, sentencing, and parole deals. Algorithmic lenders charge higher interest rates to both black and Latino applicants. Automated hiring software from some of the largest US employers such as Amazon have preferentially selected men over women. When we train machines to make decisions based on data that arise in a biased society, the machines learn and perpetuate those same biases. In situations like this, "machine learning" might better be called "machine indoctrination."

To address the major impact that algorithms have on human lives, researchers and policy makers alike have started to call for algorithmic accountability and algorithmic transparency. Algorithmic accountability is the principle that firms or agencies using algorithms to make decisions are still responsible for those decisions, especially decisions that involve humans. We cannot let people excuse unjust or harmful actions by saying "It wasn't our decision; it was the algorithm that did that." Algorithmic transparency is the principle that people affected by decision-making algorithms should have a right to know why the algorithms are making the choices that they do. But many algorithms are considered trade secrets.*

Perhaps the biggest problem with algorithmic transparencies comes back to the interpretability issue. Even if companies fully revealed the details of their algorithms, all their features and parameters, it may still be nearly impossible to understand why the algorithms make the decisions they do. Government policies can demand accountability, but they're not worth much if no one can understand what is going on well enough to explain what the algorithm is doing.†

Algorithmic biases can be particularly difficult to eradicate. Policy makers may require rules that forbid decisions based on race or gender, but it is often not sufficient to simply omit that information in the data provided to an algorithm. The problem is that other pieces of information may be correlated with race or gender, particularly when considered in concert. For example, if you build a machine to predict where the next domestic violence event will occur, the machine may choose an apartment over detached housing since those who share a

---

* Another reason to conceal the details of the algorithms is that secrecy also helps deter gaming. If Google were to release the exact details of its algorithm, search engine optimization companies would have a field day manipulating the algorithm, and the quality of Google's search results would decline.

† For example, the new General Data Protection Regulation (GDPR) in the European Union includes a "right to explanation" in Recital 71. This companion document will be influential going forward, but it is the most debated of all subjects in the GDPR, partly because of the difficulty in defining what is meant by "explain."

wall are more likely to report the event. This kind of prediction then resurfaces racial elements that you tried to remove in the first place. If you remove names from résumés as a way of eliminating gender discrimination, you may be disappointed, as Amazon was, when the machine continues to preferentially choose men over women. Why? Amazon trained the algorithm on its existing résumés, and there are features on a résumé besides a name that can reveal one's gender— such as a degree from a women's college, membership in a women's professional organization, or a hobby with skewed gender representation.

Philosophers often describe knowledge as "justified true belief." To know something, it has to be true and we have to believe it—but we also have to be able to provide a justification for our belief. That is not the case with our new machine companions. They have a different way of knowing and can offer a valuable complement to our own powers. But to be maximally useful, we often need to know how and why they make the decisions that they do. Society will need to decide where, and with which kinds of problems, this tradeoff—opacity for efficiency—is acceptable.

HOW MACHINES FAIL

In 2009, *Nature* published an article that described a new method for predicting flu outbreaks based on the search terms people use when querying Google. Terms such as "fever," "headache," "flu symptoms," and "pharmacies near me" could be used to track the spread of flu across the United States. Not only could these search frequencies and their geolocations be used to predict doctor visits, the method was both faster and cheaper than the epidemiological tracking methods employed by the Centers for Disease Control and Prevention (CDC).

The paper generated tremendous excitement and was covered by nearly every major newspaper and media outlet. Tech evangelists touted the results as an example of how big data would change the world. University professors, including one of the authors of this book, discussed the paper in their courses. Startup companies based around data analytics inserted the *Nature* paper into their pitch decks. When you have Google-scale data, argued *Wired* editor Chris Anderson, "the numbers speak for themselves." The scientific method was no longer necessary, he argued; the huge volumes of data would tell us everything we need to know. Data scientists didn't need years of epidemiological training or clinicians to diagnose flu symptoms. They just need enough data to "nowcast"* the flu and inform the CDC where to deliver Tamiflu. Or so we were told.

In all the excitement, we forget that if it sounds too good to be true, it probably is. And it was. By 2014, the headlines had turned from celebratory to monitory: "Google and the Flu: How Big Data Will Help Us Make Gigantic Mistakes," "Why Google Flu Is a Failure," "What We Can Learn from the Epic Failure of Google Flu Trends." The method worked reasonably well for a couple of years but, before long, the results started to miss the mark, not by a little but by a factor of two. Over time, the predictions continued to get worse. The results became so poor that Google axed the project and took down the Flu Trends website.

In retrospect, the study was doomed from the beginning. There was no theory about what search terms constituted relevant predictors of flu, and that left the algorithm highly susceptible to chance correlations in timing. For example, "high school basketball" was one of the top 100 predictors of a flu outbreak, simply because the search terms "flu" and "high school basketball" both peak in the winter. Like Hollywood relationships, spurious correlations fall apart on accelerated time scales. Search behavior and digital environments change— for example, Google introduced its "suggest" feature after this study was conducted.[†] Doing so likely altered people's search behavior. If you start typing "I am feeling" and the suggest feature offers "feverish," you may choose this term more often than other variants (e.g., "I am feeling hot"). This increases the frequency of certain queries, and in a vicious cycle they may become even more likely to be suggested by Google's autocomplete feature. When the frequency of search queries changes, the rules that the algorithm learned previously may no longer be effective.

If the Google Flu Trends algorithm had to predict flu cases for only

---

* "Nowcasting" is a flashy word made up to describe the practice of "predicting" aspects of the present or recent past using computer models, before anyone has time to measure them directly.

† The study included Web queries between 2003 and 2008. The suggest (autocomplete) functionality became broadly available on Google's website in 2008.

the first two years, we would still be writing about its triumph. When asked to extend beyond this time period, it failed. Sound familiar? Yep, this is overfitting. The machine likely focused on irrelevant nuances of that time period. This is where the scientific method can help. It is designed to develop theory that hyper-focuses on the key elements driving the spread of the flu, while ignoring the inconsequential. Search terms might be good indicators of those key elements, but we need a theory to help us generalize beyond two years of predictions. Without theory, predictions based on data rely on mere correlations.

When venturing into the black box, also consider the following. Many of the more complicated algorithms use dozens, hundreds, or even thousands of variables when making predictions. Google Flu Trends relied on forty-five key search queries that best predicted flu outbreaks. A machine learning system designed to detect cancer might look at a thousand different genes. That might sound like a good thing. Just add more variables; more data equals better predictions, right? Well, not exactly. The more variables you add, the more training data you need. We talked earlier about the cost of obtaining good training data. If you have ten thousand genes you want to incorporate into your model, good luck in finding the millions of example patients that you will need to have any chance of making reliable predictions.

This problem with adding additional variables is referred to as the *curse of dimensionality*. If you add enough variables into your black box, you will eventually find a combination of variables that performs well—but it may do so by chance. As you increase the number of variables you use to make your predictions, you need exponentially more data to distinguish true predictive capacity from luck. You might find that by adding the win-loss record of the New York Yankees to your list of a thousand other variables, you can better predict the Dow Jones index over the previous three months. But you will likely soon discover that this prediction success was the result of a chance alignment in the data—nothing more. Ask that variable to predict the index for the next three months, and the success rate will fall precipitously.

Researchers have not stopped trying to use data to help clinicians and solve health problems, nor should they. Researchers at Microsoft

Research are using search queries from Bing to detect people with undiagnosed pancreatic cancer, hopefully learning from the Google Flu Trends mistakes. Provided that it is collected legally, with consent, and with respect for privacy, data is valuable for understanding the world. The problem is the hype, the notion that something magical will emerge if only we can accumulate data on a large enough scale. We just need to be reminded: Big data is not better; it's just bigger. And it certainly doesn't speak for itself.

In 2014, TED Conferences and the XPrize Foundation announced an award for "the first artificial intelligence to come to this stage and give a TED Talk compelling enough to win a standing ovation from the audience." People worry that AI has surpassed humans, but we doubt AI will claim this award anytime soon. One might think that the TED brand of bullshit is just a cocktail of sound-bite science, management-speak, and techno-optimism. But it's not so easy. You have to stir these elements together just right, and you have to sound like you believe them. For the foreseeable future, computers won't be able to make the grade. Humans are far better bullshitters.

CHAPTER 9

The Susceptibility of Science

SCIENCE IS HUMANITY'S GREATEST INVENTION. OUR SPECIES HAS evolved to act within a narrow band of time scales, ranging from a few milliseconds to a few decades. We have evolved to operate within a similarly narrow band of spatial scales, ranging from micrometers to kilometers. Yet temporal and spatial scales of the universe run from unimaginably larger to incomprehensibly smaller. Science allows us to transcend these limitations. It gives us the tools to understand what happened in the first picoseconds following the Big Bang, and how the universe has evolved over the 13.7 billion years since. Science allows us to model the internal geometry of a single atom and to grapple with cosmological distances so large that we record them in light-years.

For all that it does, however, it would be a mistake to conclude that science, as practiced today, provides an unerring conduit to the heart of ultimate reality. Rather, science is a haphazard collection of institutions, norms, customs, and traditions that have developed by trial and error over the past several centuries. Science is culturally contingent on its emergence from European natural philosophy as practiced a few centuries ago, and evolutionarily contingent on the cognitive capacities of the species that practices it. Science is jury-rigged atop the evolved psychology of one particular species of ape, designed to provide members of this species with adequate incentives to work in concert toward a better understanding of the world around them. To do this, science relies on our unique human attributes—from our reasoning abilities to our modes of communication to our psychological motivations such as curiosity and status-seeking. If honeybees practiced their own form of science, it would likely be very different from our own. These observations do not demean science, but they do suggest that there may be value to lifting it down from its pedestal so that we can inspect it and evaluate its performance.

One of the reasons that science works so well is that it is self-correcting. Every claim is open to challenge and every fact or model can be overturned in the face of evidence. But while this organized skepticism makes science perhaps the best-known methodology for cutting through bullshit, it is not an absolute guarantor against such. There's plenty of bullshit in science, some accidental and some deliberate. Many scientific discoveries accurately reflect the workings of nature, but plenty of others—the notion of a geocentric universe, Giovanni Schiaparelli's Martian canals, cold fusion as an unlimited energy source—do not. In order to investigate faulty claims such as these, you'll need to be able to understand how they originate in the scientific literature.

First we want to look at what motivates scientists when they do research. Why do they put in all the hard hours and long nights working at their craft? Are all of them drawn by insatiable curiosity to probe the mysteries of nature in solitary concentration?*

* While Saint Jerome was a historian and theologian rather than a natural philosopher, Dürer's engraving captures the solitary quest for truth in our romanticized image of the scientist.

Philosophers who study science have often viewed science through this lens, focusing on how humans might ideally come to understand the natural world, while ignoring what inspires them to do so. Philosopher of science Philip Kitcher has a wonderful pair of terms for thinking about scientists and their motivations: *epistemically pure,* and *epistemically sullied.* An idealized scientist, interested only in advancing human understanding, is epistemically pure. Sir Francis Bacon, often credited as an early architect of the modern scientific method, exhorts his followers to epistemic purity in the preface of his *Instauratio Magna:*

> Lastly, I would address one general admonition to all; that they consider what are the true ends of knowledge, and that they seek it not either for pleasure of the mind, or for contention, or for superiority to others, or for profit, or fame, or power, or any of these inferior things; but for the benefit and use of life; and that they perfect and govern it in charity.

The rest of us—including every living scientist we know—are epistemically sullied. We act from the same human motivations as everyone else. This doesn't mean that scientists are irresponsible, untrustworthy, or unethical; it just means that they have other interests beyond the pure quest for understanding. To understand how science works and where things can go wrong, we need to understand what these interests are. So before addressing bullshit in science, let's look at what motivates its stewards.

While scientists tend to be intensely curious people who love solving puzzles, they are in most respects just like everyone else, striving to earn money and win status among their peers. We scientists want to understand how the world works, but we also want to impress our friends and colleagues, win the next promotion, and—if things go really, really well—make the big time with a guest appearance on the *Daily Show* or *Last Week Tonight.* Scientists seek both truth and recognition. In particular, scientists seek recognition for being the first to make a discovery. This is known in science as the *priority rule.*

Scientists build their reputations by publicizing their findings in scientific papers, typically articles of anywhere from two to fifty pages. Their results should be novel, relevant, complete, and correct.

The paper should describe experiments or observations that have not been previously reported. Its findings should tell us something we did not previously know about the world—even if they do so merely by strengthening the support for a previous argument. The article should relate to ongoing research questions that have already been deemed of interest to the community, or make a compelling case for the importance of a new research question. To be complete, a paper ought to describe the experiment or other work in enough detail that another expert in the field could reproduce the findings. Obviously a paper should not misreport findings, draw unfounded inferences, or make false claims. Finally, a paper should be of an appropriate scale. This is a matter of convention and varies across fields, but it relates to the scope of the work required to constitute a scientific publication. An afternoon's tinkering in the laboratory is insufficient, but years of efforts are typically broken into a series of publications.

Academic science relies on the process of peer review to uphold these standards. When an author wishes to publish a paper, she submits it to a scientific journal. The journal staff then send the unpublished article to a small number of referees: other scientists who have volunteered to read the paper, assess its quality, and suggest improvements. Journals occupy various positions in a prestige hierarchy. Publications in leading journals confer far more prestige than do other publications. The best journals are widely circulated, widely read, and set a high bar for the quality and importance of the articles that they publish. Other journals cater to narrower niche readership, and authors can often get papers accepted in these venues after they are rejected from the highest tier. There is even a tier of very low-quality journals that will publish more or less anything, often for a price.

Unlike industrial science, in which scientists' processes and discoveries are closely guarded, academic scientists compete to get their work into print, battle for attention on Twitter and Facebook, and vie to speak at conferences. Rewarding prestige instead of direct output is a wonderful trick for allowing a broad community of researchers to work together efficiently with minimal duplication of effort.

Findings are readily overturned when other researchers are unable to replicate them. In 1989, prominent electrochemists Martin Fleischmann and Stanley Pons announced that they had discovered cold fusion. In experiments, they combined a heavy isotope of water, known as deuterium, with palladium metal, and applied an electric current. They observed that their apparatus seemed to periodically generate more energy, in the form of heat, than they had put into their system. They speculated that this was a consequence of room-temperature nuclear fusion occurring among deuterium molecules within the palladium metal. If they had been right, their discovery would have provided a world-changing, readily accessible source of clean power. But, sadly, this was not to be. Many leading research labs attempted to replicate their findings, but none could. Within the year, the research community determined that cold fusion was not a real phenomenon, and the issue was put to rest.

Even science's deepest foundations can be questioned, and at times replaced, when they prove incompatible with current discoveries. Geneticists and evolutionary biologists had long assumed that genes were the sole molecular vehicles of inheritance. Offspring resemble their parents because they share the same DNA sequences in their genomes. But when genetic sequencing became inexpensive and new molecular biology techniques gave us ways to measure how genes were being activated, strong evidence began accumulating that this was not the full picture. In addition to passing their genes to their offspring, parents sometimes pass a second layer of nongenetic information about what genes to activate, when. This became known as epigenetics. Because our scientific understanding of the world can change in light of new evidence, science has proven resilient to the occasional wrong turn and even to deliberate misdirection in the form of scientific fraud.

Around the turn of the twenty-first century, replication problems began to crop up in a number of fields at unexpectedly high rates. Occasionally these problems were the result of fraud or incompetence, but far more often there were no simple explanations. Solid work by respected investigators simply could not be replicated.

In 2012, a paper in the leading scientific journal *Nature* suggested that replication failures might be more common than most suspected. Authors C. Glenn Begley and Lee Ellis reported that scientists working in a commercial lab were able to reproduce only 6 of 53 important cancer biology studies published in the recent scientific literature. Shortly thereafter, the Open Science Collaboration—a large-scale collective effort among dozens of researchers—reported that they were able to replicate only 39 out of 100 high-profile experiments in social psychology. In experimental economics, meanwhile, a similar effort was under way. One study revealed that only 11 of 18 experimental papers published in the very best economics journals could be replicated. Was science, one of our most trusted institutions, somehow generating inadvertent bullshit on a massive scale? And if so, why?

Scientific results could be irreproducible for a number of reasons. Perhaps the most obvious is outright fraud. If researchers have faked their data, we wouldn't expect to be able to replicate their experiments. Fraud generates enormous publicity, which can give a misleading impression of its frequency.* But outright fraud is rare. It might explain why one study in a thousand can't be replicated. It doesn't explain why half of the results in fields are irreproducible. How then do we explain the replication crisis? To answer this, it is helpful to take a detour and look at a statistic known as a p-value.

THE PROSECUTOR'S FALLACY

As we've seen, most scientific studies look to patterns in data to make inferences about the world. But how can we distinguish a pattern from random noise? And how do we quantify how strong a particular pattern is? While there are a number of ways to draw these

---

* Just a few examples from the past decade: Social psychologist Diedrich Stapel became a superstar within his field by concocting fake data for dozens of experiments that he never actually conducted. His misdeeds were striking in their sheer scale. He now has fifty-eight retracted papers, with more likely to follow. Readers may be interested in *Faking Science,* Stapel's exploration of how his own psychology led him to this large-scale fraud. As an author, Stapel appears disarmingly honest in exploring his own flaws, so the book is hard to put down. But as the socially skilled perpetrator of such a massive-scale fraud, how can we not view Stapel as something like the ultimate unreliable narrator?

The highest echelons of Japanese biomedical research were deeply shaken when other researchers failed to replicate work by young research superstar Haruko Obokata. An investigation revealed that Obokata had inappropriately manipulated images in her scientific papers, raising false hopes for stem cell researchers everywhere. In a tragic turn, Obokata's supervisor, Yoshiki Sasai, subsequently committed suicide amid the fallout from the scandal.

UCLA political scientist Michael LaCour misled the scientific community, including his coauthor, with fabricated data suggesting that direct interaction with gay canvassers can have a drastic effect on attitudes toward gay marriage. The work was widely reported by national and international media outlets before the deception was uncovered.

distinctions, the most common is the use of *p-values*. Loosely speaking, a *p*-value tells us how likely it is that the pattern we've seen could have arisen by chance alone. If that is highly unlikely, we say that the result is *statistically significant*. But what does this really mean, and how should we interpret it? We will explore these questions by means of a short story.

Imagine that you are a prominent defense attorney, defending a mild-mannered biologist against the charge that he has committed the greatest art heist of the new century.

The crime was a spectacular one. A wealthy collector shipped her private collection of thirty European masterpieces, by guarded railcar, from her home in Santa Clara to an auction house in New York City. When the train reached its destination, the boxes were taken to the auction house to be unpacked. The journey had passed uneventfully and the boxes appeared untouched, but to everyone's shock, the four most valuable paintings had been cut from their frames and were missing! Neither the police nor the insurance investigators were able to find a single clue—save for one fingerprint on the frame of one of the missing paintings. The stolen paintings were never found.

Without any other leads, the police ran the fingerprint through the FBI's massive new fingerprint database until they found a match: your client. (He had provided his fingerprints to the Transportation Safety Administration in exchange for the convenience of leaving his shoes on when passing through airport security.) Upon questioning, your client was discovered to have no alibi: He claimed that he had been cut off from human contact for two weeks, tracking radio-collared grouse through the High Sierras as part of a research project.

Lack of alibi notwithstanding, you are convinced that your client could not be the culprit. He is more of a bumbling academic than a steely-nerved art thief. He already has two NSF grants to fund his work on grouse breeding and seems to have little desire for additional income. And as best as you can tell, he doesn't know a damn thing about art—he thinks Donatello is a Ninja Turtle, for goodness' sake.

Yet the case goes to trial, and you face a brilliant up-and-coming prosecutor. After presenting all of the other evidence against your client—weak and circumstantial as it may be—she moves on to her trump card, the fingerprint. She describes the computerized fingerprint matching process to the jury, and closes her statement by declaring "There is absolutely no chance of getting a fingerprint match this good simply by accident."

You counter. "You said there is absolutely no chance of a match this good. That can't be possible. Every test has at least some chance of being mistaken."

"Well, sure," she concedes, "the test *could* be mistaken in principle. But for all practical purposes, there is zero chance of it actually happening. The FBI's own studies have shown a one-in-ten-million chance that two different fingerprints would match as well as the ones we have here. One in ten million: That's certainly far beyond any reasonable doubt!"

This is just what you were looking for. You turn to the jury and sketch out a two-by-two table on a large pad of paper. It looks something like this:

	MATCH	NO MATCH
Guilty		
Innocent		

"I think we all agree," you continue, "that this crime was indeed committed by someone. And let us also assume that the true culprit is in the fingerprint database. He might not be," you say to the prosecutor, "but that would only weaken your case. So let's assume for now that he or she is included."

The prosecutor nods.

"Then the table looks something like this." You fill in the top row with a large red marker.

	MATCH	NO MATCH
Guilty	1 person	0 people
Innocent		

Turning to the prosecutor, you inquire, "Now how many people are in that FBI database of yours?"

She breaks in: "Objection, Your Honor! How is that possibly relevant?"

"Actually, it's the heart of the matter," you respond. "I think I'll make that very clear in the next few minutes."

"Objection overruled."

Your opponent concedes that with all US criminal prints, all civil background-check prints, and all of the prints from the TSA, there are approximately fifty million Americans represented in the database. And of course the majority of those people will have prints that do not match the fingerprint on the painting's frame.

"So now we can fill in more of the table," you respond. You add a 50,000,000 to the lower right corner.

	MATCH	NO MATCH
Guilty	1	0
Innocent		50,000,000

Now you point at the lower left corner—innocent people who nonetheless match—and you ask, "What do you think goes here?"

You look right at the prosecutor. "You said that there is a one in ten million chance that the algorithm finds a false match. That means that with fifty million people in the database, there should be about five people who match the fingerprint found at the scene of the crime. So we can complete our table as follows."

	MATCH	NO MATCH
Guilty	1	0
Innocent	5	50,000,000

"So look at this," you say, turning to the jury. "The prosecutor is trying to distract you by calling your attention to this comparison." You point along the bottom row (shaded above). "There is a one-in-ten-million chance of seeing a match by accident. But that's not relevant to what we're doing here in the courtroom. We don't care what the chance is of having a match, given that my client is innocent. We already *know* that we've got a match."

	MATCH	NO MATCH
Guilty	1	0
Innocent	5	50,000,000

"No, we want to know what chance there is that my client is innocent given that we've got a match." Now you point to the left-hand column. "That is a completely different matter, and it is illustrated by the left-hand column. We expect there to be about five innocent matches in the database, and one guilty person. So given a match, there is about a one-sixth chance that the accused actually committed the crime.

"Now, I can't prove beyond a shadow of a doubt that my client is innocent. All I've got is his word that he was following . . . dammit, what kind of bird was that again? Never mind. The point is that I don't have to *prove* that my client is innocent. Here in America, he is innocent until presumed guilty, and the standard of proof for guilt is 'beyond a reasonable doubt.' If there are five chances in six that my client is innocent, we're clearly nowhere near that standard. You must acquit."

In the story we've just told, your argument is not sophistry; it is correct. If your client had been found simply by scanning through the FBI's database until a match was made, there would be something like a five in six chance that he did not leave the fingerprint.*

You and the prosecutor have each stressed different *conditional probabilities*. A conditional probability is the chance that something is true, given other information. The prosecutor asks what the chance

---

* While our story here is fiction, our society will be confronting similar issues with increasing frequency as larger and larger databases of DNA evidence become available. Such information is particularly useful to investigators—but also particularly problematic from a false-accusation perspective—because the suspect himself or herself need not be in the database. His or her identity can be triangulated from DNA contributed by relatives. In one prominent case, the so-called Golden State Killer was identified in 2018 by screening a DNA sample against about two hundred thousand entries contributed voluntarily to a genealogy website. Before finding what appears to be the correct match, investigators initially fingered the wrong suspect who happened to share rare genes with the killer. Facial recognition systems suffer from similar problems. One system, tested by London's Metropolitan Police, was described as having a 0.1 percent error rate based on its rate of correctly identifying true negatives. But only eight of the twenty-two suspects apprehended by using the system were true positives, for a whopping error rate of 64 percent among the positive results returned.

is that there is a false match, given an innocent person chosen at random.* We can write this as P(match|innocent). You are asking the converse: What is the chance that your client is innocent, given that there is a match, which we write as P(innocent|match). People often assume that these two probabilities must be the same, but that is not true. In our example, P(match|innocent) = 1/10,000,000 whereas P(innocent|match) = 5/6.

This confusion is so common that it has its own name, the prosecutor's fallacy. Our story illustrates why. It can be a matter of life and death in the courtroom, but it's also a common source of confusion when interpreting the results of scientific studies.

When Carl was a kid, he and his friends wanted to believe that their minds might have unrecognized powers, so they tried experimenting with mind reading and ESP. One time he opened a deck of playing cards, shuffled thoroughly, and had a friend turn over the cards one by one. Carl tried to call out the unseen suit of each card. He was hopeless—nowhere near 100 percent—so they quickly gave up. But suppose we wanted to go back today and analyze the results from that little experiment. It wouldn't take anything like 100 percent success to suggest something interesting was happening. Because there are four suits of cards, you would expect to get only one in four of the guesses right. If instead you got one in three correct, that might suggest that something curious was going on. But it's not at all obvious how much better than one in four Carl would have had to do to suggest that there was something other than random guessing at play. Suppose he correctly guessed the suit of 19 of the 52 cards. That's more than expected; on average one would guess only 13 correctly. But is 19 different enough from 13 to be meaningful?

This is where *p*-values come in. We can think of our task as trying to distinguish between two different hypotheses. The first, called the *null hypothesis* and written H0, is that Carl's guesses were no better than random. The second, called the *alternative hypothesis* and written H1, is that Carl was able to identify the cards at a rate higher than chance. The *p*-value associated with the experiment tells us how likely

---

* Note straight off that your client isn't a randomly chosen person; he was chosen specifically because the computer found a match.

it is that by guessing at random Carl would get 19 or more cards correct. We can use statistical theory to calculate the appropriate p-value. In this particular case, it turns out that there is only a 4.3 percent chance that one would do this well at random,* so we say that the p-value is 0.043.

So guessing at random, 95.7 percent of the time one would fail to get 19 or more correct. But the key thing to notice here is that this does not mean that we are 95.7 percent sure that H0 is false. These are two very different claims—and they closely parallel the two claims we looked at in the art heist example.

In the courtroom drama, the prosecutor calls the jury's attention to the probability of a match by chance, i.e., given that the client is innocent: one in ten million. This is analogous to the probability of getting 19 or more cards right simply by chance. But in the courtroom, we already knew our client matched, and in the ESP example, we already know that Carl got 19 cards right. So these probabilities are not the ones we want to calculate. Rather, we want to figure out what to believe after the experiment is done. In the courtroom we wanted to determine the probability that your client was guilty given a match. To assess the results of the mind-reading test we want to know the probability that something other than random chance was responsible for Carl's score.

So here's the dirty secret about p-values in science. When scientists report p-values, they're doing something a bit like the prosecutor did in reporting the chance of an innocent person matching the fingerprint from the crime scene. They would like to know the probability that their null hypothesis is wrong, in light of the data they have observed. But that's not what a p-value is. A p-value describes the probability of getting data at least as extreme as those observed, if the null hypothesis were true. Unlike the prosecutor, scientists aren't trying to trick anybody when they report this. Scientists are stuck using p-values because they don't have a good way to calculate the probability of the alternative hypothesis.

The image following illustrates the parallel. What the jury wants to know is the probability that the defendant is innocent, given the

---

* This assumes that the deck is shuffled between each guess, so that Carl can't gain a slight edge by counting cards.

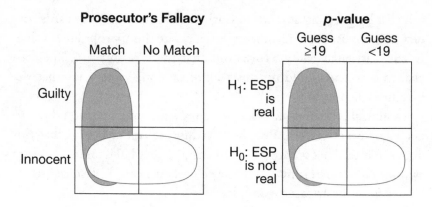

match. This is a matter of comparing the probabilities in the shaded vertical oval. Instead, the prosecutor tells them the probability of a match, given that the defendant is innocent. This is the comparison in the unshaded horizontal oval. Scientific *p*-values are the same. We want to know what the probability is that ESP is not real, given that Carl guessed at least 19 cards right. The shaded vertical oval illustrates this comparison. Instead, we are told the probability that Carl would guess at least 19 cards right, assuming that ESP is not real. The unshaded horizontal oval represents this comparison.

Why is it difficult to calculate the probability of the alternative hypothesis? That probability depends on how likely we thought it was before we did the experiment—and people seldom agree on that issue. Suppose the alternative explanation to random chance is:

> H1a: *There really is such a thing as ESP, but despite years of looking, occultists and spiritualists and even scientists never managed to observe it until two kids came along and did an experiment with playing cards in a suburban living room in Ann Arbor, Michigan, in the late 1970s.*

How likely would you have thought this H1a was before you knew that Carl correctly guessed 19 of 52 cards? A one-in-a-million chance? One in a billion? One in a trillion? Something extremely improbable, in any case. Given that, even after you know that he guessed 19 of 52 cards correctly, you have little reason to suspect that H1 is true. The odds that Carl and his friend were the first to observe human telepathy are vanishingly small, whereas at nearly 5 percent the probability of getting 19 right by chance is far higher.

But suppose instead that we consider a different alternative hypothesis for how Carl did so well.

H1b: *Carl's friend wanted to make him believe in ESP, so he sometimes reported that Carl had guessed correctly, even when he hadn't.*

If you'd known Carl's friend (who cheated at everything from basketball to solitaire), you would almost expect him to do something like this. So in this case, after you found out that Carl guessed 19 cards right, you'd say "That figures—Arnie probably lied about his score." The point here is that the probability of the alternative hypothesis after we see the data, $P(H_1 \mid \text{data})$, depends on the probability of the alternative hypothesis before we see the data, and that's something that isn't readily measured and incorporated into a scientific paper. So as scientists we do what we can do instead of what we want to do. We report $P(\text{data at least as extreme as we observed} \mid H_0)$, and this is what we call a *p*-value.

So what does all of this have to do with bullshit? Well, even scientists sometimes get confused about what *p*-values mean. Moreover, as scientific results pass from the scientific literature into press releases, newspapers, magazines, television programs, and so forth, *p*-values are often described inaccurately. For example, in 2012 scientists using the Large Hadron Collider in Geneva reported exciting results that supported the existence of the Higgs boson, an elementary particle that had long been predicted but never observed directly. Reporting on the story, *National Geographic* wrote that scientists "are more than 99 percent certain they've discovered the Higgs boson, aka the God particle—or at least a brand-new particle exactly where they expected the Higgs to be." What *National Geographic* should have reported is that the *p*-value for the experiment was 0.01. The results obtained with the Large Hadron Collider would have had a 1 percent probability of appearing by chance even if there had been such a thing as a Higgs boson. This does not mean that scientists were 99 percent sure that the Higgs boson was real. In the case of the Higgs boson, there were already good reasons to expect that the Higgs boson would exist, and its existence was subsequently confirmed. But this is not always the case.* The important thing to remember is that a very unlikely hypothesis remains unlikely even after someone obtains experimental results with a very low *p*-value.

P-HACKING AND PUBLICATION BIAS

Purely as a matter of convention, we often use a *p*-value of 0.05 as a cutoff for saying that a result is *statistically significant*.† In other words, a result is statistically significant when $p < 0.05$, i.e., when it would have less than 5 percent probability of arising due to chance alone.

Researchers are more interested in reading about statistically significant "positive" results than nonsignificant "negative" results, so both authors and journals have strong incentives to present significant results. Why are researchers and journals uninterested in negative results? It's not entirely clear to us, but there are a number of plausible contributing factors. Some of it may lie in our own psychology; to most of us negative results feel sort of boring. "These two groups don't differ." "This treatment doesn't change the outcome." "Knowing x doesn't help us predict y." Reading sentences like these, we feel like we're right back where we started, instead of learning something interesting about the world.

Negative results may also be associated with the inability to carry out a technical experiment. When Carl was working in a microbiology lab, he was often unable to grow his study organism *E. coli* on an agar plate. This wasn't an interesting scientific result; it just demonstrated his utter incompetence in a laboratory environment.

---

* In 2019, CNN reported on a physics paper that claimed to have evidence for a fifth fundamental force of nature. Referring to a *p*-value of one in one trillion, the article alleges that "there was only a one-in-a-trillion chance that the results were caused by anything other than the X17 particle, and this new fifth force." This is completely wrong. As in the Higgs boson example, the statement confuses the *p*-value for the probability of the hypothesis. But here it does so with a stronger *p*-value in support of a hypothesis that scientists find considerably less likely. Worse still, it implies that the existence of a fifth fundamental force is the *only* possible explanation for the results other than experimental error. That is not a valid inference. Something out of the ordinary seems to have happened in the experiment, but rejecting the null hypothesis does not guarantee that a researcher's favorite alternative hypothesis is true.

† Since the choice of 0.05 as the threshold for statistical significance is an arbitrary one, there is no reason it could not be set to some other value. A debate has recently emerged in the scientific literature about whether the cutoff value of 0.05 is a reasonable choice, or whether we should be using a more stringent cutoff such as 0.005.

A third possibility is that negative propositions are a dime a dozen. It's easy to state hypotheses that aren't true. Assemble words into sentences at random, and they'll usually be false. "Tulips bite." "Snowflakes melt iron." "Elephants are birds." Finding true statements in this sea of false ones is like looking for a needle of meaning in a haystack of nonsense. Think of it like the old board game Battleship. Most of the spaces on the grid are open water, so you don't learn much when you miss. But when you hit, you learn a great deal—and you can work from there to learn even more.

For all of these reasons, negative results simply do not get a huge amount of attention. We've never seen someone secure a job or win a prize by giving a lecture solely about the things she couldn't get to work in the lab.

Very few scientists would commit scientific fraud to get the *p*-values they want, but there are numerous gray areas that still undermine the integrity of the scientific process. Researchers sometimes try different statistical assumptions or tests until they find a way to nudge their *p*-values across that critical $p = 0.05$ threshold of statistical significance. This is known as *p*-hacking, and it's a serious problem. Or they will alter the outcomes they are testing. A clinical trial may set out to measure the effect of a new drug on survival after five years, but after finding no change, the researchers might mine the data and pull out an apparent improvement after three years in quality of life.

When you analyze data you have collected, you often get to make a large set of choices about what exactly to include in your study. For example, suppose I want to study how election results influence painkiller consumption in the US. I might tabulate election results, collect survey reports about painkiller use, and acquire data on painkiller sales over time. There are many degrees of freedom here. What elections do I look at? US president, US senator, US representative, state governor, state senator, state representative, mayor, city council member, etc.? Do I look at consumption by men, women, or both? Consumption by young adults, middle-aged adults, those over sixty-five, teens, all of the above? Am I looking at the effect of Democratic versus Republican candidates taking office, or am I looking at the effects of having a preferred versus nonpreferred candidate in office? In other words, do I control for the political stance of the user? And what counts as a painkiller? Aspirin, Advil, Tylenol, hydrocodone, OxyContin? Do I want to compare painkiller use in one location before and after the election, or do I want to look only after the election and compare different locations? There are a huge number of decisions I need to make before I can analyze my data. Given the many combinations, the likelihood is high that at least one of those combinations will show a statistically significant result—even if there is no causal relationship between election results and painkiller use.

To avoid this pitfall, researchers ought to specify all of these choices before they look at the data, and then test the one hypothesis they've committed to in advance.* For example, I might decide to test whether adult men and women of voting age take more painkillers after their preferred gubernatorial candidate has lost an election. Or I might test to see whether Children's Tylenol sales drop in districts where a Republican is elected to replace a Democrat in the US House of Representatives. Whatever it is that I choose to look at, the important thing is that I specify it clearly before I analyze the data. Otherwise by looking at enough different hypotheses, I'll always find some significant results, even if there are no real patterns.

But look at it from the researcher's perspective. Imagine that you have just spent months collecting a massive data set. You test your main hypothesis and end up with results that are promising—but nonsignificant. You know you won't be able to publish your work in a good journal this way, and you may not be able to publish at all. But surely the hypothesis is true, you think—maybe you just don't have quite enough data. So you keep collecting data until your p-value drops below 0.05, and then stop right away lest it drift back above that threshold.

Or maybe you try a few other statistical tests. Since the data are close to significant, the right choice of measures and of tests might allow you to clear the critical $p = 0.05$ bar. Sure enough, with a bit of tinkering, you find an approach that gives you a significant result.

Or maybe your hypothesis appears to be correct only for men, and the meaningful pattern is getting swamped out by including women

* If researchers want to test multiple hypotheses, there are statistical methods such as the Bonferroni correction that allow this. Each individual test then requires stronger evidence to be considered significant, so that there is roughly a one-in-twenty chance that *any* of the tested hypotheses would appear significant if the null hypothesis were true.

in your sample. You look—and lo and behold, once you look at men only, you've got a statistically significant result. What are you going to do? Scrap the whole project, abandon thousands of dollars invested, ask your graduate student to delay her graduation by another six months . . . or just write up the result for men and submit to a top journal? Under those circumstances it may feel easy to rationalize the latter approach. "I'm sure the trend is really there," you might tell yourself. "I was thinking about omitting women from the study right from the start."

Congratulations. You've just *p*-hacked your study.*

IMAGINE A THOUSAND RESEARCHERS of unimpeachable integrity, all of whom refuse to *p*-hack under any circumstances. These virtuous scholars test a thousand hypotheses about relationships between political victories and analgesic use, all of which are false. Simply by

---

* To illustrate how powerful *p*-hacking techniques can be, Joseph Simmons and colleagues Leif Nelson and Uri Simonsohn tested a pair of hypotheses they were pretty sure were untrue. One was an unlikely hypothesis; the other was impossible.

The unlikely hypothesis was that listening to children's music makes people feel older than they really are. Volunteers listened to either a children's song or a control song, and later were asked how old they felt. With a bit of *p*-hacking, the researchers concluded that listening to a children's song makes people feel older, with statistical significance at the $p < 0.05$ level.

While suggestive, the initial study was not the most persuasive demonstration of how *p*-hacking can mislead. Maybe listening to a children's song really does make you feel old. So the authors raised the bar and tested a hypothesis that couldn't possibly be true. They hypothesized that listening to the classic Beatles song "When I'm Sixty-Four" doesn't just make people feel younger, it literally makes them younger. Obviously this is ridiculous, but they conducted a scientific experiment testing it anyway. They ran a randomized controlled trial in which they had each subject listen either to the Beatles song or to a control song. Remarkably, they found that while people who listened to each song should have been the same age, people who heard "When I'm Sixty-Four" were, on average, a year and a half younger than people who heard the control. Moreover, this difference was significant at the $p < 0.05$ level! Because the study was a randomized controlled trial, the usual inference would be that the treatment—listening to the song—had a causal effect on age. Thus the researchers could claim (albeit tongue in cheek) to have evidence that listening to "When I'm Sixty-Four" actually makes people younger.

To reach these impossible conclusions, the researchers deliberately *p*-hacked their study in multiple ways. They collected information about a number of characteristics of their study subjects, and then controlled for the one that happened to give them the result they were looking at. (It was the age of the subject's father, for what that's worth.) They also continued the experiment until they got a significant result, rather than predetermining the sample size. But such decisions would be hidden in a scientific report if the authors chose to do so. They could simply list the final sample size without acknowledging that it was not set in advance, and they could report controlling for the father's age without acknowledging that they had also collected several additional pieces of personal information, which they ended up discarding because they did not give the desired result.

The paper makes a compelling case. If *p*-hacking can reverse the flow of time, what can it not do?

chance, roughly fifty of these hypotheses will be statistically supported at the $p = 0.05$ level. The fifty lucky researchers will write up their results and send them to journals where they are accepted and published. Of the other 950 researchers, only a handful will bother to write up their negative results, and of these only a few will be able to get their negative results published.

When a reader comes along and looks at the literature, she'll see fifty studies showing links between political outcomes and painkiller consumption, and perhaps a handful that find no association. It would be natural for her to conclude that politics heavily influences the use of painkillers, and the studies that didn't work must have simply measured the wrong quantities or looked for the wrong patterns. But the reality is the other way around. There was no relationship. The appearance of a connection is purely an artifact of what kinds of results are considered worth publishing.

The fundamental problem here is that the chance that a paper gets published is not independent of the p-value that it reports. As a consequence, we slam head-on into a selection bias problem. The set of published papers represents a *biased sample* of the set of all experiments conducted. Significant results are strongly overrepresented in the literature, and nonsignificant results are underrepresented. The data from experiments that generated nonsignificant results end up in scientists' file cabinets (or file systems, these days). This is what is sometimes called the *file drawer effect*.

Remember Goodhart's law? "When a measure becomes a target, it ceases to be a good measure." In a sense this is what has happened with p-values. Because a p-value lower than 0.05 has become essential for publication, p-values no longer serve as a good measure of statistical support. If scientific papers were published irrespective of p-values, these values would remain useful measures of the degree of statistical support for rejecting a null hypothesis. But since journals have a strong preference for papers with p-values below 0.05, p-values no longer serve their original purpose.[*]

In 2005, the epidemiologist John Ioannidis summarized the consequences of the file drawer effect in an article with the provocative title

---

[*] This is not a new insight. The statistician Theodore Sterling observed in 1959 that when we read a paper that has been selected for publication, "the risk [e.g., the p-value] stated by the author cannot be accepted at face value once the author's conclusions appear in print."

"Why Most Published Research Findings Are False." To explain Io-annidis's argument, we need to make a slight digression and explore a statistical trap known as the *base rate fallacy*.

Imagine that you are the physician treating a young man who is concerned that he may have contracted Lyme disease while on a fishing trip in Maine. He has felt poorly ever since but has not had the characteristic circular rash associated with Lyme. Mostly to relieve his concern, you agree to test his blood for antibodies against the bacteria that cause the disease.

To his dismay and yours, the test comes back positive. The test itself is reasonably accurate, but not exceptionally so. It shows a false positive about 5 percent of the time. What are the chances that your patient has Lyme disease?

Many people, including many physicians, would expect the answer to be somewhere around 95 percent. This is incorrect. Ninety-five percent is the chance that someone who doesn't have Lyme disease would test negative. You want to know the chance that someone who tests positive has Lyme disease. It turns out that this is a low probability, because Lyme disease is quite rare. In areas where it is endemic, only about one person out of one thousand is infected. So imagine testing 10,000 people. You'd expect to have about 10 true positives, and about $0.05 \times 10,000 = 500$ false positives. Fewer than 1 in 50 of those who test positive are actually infected. Thus you expect your patient would have less than a 2 percent chance of having the disease, *even after testing positive*.

This confusion—thinking that there is an about 95 percent chance that the patient is infected when actually the chances are less than 2 percent—should be a familiar mistake. This is our old friend, the prosecutor's fallacy, dressed up in new clothes. We sometimes call it the *base rate fallacy* because it involves ignoring the base rate of the disease in a population when interpreting the results of a test.

Recall our table from the prosecutor's fallacy:

	MATCH	NO MATCH
Guilty	1	0
Innocent	5	50,000,000

The analogous table for the base rate fallacy is as follows:

	POSITIVE TEST	NEGATIVE TEST
Infected	10	0
Uninfected	500	10,000

In each case, the mistake is to compare probabilities along the bottom row instead of down the left column.

The base rate fallacy is less of an issue if you are testing for a condition that is very common. Suppose you are treating a young Caucasian woman from the upper Midwest for stomach problems, and you decide to test for the presence of *Helicobacter pylori,* a stomach pathogen associated with peptic ulcers. As with the antibody test for Lyme disease, about 5 percent of uninfected people test positive when they use the urea breath test. If your patient tests positive, what are the chances that she is carrying *Helicobacter*? Is it also 1 in 100? No, it's far greater, because *Helicobacter* is a common pathogen. In the United States, about 20 percent of Caucasians carry *Helicobacter*. So imagine testing 10,000 people for this pathogen. You would see about 2,000 true positives, and about 5 percent of the remaining 8,000 people, i.e., about 400 people, would get false positive results. Thus among US Caucasians, roughly 5 in 6 of those who test positive for *Helicobacter* are actually carrying it.

With that out of the way, let's come back to Ioannidis. In his paper "Why Most Published Research Findings Are False," Ioannidis draws the analogy between scientific studies and the interpretation of medical tests. He assumes that because of publication bias, most negative findings go unpublished and the literature comprises mostly positive results. If scientists are testing improbable hypotheses, the majority of positive results will be false positives, just as the majority of tests for Lyme disease, absent other risk factors, will be false positives.

That's it. That's the whole argument. We can't really argue with Ioannidis's mathematics. His conclusions are correct, given his model. He also has some empirical support from the papers we discussed earlier, those demonstrating that many experiments published in good journals cannot be reproduced. If many of the positive findings for those experiments were false positives, this is exactly what we would expect.

What we can argue about are Ioannidis's assumptions. For most published findings to be false, scientific experiments would have to be like rare diseases: highly unlikely to generate a true positive result. Science doesn't work like that, because scientists get to *choose* what hypotheses they want to test. We've seen that scientists are finely attuned to the reward structure of their professional world, that rewards accrue mostly for publishing interesting work, and that it is difficult to publish negative results. So we would expect scientists to test hypotheses that, while undecided, seem reasonably likely to be true. This moves us toward the domain of the *Helicobacter pylori* example, where the majority of positive results are true positives. Ioannidis is overly pessimistic because he makes unrealistic assumptions about the kinds of hypotheses that researchers decide to test.

Of course, this is all theoretical speculation. If we want to actually measure how big of a problem publication bias is, we need to know (1) what fraction of tested hypotheses are actually correct, and (2) what fraction of negative results get published. If both fractions are high, we've got little to worry about. If both are very low, we've got problems.

We've argued that scientists will tend to test hypotheses with a decent chance of being correct. The chance may be 10 percent or 50 percent or 75 percent, but it is unlikely to be 1 percent or 0.1 percent. What about publishing negative results? How often does that happen? Across the sciences at large, about 15 percent of the results published are negative. Within biomedicine, 10 percent. Social psychology, a mere 5 percent. The problem is that we don't know from these data whether psychologists are less likely to publish negative results, or whether they are choosing experiments that are more likely to generate positive results. The fraction of published results that are negative is not what we really want to know. We want to know the fraction of negative results that are published.

But how can we get at that? We would have to somehow know about all of the unpublished results of experiments—and these tend to be buried in file drawers. Erick Turner at the US Food and Drug Administration (FDA) found an ingenious way to get around this problem. In the United States, whenever a team of investigators wants to run a clinical trial—an experiment using human subjects to test outcomes of medical treatments—they are required by law to register this trial with the FDA. This involves filing paperwork that explains what the trial is designed to test, how the trial will be conducted, and how the outcomes will be measured. Once the trial is completed, the team is also required to report the results to the FDA. However, they are not required to publish the results in a scientific journal.

This system provided Turner and his colleagues with a way of tallying both the published and unpublished trials in one particular area of research. Turner compiled a list of 74 clinical trials aimed at assessing the effectiveness of 12 different antidepressant medications. Results from 51 of these trials were published, 48 with positive results (the drug is effective) and 3 with negative results. Looking at the published literature, a researcher would conclude that these antidepressant drugs tend to work. But with access to the experiments as initially registered, the FDA sees a very different picture. They see 74 trials of which 38 yield positive results, 12 yield questionable results, and 24 yield negative results. From those numbers one would reach a more pessimistic conclusion—that some antidepressants seem to work somewhat under some circumstances.

What happened? How did clinical trials with a 51 percent success rate end up being reported as successful in 94 percent of the published papers? For one thing, almost all of the positive results were published, whereas fewer than half of the questionable or negative results were published. Yet more problematically, of the 14 questionable or negative results that were published, 11 were recast as positive findings.*

Turner illustrates these results with a graph that looks something like the upcoming graph. The dark rectangles represent negative results, the open ones positive results. Lightly shaded rectangles represent studies that originally returned questionable or negative results, but were published as positive findings.

---

* We caution against overly extrapolating from Turner's study. Clinical trials differ considerably from many other types of experiments, and they may be more—or less—subject to publication bias. On one hand, commercial interests may be involved to an unusual degree and may have some role in deterring the publication of negative results or encouraging that these results are reframed as positive. On the other hand, clinical research tends to be expensive, time-consuming, and generally involves a large number of investigators—so there may be strong incentives to publish results, whatever they may be.

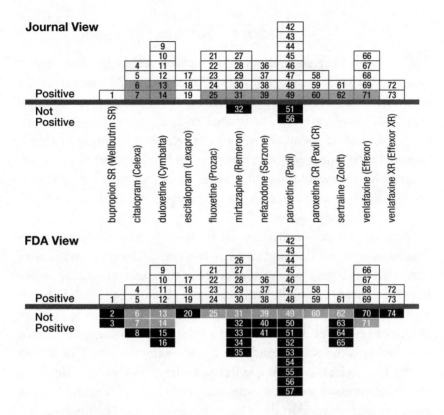

Just as a sailor sees only the portion of the iceberg above the water's surface, a researcher reads only the positive results in the scientific literature. This makes it difficult to tell how many negative results are lying beneath the waterline. They are rarely published and, if they do appear, are often spun to appear in the guise of positive results. If there isn't much below the waterline, we have strong support for whatever is being tested. But if there is considerable mass lurking below the surface, the impression one gathers from viewing only the surface can be highly misleading.

Fortunately, there are ways to estimate the size of the submerged piece of the iceberg. One of the most powerful approaches involves meta-analysis: looking at multiple studies simultaneously. Doing so, we may be able to see when the published literature is likely to be representative of the set of all experiments conducted, and when, instead, the published literature reflects problematic practices such as *p*-hacking or publication bias. Figuring out how best to do this has become a hot area in statistics research.

CLICKBAIT SCIENCE

Members of the general public are sometimes skeptical of professional scientists and their opinions. For example, 88 percent of the members of the AAAS—a professional association for scientists—feel that GMO foods are safe, compared with 37 percent of US adults overall. Of AAAS members, 87 percent believe that climate change is mostly due to human activity, compared with 50 percent of US adults overall. An overwhelming 98 percent of AAAS members are convinced that humans have evolved over time, compared with 65 percent of the US population.

Some of this public distrust can be attributed to deliberate, well-funded campaigns to manufacture uncertainty. The tobacco industry spent decades trying to sow doubts about the evidence linking smoking with cancer. The oil industry continues to attack the link between carbon emissions and climate change. Religiously motivated groups attempt to create public mistrust of evolutionary biology, in favor of so-called creation science and intelligent design theory. This is how cover-ups work at scale. People like to believe in massive conspiracies that keep some story—alien corpses on ice in Area 51, a moon landing staged in a Hollywood studio, CIA involvement in 9/11—undercover. But no one can keep a secret that big. Rather, the really big cover-ups take place out in the open, as climate denial does. The smoking gun is there for everyone to see; the cover-up is providing people with alternative reasons to believe it might be smoking.

Still, a fair share of the blame lies squarely on the shoulders of scientists and science reporters. For one thing, science reporting amplifies the publication bias problem that we see in the scientific literature. Newspapers and other sources of science news eagerly report potential breakthroughs, but many of these studies fail to pan out. This isn't necessarily a problem. Science works like that—only a few of the exciting new leads that we uncover withstand subsequent experiments. The problem arises because news sources often fail to clearly indicate the preliminary nature of the findings that they report, and worse yet, they seldom report when the studies covered previously fail to pan out.

Estelle Dumas-Mallet and her colleagues attempted to estimate the magnitude of this bias in news reporting. They looked at over five thousand papers about disease risk, of which 156 were reported in the popular press. All of the papers that received press attention reported positive results, in the sense that they suggested links between disease and genetic or behavioral risk factors. Thirty-five of these papers (about which 234 news articles had been written) were disconfirmed by subsequent research. Yet when that happened, only four news articles were published pointing out that the original stories were incorrect. Negative results simply aren't exciting.

Think about the endless parade of newspaper stories about the health effects of red wine. One week, a single daily glass of wine increases heart disease risk, and the next week that same glass of wine decreases this risk. So long as a research study on this topic finds a relationship, it seems newsworthy. But when a follow-up study finds that the relationship was spurious, the popular press isn't interested. No wonder members of the public feel jerked around by the scientists who can't decide whether wine is good or bad, and no wonder they quickly become cynical about the entire enterprise.

Popular science writing often allows, if not actively encourages, a fundamental misunderstanding about what the results of a single study mean for science. In the news media and even in textbooks, scientific activity is often portrayed as a *collecting process,* and a scientific paper as the report of what has been collected. By this view, scientists search out the facts that nature has hidden away; each uncovered fact is published in a scientific paper like a stamp laid in a collector's album; textbooks are essentially collections of such facts.

But science doesn't work like this. The results of an experiment are not a definitive fact about nature. The results of experiments involve chance, as well as a web of assumptions about how such results are properly assessed. The interpretation of experimental results involves a yet more complex network of models and assumptions about how the world works. Rather than representing a definitive fact about nature, each experiment or collection of observations merely represents an argument in favor of some particular hypothesis. We judge the truth of hypotheses by weighing the evidence offered from multiple papers, each of which comes at the issue from a different perspective.

This distinction has important implications for how we ought to interpret media reports about scientific studies. Suppose a new study reports cardiac benefits associated with moderate consumption of red wine. This is not a new fact to be engraved in our canon of knowledge. Rather, it represents yet one additional contribution to an oft-studied question, marginally shifting our beliefs in the direction of the hypothesis "red wine has cardiac benefits." A single study doesn't tell you much about what the world is like. It has little value at all unless you know the rest of the literature and have a sense about how to integrate these findings with previous ones.

Practicing scientists understand this. Researchers don't make up their minds about a complex question based on an individual research report, but rather, weigh the evidence across multiple studies and strive to understand why multiple studies often produce seemingly inconsistent results. But the popular press almost never reports the story in this way. It's boring.

Even when popular science articles discuss multiple studies, they do not always do so in a representative fashion. The epithet "cafeteria Catholic" suggests a worshipper who picks and chooses from the tenets of the faith, ignoring those that are uncomfortable or unpleasant. Science writers sometimes engage in an analogous practice that we call cafeteria science. They pick and choose from a broad menu of studies, to extract a subset that tells a consistent and compelling story.

Scientists are not altogether innocent of this practice either. In 1980, two researchers published a brief hundred-word note in *The New England Journal of Medicine,* reporting a low rate of addiction to narcotic painkillers based on medical records of hospitalized patients. Following the release of the opioid painkiller OxyContin, this paper was widely cited in the medical literature as evidence that opioids rarely cause addiction—a massive overstatement of its findings. Some scholars go so far as to ascribe a portion of the ongoing opioid crisis to the uncritical use of the paper to minimize concerns about addiction. In 2017, the editors of the *New England Journal* took the highly unusual step of issuing a warning that now appears atop the article. While the warning does not question the paper's findings, it cautions: "For reasons of public health, readers should be aware that this letter has been 'heavily and uncritically cited' as evidence that addiction is rare with opioid therapy."

Worse still, there is a powerful selection bias in what scientific studies we end up hearing about in the popular press and on social media. The research studies that are reported in the popular press are not a random sample of those conducted, or even of those published. The most surprising studies are the ones that make the most exciting articles. If we fail to take this into account, and ignore all of the less surprising findings from related studies, we can end up with an unrealistic picture of how scientific knowledge is developing.

When science writers cast scientific studies in popular language, they sometimes omit important caveats, offer stronger advice than is justified, present correlations as causal relationships, or extrapolate from findings in lab animals to suggest immediate application in humans. Very often these errors are not introduced by the reporters; they are already present in the press releases issued by universities and scientific journals. Charged with producing more and more material in less and less time, science writers often rely heavily on these releases as source material. Less reputable news outlets and blogs often go one step further, republishing press releases in the guise of original reporting.

In the spring of 2015, astronaut Scott Kelly boarded a rocket for a trip to the International Space Station. Three months later he returned to Earth a changed man. A NASA press release reported that

> Researchers now know that 93% of Scott's genes returned to normal after landing. However, the remaining 7% point to possible longer term changes in genes related to his immune system, DNA repair, bone formation networks, hypoxia, and hypercapnia.

Major news networks interpreted this as meaning that Kelly's genome changed by 7 percent. "Astronaut's DNA No Longer Matches That of His Identical Twin, NASA Finds," announced CNN. "NASA Twins Study Confirms Astronaut's DNA Actually Changed in Space," reported *Newsweek*. "After Year in Space, Astronaut Scott Kelly No Longer Has Same DNA as Identical Twin," declared the *Today* show. On Twitter, Scott Kelly joked, "What? My DNA changed by 7%! Who knew? I just learned about it in this article. This could be good news! I no longer have to call @ShuttleCDRKelly my identical twin brother anymore."

But wait—this doesn't even pass a very basic plausibility check. A chimpanzee's genome is only 2 percent different from a human's. In fact, Kelly's genes themselves didn't change. The way his genes were expressed did. In other words, there were persistent changes in the rates at which about 7 percent of his (unchanged) genes were being translated into proteins. This is unsurprising. Changes in environmental conditions commonly drive changes in gene expression. Geneticists and other biologists responded immediately, trying to correct the misinformation on social media and in news interviews. NASA issued a correction to its press release. Some news outlets wrote entire stories about the debacle. But most people had moved on and the corrections received only a fraction of the attention given to the original story. Jonathan Swift had it right: "Falsehood flies, and truth comes limping after it."

THE MARKET FOR BULLSHIT SCIENCE

In a typical economic market for consumer goods, money flows in one direction; goods flow in the other. A steel company provides raw materials to an auto manufacturer, which assembles cars and sells them to consumers. The consumers pay the manufacturer, which in turn pays the steel company. The market for scholarly journals is different. A scholar pours her heart and soul into writing a scholarly paper. She provides her work to an academic publisher, which collects a number of such articles and bundles them together as a journal issue. The publisher charges libraries to subscribe, but doesn't pass any of the revenue on to the authors.

Some journals even require that the author pay to have her work published. Why would anyone pay? Recall what motivates academic scholars. As we discussed earlier in the chapter, scholars are rewarded

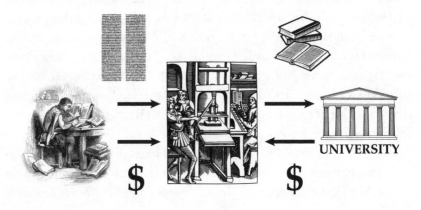

UNIVERSITY

for the reputations they accrue, and publishing is how reputations are made.

To be clear, there's nothing inherently wrong with the idea of charging authors to publish their work. Many scientists enthusiastically support *open access* publishing, in which journal publishers take money from the authors and dispense with subscription fees entirely. This has a number of advantages. The papers published in this way are free for anyone in the world to read at any time. With open access, scientists at institutions in the developing world do not have to struggle to access the papers they need; medical patients and their families can view the latest papers about the relevant diseases; the public can read about the research results that they have already funded through government-sponsored research grants. And increased readership is a good thing for the authors.

That's the full half of the half-full glass. There's an empty half as well. Open access publishing creates a niche for low-quality journals that do not impose adequate standards. When a journal charges for subscriptions, its editors have strong incentives to publish high-quality articles that have been thoroughly vetted through peer review. Journals filled with low-quality articles sell few subscriptions. When a journal charges academics who are eager to publish for the service of publishing their work, multiple business models come into play. Most open access journals seek to build their reputations by publishing only high-quality work. But for some, money is money—they'll publish anything provided that the check clears.

Here is Goodhart's law's again: When a measure becomes a target, it ceases to be a good measure. This has happened to a substantive swath of the scientific literature. When scientists started judging one another by the number of papers published, a market sprung up for journals willing to publish low-quality work. At the bottom of that particular barrel are journals produced by so-called predatory publishers. These parasites on the scientific publishing system provide little to nothing by way of rigorous peer review. Today they are sucking tens of millions of dollars from the academic system and polluting the literature with millions of unreliable articles.

It could be useful to have a central authority validating journals as "scientific," but none exists. In the age of print, the cost of publishing a physical journal and the need to sell subscriptions to libraries created barriers that prevented scammers from entering the publishing game. Now that journals are viewed online, articles are delivered electronically, and publishers can bill authors rather than libraries, those barriers are gone. Today, a rudimentary understanding of Web design and a willingness to defraud people is all it takes to become a predatory publisher.

While the primary customers for predatory journals may be marginal academics looking to boost their résumés with additional publications, other parties take advantage of these journals' services as well. Climate skeptics, antivaxxers, creationists, and HIV denialists publish their work in predatory journals and then point to these papers as "peer-reviewed" science supporting their fringe beliefs. Con artists publish fabricated data purporting to show the power of their snake-oil diet supplements or disease cures. Unscrupulous political operatives publish unfounded claims about their political opponents in an effort to rally support. Conspiracy theorists document the collaborations between the CIA, the Illuminati, and the aliens that built the great pyramids. Crackpots can publish grand theories of quantum gravity and the universal consciousness permeating all of space-time, or incantations written in lost languages that will summon a demonic archon to oversee the destruction of the world.

To make money, predatory journals need to attract submissions. Here they turn to sending spam email. If you publish an academic paper or two, your email in-box will start to fill up with messages from predatory journals, each saying something along the lines of: "With great interest we read your paper [paper title] in the journal [journal title]. We congratulate you on this excellent work. If you have additional research in this area, we would urge you to consider our journal for your next publication. . . ." Of course, no one from the journal has actually read your paper; its title and your email address have simply been scraped from the Internet—but if you are new to academic publishing, you wouldn't necessarily know this. Sometimes these communications list the publication fees, but many predatory journal publishers hide these fees until after a paper has been accepted.

In a typical week we each get a few dozen of these emails. Some of our colleagues have found amusing ways to fight back. Scientific editor John McCool was invited to publish in the *Urology & Nephrology*

Open Access Journal. McCool has no medical background, but he is a devoted *Seinfeld* fan, and he recalled an episode that might be of interest to the journal in question. In season three's episode "The Parking Garage," Jerry Seinfeld forgets where he parked his car, and after hours of searching without a bathroom break he is arrested for public urination. At the police station, he tries to talk his way out of his predicament. "Why would I [urinate in public] unless I was in mortal danger? I know it's against the law," Jerry tells the officer who is booking him into jail. He then answers his own question: "Because I could get uromycitisis poisoning and die! That's why." Of course there is no such thing as uromycitisis. Seinfeld just made up a scary-sounding word off the top of his head.

McCool's paper, "Uromycitisis Poisoning Results in Lower Urinary Tract Infection and Acute Renal Failure: Case Report," lays out a complete summary of the episode's plot in the guise of a case report. It begins: "A 37-year-old white male was in a large suburban mall parking garage and was unable to locate his car. After more than an hour of walking up and down flights of stairs and through row after row of cars, searching fruitlessly for his own car, he felt a powerful urge to urinate. With no restroom available in the garage, and knowing that he suffers from uromycitisis, he feared that if he did not urinate immediately he would develop uromycitisis poisoning." The peer reviewers, if such existed at all, must not be *Seinfeld* fans (or critical thinkers). The ridiculous case report was accepted for publication in a matter of days, in hope that McCool would pay the $799 author fee. He never did.

So how do you tell whether a scientific article is legitimate? The first thing to recognize is that *any scientific paper can be wrong.* That's the nature of science; nothing is above questioning. No matter where a paper is published, no matter who wrote it, no matter how well supported its arguments may be, any paper can be wrong. Every hypothesis, every set of data, every claim, and every conclusion is subject to reexamination in light of future evidence. Linus Pauling was a brilliant scientist who remains the only person to have received two unshared Nobel Prizes, the prize in chemistry and the peace prize—but he also published papers and books that turned out to be completely wrong, from his proposed triple-helix structure of DNA to his views about the benefits of high doses of vitamin C. *Nature* and *Science* are the two most prestigious journals in the basic sciences, but they too have published some howlers. In 1969, *Science* published a paper about a nonexistent polymer of water known as polywater, which contributed to fears among defense researchers of a "polywater gap" between the US and Russia. *Nature* published an erroneous paper in 1988 purporting to show that homeopathy can be effective.

The second thing to understand is the role of peer review. While it's an important part of the scientific process, *peer review does not guarantee that published papers are correct*. Peer reviewers carefully read a paper to make sure its methods are reasonable and its reasoning logical. They make sure a paper accurately represents what it adds to the literature, and that its conclusions follow from its results. They suggest ways to improve a paper, and sometimes recommend additional experiments. But peer reviewers can make mistakes and, more important, peer reviewers cannot possibly check every aspect of the work. Peer reviewers don't redo the laboratory experiments, repeat the field observations, rewrite the computer code, rederive all of the mathematics, or even delve too deeply into the data in most cases. Though helpful, peer review cannot catch every innocent mistake, let alone uncover well-concealed acts of scientific misconduct.

As a result, there is no surefire way for you, as the reader, to know, beyond a shadow of a doubt, that any particular scientific paper is correct. Usually the best you can hope to do is to determine that a paper is *legitimate*. By legitimate, we mean that a paper is (1) written in good faith, (2) carried out using appropriate methodologies, and (3) taken seriously by the relevant scientific community.

A quick way to evaluate the legitimacy of a published paper is to find out about the journal in which it is published. A number of websites purport to rank journal quality or prestige, typically based on citations.* Highly cited journals are thought to be better than their

---

* Clarivate's journal impact factor is the most commonly used of these metrics. Journal impact factor measures the ratio of citations received over a two-year window to the number of "citable" articles published in that same window. Unfortunately, impact factor scores are available only in bulk via a subscription service known as the Clarivate *Journal Citation Reports* (JCR). While what constitutes an impressive impact factor varies from one field to another, it is a reasonable rule of thumb to consider that any journal listed in the JCR is at least somewhat reputable, any journal with an impact factor of at least 1 is decent, and any journal with an impact factor of at least 10 is outstanding. Several free alternatives to journal impact factor are also available. We the authors provide a set of journal indicators at http://www.eigenfactor.org. These metrics cover the same set of journals included in the JCR. The large commercial publisher Elsevier provides an alternative set of

seldom-cited competitors. Knowing the publisher is helpful as well. Major publishers and reputable scientific societies usually ensure that the articles in their journals meet basic standards of quality.

Another issue to be on the lookout for is whether the claims in a paper are commensurate with the venue in which it is published. As we mentioned, journals occupy different positions in a hierarchy of prestige. All else equal, papers published in top journals will represent the largest advances and have the highest credibility. Less interesting or less credible findings will be relegated to less prestigious outlets. Be wary of extraordinary claims appearing in lower-tier venues. You can think of this as the scientist's version of "if you're so smart, why aren't you rich?"

Thus if a paper called "Some Weights of Riparian Frogs" lists the weights of some frogs in the little-known *Tasmanian Journal of Australian Herpetology*, there is relatively little cause for concern. A table of frogs' weights, while possibly useful to some specialists in the area, is far from a scientific breakthrough and is well suited for the journal in question. If, however, a paper called "Evidence That Neanderthals Went Extinct during the Hundred Years' War" appears in the equally low-profile *Journal of Westphalian Historical Geography*, this is serious cause for concern. That finding, if true, would revolutionize our understanding of hominin history, and shake our notion of what it means to be human. Such a finding, if true, would appear in a high-profile journal.

While the examples above are hypothetical, real examples abound. For example, in 2012 television personality Dr. Mehmet Oz used his show to promote a research paper purporting to demonstrate that green coffee extract has near miraculous properties as a weight-loss supplement. Despite this remarkable claim, the paper did not appear in a top medical journal such as *JAMA, The Lancet,* or *NEJM.* Rather, it appeared in a little-known journal titled *Diabetes, Metabolic Syndrome and Obesity: Targets and Therapy* from a marginal scientific publisher called Dove Press. The journal is not even listed in some of the major scientific indices. This should set off alarm bells for any reader—and

---

metrics based on their Scopus database. Scopus covers a larger set of journals than the JCR, but we have concerns about the possible conflicts of interest that arise when a major journal publisher begins ranking its own journals against those of its competitors. Google Scholar provides journal rankings of its own as well.

indeed a look at the paper reveals that the results are based on a clinical trial with an absurdly small sample size of sixteen, too small a sample to justify the strong claims that the paper makes. The small sample size and inglorious venue turned out to be only part of the story. The paper was subsequently retracted because its data could not be validated.

While retractions are uncommon, it can be a good idea to check for a retraction or correction before staking too much on the results of a scientific paper. The easiest way to do this is simply to check the paper on the publisher's website or—if it is a paper in biology or medicine—in the PubMed database.*

WHY SCIENCE WORKS

We've run through a fairly long litany of problems that plague contemporary science. It would be easy to feel overwhelmed, and start to wonder whether science works at all. Fortunately, there are a number of reasons why the institutions of science are effective despite everything we've discussed in this chapter.

We've already discussed how most of the hypotheses that get tested are *a priori* reasonably likely to be correct. Scientists tend to test hypotheses that have a decent chance of being true rather than wasting their time on long shots. When such is the case, most positive findings will be true positives, not false positives.

Science is a cumulative process. Even though experiments are not often directly replicated, science proceeds when researchers build upon previous results. If a result is false, people cannot build on it effectively. Their attempts will fail, they'll go back and reassess the original findings, and in this way the truth will come out. Suppose that while studying fruit flies, I discover a biochemical pathway that makes it easy to edit an organism's genes. Other researchers may not try to directly replicate my experiment, but people working with mice or nematodes or other model organisms will want to see if the same mechanism works in their systems. Or perhaps people interested in technological applications may try to work out better methods of using this pathway in a directed fashion. If I were wrong in the first

---

* PubMed is freely available online at https://www.ncbi.nlm.nih.gov/pubmed/.

place, none of this will work and my mistakes will be corrected. If I am right, the successes of these subsequent researchers will confirm my discovery.

Experiments often test not only whether there is an effect but the direction of the effect. Suppose several research teams test whether a new antidepressant also helps with memory loss among seniors. If this drug has no real effect on memory, there are two different kinds of false positive results we could find: The drug could improve or decrease performance on memory tests. Because in either case the treatment group taking the drug differs from the control group taking a placebo, either result could be published. If a treatment has mixed effects in the published literature, some beneficial and some harmful, we have reason to suspect that we are looking at statistical noise instead of a true signal.

As science moves toward accepting some claim as a fact, experiments that contradict that claim become noteworthy, are treated almost as positive results, and become far easier to publish. For example, physicists have typically assumed that the speed of light in a vacuum is a fundamental constant of physics and is the same everywhere and at all times in the universe. If a few decades ago someone tried to measure differences in the speed of light across time and space and found no difference, this would have been a negative result and difficult to publish in a high-profile journal. But recently several lines of evidence have accumulated suggesting that the speed of light in a vacuum may vary. Now that these claims are being discussed in the physics community, careful experiments showing no difference would be of substantial interest.

Finally, irrespective of the problems we have discussed in this chapter, science just plain works. As we stated at the start of this chapter, science allows us to understand the nature of the physical world at scales far beyond what our senses evolved to detect and our minds evolved to comprehend. Equipped with this understanding, we have been able to create technologies that would seem magical to those only a few generations prior. Empirically, science is successful. Individual papers may be wrong and individual studies misreported in the popular press, but the institution as a whole is strong. We should keep this in perspective when we compare science to much of the other human knowledge—and human bullshit—that is out there.

CHAPTER 10

Spotting Bullshit

I N SEPTEMBER 2017, A SHOCKING PHOTOGRAPH MADE THE ROUNDS on social media. Set in the locker room of the Seattle Seahawks football team, the picture appeared to show former Seahawks defensive lineman Michael Bennett bare-chested and brandishing a burning American flag. Circled around Bennett and cheering jubilantly were his Seahawks teammates and coaching staff.

This photograph was, of course, a fake. No Seahawk ever burned an American flag during a team meeting—or any other time. The photo (minus the burning flag) had been taken nearly two years earlier, when the Seahawks were celebrating a crucial victory against the rival Arizona Cardinals. But it spoke volumes about an ongoing cultural battle that had swept up the National Football League. San Francisco quarterback Colin Kaepernick led a growing number of players across the league in taking a knee during the national anthem as a protest against police brutality. Donald Trump branded these players as unpatriotic, antimilitary, and altogether un-American. The image of Michael Bennett with the burning flag, first posted to the Facebook page of an organization called "Vets for Trump," provided an extreme expression of Trump's narrative. Many viewers overlooked the low-quality image manipulations and shared the photograph, with angry invectives directed at the Seahawks players. The anger and disgust that many felt in seeing the image likely overshadowed any inclination to critically evaluate its authenticity and primed them to fall for the bullshit.

If bullshit is everywhere, how can we avoid being taken in? We think it is crucial to cultivate appropriate habits of mind. After all, our habits of mind keep us safe on a daily basis. We don't think about it, necessarily, but as we drive to work, our eyes are scanning for a driver about to run a red light. Walking alone at night, we are aware of our surroundings and alert for signs of danger. Spotting bullshit is the same. It takes continual practice, but with that practice one becomes adept at spotting misleading arguments and analysis. While developing a rigorous bullshit detector is a lifelong project, one can go a long way with a few simple tricks that we will introduce in this chapter.

1. QUESTION THE SOURCE
OF INFORMATION

Journalists are trained to ask the following simple questions about any piece of information they encounter:

> Who is telling me this?
> How does he or she know it?
> What is this person trying to sell me?

These questions are second nature to us under some circumstances. When you walk into a used-car dealership and the salesman starts talking about how the car in the corner of the lot had only a single owner, a little old lady who drove it once a week to church on Sunday, you are, of course, thinking this way: Who is this person? A used-car salesman! How does he know this? Well, maybe he heard it straight from the little old lady herself. Or maybe, he heard it from the dealer across town who sold him the car. Or, just maybe, there never was a little old lady to begin with. What's he trying to sell you? That one's obvious. The 2002 Pontiac Aztek you made the mistake of glancing toward as you walked on the lot.

When we scan through our social media feeds, or listen to the evening news, or read the latest magazine page about how to improve our health, we need to ask the same questions.

In the process of writing this chapter, we read online that crystals "retain all the information they have ever been exposed to. Crystals absorb information—whether a severe weather pattern, or the experience of an ancient ceremony—and pass it to anyone that comes into contact with them." Now this doesn't even remotely jibe with our understanding of physics, so it's worth asking ourselves these three questions about this claim.

Answering the first question is relatively straightforward. Who is telling us this? This text comes from an interview about healing crystals from the website of the lifestyle brand Goop. The interviewee is Colleen McCann, a "fashion stylist turned energy practitioner" and "certified shamanic energy medicine practitioner" who "utilizes a combination of crystals, color theory, chakra systems, astrology, naturopathy, and Feng Shui principles."

Answering the second question, "How does she know it?," can be harder to ascertain. In this case, however, McCann's website gives us enough material to make some educated guesses. In her bio, we learn that McCann "started hearing voices, also known as *Clairaudience,* in a Brooklyn bodega" and that the "reputable Manhattan psychic" she subsequently consulted "gently broke the mystical bomb to her that she too was psychic. The voices were in fact her Spirit Guides saying hello." She then "jumped heels first into the crystal-laden rabbit hole with three years of private mentorship with an Intuitive Healer. Her journey then led her to train at The Four Winds Society in Peruvian Shamanic Studies." Finally, we learn that she "has spent a decade studying with a Buddhist Feng Shui master to learn Crystal Healing and Space Clearing." Perhaps it was through these experiences, or others like them, that McCann picked up the information that she shared in this interview.

And the third question, "What are they trying to sell us?" Here again we have to guess a little bit, but only a little bit. The Goop company and the interviewee may be selling slightly different things, of course. McCann may be aiming to sell us on a set of ideas or a philosophy. In addition, and perhaps not coincidentally, her website reveals that she also sells crystals and provides services including "intuitive crystal readings," "crystal gridding," and "crystal luxtration." The Goop company, for their part, might argue that they are promoting a lifestyle. But they also sell a so-called Goop Medicine Bag, wherein for eighty-five dollars one receives a set of eight "chakra-healing crystals." To us these seem nearly indistinguishable from the polished gems and such that you would get for five dollars a bag at tourist shops—but think again. The Goop stones have been "cleansed with sage, tuned with sound waves, activated with mantras, and blessed with Reiki."

In short, people may be trying to sell you used cars or life insurance or beauty treatments—or they be trying to sell you ideas, viewpoints, and perspectives. Some sales jobs get you to part with your hard-earned money. Other sales jobs convince you to believe something that you didn't believe before, or to do something you wouldn't have done otherwise. Everyone is trying to sell you something; it is just a matter of figuring out what.

We could also ask these questions about the photograph of Michael Bennett with a burning flag. Who is telling me this? The Facebook group called Vets for Trump. How do they know it? Since the photo appeared only on Facebook and was not reported in any traditional media outlet, the only possible story would be that someone had a camera in a locker room, but somehow the media was either not present or they all agreed not to report on what had happened—and none of the Seahawks players or staff spoke up about it afterward. That seems highly implausible. What are they trying to sell us? They want to convince us that the NFL players who are protesting racial injustice hold anti-American sentiments and may be a threat to the country. Even without the giveaway signs of a poor photoshopping job, the answers to these three questions should be enough to make us question the authenticity of such a shocking and unexpected picture.

2. BEWARE OF UNFAIR COMPARISONS

"Airport Security Trays Carry More Germs Than Toilets!" Media outlets around the world ran some version of this headline after a research study was published in September 2018, confirming the fears of every germophobe who has ever suffered through the airport security screening process.

But the claim is somewhat disingenuous. The scientists who did this study looked only at respiratory viruses, the kind transmitted through the air or through droplets on people's hands when they cough or sneeze. It isn't surprising that security trays have more respiratory viruses than toilet seats. People don't usually cough or sneeze onto toilet seats, nor do they tend to touch them extensively with their hands. Toilet seats have plenty of germs, just not of the kinds that the researchers were tallying.

Airline trays may be important vectors for colds and flus, but when the headlines bring toilet seats into the picture, they are making an unfair comparison for shock value. Trays don't have more germs than toilet seats, they just have more germs of the type likely to land on trays.

Let's look at another example. People have always enjoyed ranked lists. In a clickstream economy, where advertising revenues depend on page views, they're gold. A single top-ten list can generate ten page views per reader by putting each list item on a separate page. Farewell Casey Kasem, hello "12 Reasons Why Sam, the Cat with Eyebrows, Should Be Your New Favorite Cat."

One form of list that continuously reappears is some variant of "America's Most Dangerous Cities." Recently we came across such a list, released by financial news outlet *24/7 Wall St.* and based on a compilation by the FBI. At the top of the list were

1. St. Louis, MO
2. Detroit, MI
3. Birmingham, AL
4. Memphis, TN
5. Milwaukee, WI

Well, that got personal quickly. Carl was born in St. Louis; he spent much of his later teens exploring the neighborhoods of Detroit. Are these cities really all that bad? he wondered. The rankings are based on hard numbers from a trusted government agency. But is this really a fair comparison? Or is there something funny going on that sends St. Louis and Detroit to the top of the list? The first question we could ask is how they have quantified how dangerous a city is. Biggest potholes? Most bedbugs? Greatest number of golfers hit by lightning?

In this case, the metric of danger is the number of violent crimes per capita. We might try to argue that this measure does not do a good job of characterizing how dangerous a city is. Perhaps violent crime reporting is accurate in St. Louis and Detroit, but such events are severely underreported in other places. Perhaps St. Louis and Detroit have high assault rates but few murders. Or perhaps the data used to compute violent crimes per capita underestimate the populations of St. Louis and Detroit due to recent population growth.

A more likely problem is that there is something arbitrary in how cities are defined. City limits are political boundaries. Some cities include primarily a central urban region and exclude the outlying suburbs. Others encompass the majority of the surrounding metropolitan area. This could make a huge difference when tallying violent crime rates. For complex reasons, crime rates within many US cities tend to be high in the historical urban core of a city and lower in the suburbs.

Why does this matter? It matters because the crime rate in a city will depend on how tightly the city boundary encircles the urban core. And because the locations of city boundaries depend on a city's history and politics, we see a great deal of variation in how tightly the boundaries circumscribe the city center. At this point we have a hypothesis—that city boundaries have a substantial effect on the violent crime rate—but no hard evidence. We have some grounds for skepticism about top ten most-dangerous lists,* but if we hope to argue that the way city limits are defined impacts the results, we need to collect additional data and test this hypothesis directly. Violent crime data are readily available, as are population data. But how do we control for whether the city boundaries include the suburbs?

The US government compiles a list of *metropolitan statistical areas* and assembles statistical and demographic data about each. Each metropolitan area comprises a core city or multiple core cities, surrounded by outlying suburbs. If differences in violent crime rates are influenced by differences in the way city boundaries are drawn, we would expect cities that are small compared to the surrounding metropolitan areas to have higher crime rates, on average, than cities that are big compared to their surrounding metropolitan areas.

In the scatter plot below, each dot represents one city. On the verti-

---

* The FBI itself urges this sort of caution in interpreting their own data: "Each year when *Crime in the United States* is published, some entities use the figures to compile rankings of cities and counties. These rough rankings provide no insight into the numerous variables that mold crime in a particular town, city, county, state, tribal area, or region. Consequently, they lead to simplistic and/ or incomplete analyses that often create misleading perceptions adversely affecting communities and their residents. Valid assessments are possible only with careful study and analysis of the range of unique conditions affecting each local law enforcement jurisdiction. The data user is, therefore, cautioned against comparing statistical data of individual reporting units from cities, metropolitan areas, states, or colleges or universities solely on the basis of their population coverage or student enrollment."

cal axis, we show the violent crime rate (measured as the number of violent crimes reported per 100,000 people per year). On the horizontal axis we show the fraction of the metro's population that resides within its major city.* This gives us a measure of how narrow or expansive the city's boundaries are.

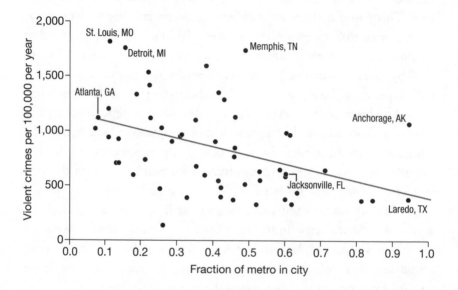

As we suspected, the higher the fraction of the metropolitan area that lies within the city limits, the lower the violent crime rate tends to be. Cities that have narrow boundaries tend to have higher crime rates, and cities with expansive boundaries tend to have lower crime rates. If we fit a line representing crime rates through the points, that line slopes downward. Statistical tests show that this slope is likely to be meaningful rather than merely the result of chance.† Thus there is a correlation between the violent crime rate in a city and the way the city boundaries are drawn. The overall amount of crime in a metropolitan area influences whether a city appears dangerous or safe—but so does the way in which the city's boundaries are drawn. People are making apples-to-oranges comparisons when comparing cities such as

* We look only at cities with populations of at least four hundred thousand people. We omit major metropolitan areas that contain two or more cities of this size, because the ratio of city size to metro size will be an underestimate of the fraction of the population living in an urban core.

† The slope of a linear regression through these points is significantly different from zero at the $p = 0.005$ level. $R^2 = 0.17$.

St. Louis or Detroit, which include only the urban core, with cities such as Anchorage or Laredo, which include the suburbs as well.

This example of violent crime rates serves to illustrate a more general principle: Ranked lists are meaningful only if the entities being compared are directly comparable.

3. IF IT SEEMS TOO GOOD OR TOO BAD TO BE TRUE . . .

Early in 2017, the Trump administration instituted a set of policies restricting travel and immigration to the United States. Trump's policies influenced many aspects of American life, including higher education. In March 2017, NBC News sent out a message on Twitter about the consequences of these policy changes: "International student applications are down nearly 40 percent, survey shows."

The tweet linked to a news story and was widely shared on Twitter. But the claim it put forth seems implausible. Sure, Trump's travel ban and associated changes to US immigration policy were unlikely to make the US seem more welcoming to international students. But a catastrophic 40 percent drop in applications struck us as too large to be real. Not only is the size of the effect massive, its timing is suspect. Applications to many US universities would have been due in December or January, before Trump took office. We were skeptical.

Our skepticism follows from a general principle for spotting bullshit: *If a claim seems too good—or too bad—to be true, it probably is.* We all apply this rule of thumb on a regular basis in our daily lives. How many people actually think they've won a free vacation when they get the robocall from a telephone solicitor?

So how do we figure out whether the 40 percent statistic that NBC provides is actually bullshit? Simple: *Dig to the source.* Don't trust the tweet. In a world dominated by social media where any information we receive has already been rewritten, rearranged, and reprocessed, it's important to cultivate the habit of digging to the source.

The NBC tweet provided a link to its source, an *NBC Nightly News* story titled "Survey Finds Foreign Students Aren't Applying to American Colleges." This story explains that foreign applications are down at a number of schools, and attributes this decline to Trump's travel ban and anti-immigration rhetoric:

Applications from international students from countries such as China, India and in particular, the Middle East, are down this year at nearly 40 percent of schools that answered a recent survey by the American Association of Collegiate Registrars and Admissions Officers.

Educators, recruiters and school officials report that the perception of America has changed for international students, and it just doesn't seem to be as welcoming a place anymore. Officials point to the Trump administration's rhetoric surrounding immigration and the issuing of a travel ban as having an effect.

But hold on! This article is telling a different story than the tweet suggested. The tweet claimed applications were down by 40 percent. The story suggests that applications are down *at 40 percent of schools*. That's a different matter altogether. Applications could be down just a small percentage at those schools, for example, resulting in a very small overall drop in foreign applications. Already we've found a discrepancy between the tweet and the news story it advertises.

But which is right? The tweet or the news story? To figure that out, we have to keep digging. The news story cites a bulletin from the American Association of Collegiate Registrars and Admissions Officers; a bit of searching leads us to this report, posted eleven days before the NBC story, which provides a critical detail.* Yes, international applications decreased at 39 percent of universities—but they increased at 35 percent of universities. Taken together this isn't news, it's statistical noise. Given the information presented in the article, there is no meaningful indication of a "Trump effect" on international applications. Most likely, these numbers merely reflect chance fluctuations in the number of applications to different US schools.

So how did all of this happen? There seem to have been lapses at multiple levels. First, the NBC article is misleading because it describes only the fraction of schools with declining applications, and fails to mention that a comparable fraction of schools received an in-

---

* Even the original American Association of Collegiate Registrars and Admissions Officers article suffers from a misleading headline, "International Student Applications Decline, Concerns about Visa and US Political Climate Rise." The data reported do not demonstrate a net decrease in US international student applications, nor is the fraction of institutions with increased enrollment substantially different from that with decreased enrollment.

creasing number of applications. We can imagine how that would have come about. A large-scale survey reveals no evidence of systematic change in international applications in response to Trump policies; that's hardly an exciting news story. Either to liven up the story, or simply because writers or editors lack quantitative sophistication, they highlight the decline in applications at 39 percent of schools and ignore or downplay the increase in applications at 35 percent of schools. Here is an example of how a statement can be true and still qualify as bullshit. It is true that applications declined at 39 percent of schools. But the absence of context is bound to mislead the reader.

The new story was then presumably misinterpreted by whoever runs the social media feed for NBC, and a decline *at* 40 percent of schools was transposed into a decline *by* 40 percent. This improbably large effect is where the "if it sounds too good or bad to be true . . ." rule of thumb comes into play. We find that this third rule is particularly good for spotting bullshit that spreads across social media. In a social media environment, the posts that are spread most widely are often those that shock, spark a sense of wonder, or inflame feelings of righteous indignation: namely, those that make the most extreme claims. And the most extreme claims are often too good or too bad to be true.

4. THINK IN ORDERS OF MAGNITUDE

Think back to philosopher Harry Frankfurt's distinction between bullshit and lies. Lies are designed to lead away from the truth; bullshit is produced with a gross indifference to the truth. This definition gives us a considerable advantage when trying to spot bullshit. Well-crafted lies will be plausible, whereas a lot of bullshit will be ridiculous even on the surface. When people use bullshit numbers to support their arguments, they are often so far off that we can spot the bullshit by intuition and refute it without much research.

The National Geographic Society sent out a mailer warning that plastic waste is polluting our oceans. "9 Billion Tons of Plastic Waste End Up in the Ocean Every Year," the headline proclaimed. That sounds dreadful, but pause and think for a moment. There are fewer than eight billion people on the planet. Is it really possible that each person puts an average of one ton of plastic waste into the ocean each year? That seems unlikely. In fact, the total production of plastic *throughout all history* is only about eight billion tons—and not all of that ends up in the oceans. Clearly the figure of nine billion tons per year is in error. What is the correct figure? *National Geographic* themselves recently reported that nine million tons of plastic waste go into the ocean each year. Plastic pollution of our oceans is surely an ecological disaster in the making—but inflating the magnitude a thousandfold doesn't help anyone. It merely undermines the credibility of pro-environmental sources. Not that there is any reason to suspect that the mistake was intentional; we suspect that in the production of the mailer, someone accidentally typed "billions" instead of "millions."

Because the nine billion tons of plastic waste per year is readily compared with the eight billion people on Earth, this mistake is pretty easy to catch without doing any mental math. Often, however, one needs to do a few simple mental calculations to check a numerical claim. For example, suppose a friend claims there are more than 121,000 men in the UK named John Smith. Does that sound right? We think that the key to working out these kinds of questions quickly, without even pencil and paper, is to break down a number into components that you can estimate. The estimates can be very loose; it is usually good enough to estimate to the nearest power of ten (sometimes called an "order of magnitude"). Here we might ask, "How many people are there in the UK? What fraction of those are named John? What fraction of the UK Johns have the surname Smith?"

So how many people are in the UK? About 1 million? 10 million? 100 million? 1 billion? Most of us know that 100 million is the best estimate from among these (the true value in 2018 was about two-thirds of that, 67 million).

How many of those people have the first name John? One in ten? Well, since few women are named John, that would require that about one in five men be named John. Not even close. (Remarkably, until around 1800 one in five men in England *was* named John—but that isn't true today.) One in a thousand? Clearly the name John is a lot more common than that. One in a hundred sounds about right.

How many people in the UK have the last name Smith? Again, one in ten seems too many and one in a thousand seems too few, so one in a hundred makes for a good guess.

So how many John Smiths do we expect in the UK? To make the calculation easy we will assume that people with the surname Smith are just as likely as anyone else to have the given name John, though in practice this is probably not quite right. But we are only approximating; it should be fine to make this assumption. Therefore we have roughly 100 million people in the UK, of whom one in a hundred are named John. This gives us 1 million Johns. Of these, we estimate that one in a hundred is named Smith, giving us an estimate of ten thousand John Smiths in the UK.

This estimate turns out to be pretty good. In practice, there are about 4,700 people named John Smith living in the UK today. If we'd used the actual UK population of 67 million, we'd have had an even closer estimate of 6,700. But either way, we can see that our friend's claim of 121,000 John Smiths is off by a factor of ten or more.

This process of making back-of-the-envelope approximations is known as Fermi estimation, after the physicist Enrico Fermi, who was famous for estimating the size of an atomic blast using these simple methods.* For spotting bullshit on the fly, we suggest that making these approximations in powers of ten is often good enough. Freeing yourself up to be within a power of ten in your estimates encourages you to think through a problem quickly, using information you already know, instead of getting hung up on calculating the number of seconds in a fortnight (1,209,600 seconds) or using a search engine to find how many gallons of water the average New Yorker uses in a day (115 gallons). Even if you're off by 50 percent here and there, your final estimate is very likely to be within tenfold of the true value, which is often sufficient to spot bullshit. Of course, if your estimate leads you to believe a figure is nonsense, and you want to be sure, you can always look up the true numbers or make a more accurate estimate using pen and paper.

At a May 2018 hearing of the US House Committee on Science, Space and Technology, Representative Mo Brooks (R-Ala.) speculated that perhaps rising sea levels could be attributed to rocks falling into the ocean. For example, he asked his constituents to consider the continuously eroding White Cliffs of Dover. These

---

* For a delightful introductory course on Fermi estimation, see Lawrence Weinstein and John A. Adam, *Guesstimation* (Princeton, N.J.: Princeton University Press, 2008).

have to be filling up the ocean over time, and all the water that they displace must be going somewhere. It is comforting that like Aesop's crow,* Representative Brooks understands the consequences of putting rocks in water. But this is an entirely inadequate explanation that belies Representative Brooks's ability to grasp how vast the oceans are.

The oceans take up roughly two-thirds of the earth's surface and run to an average depth of about two miles. That is an enormous amount of water, spread over an almost unimaginably large area. Given that, how much of an effect could collapsing cliffs have?

We can work this out in straightforward fashion. Imagine that tomorrow the entire White Cliffs of Dover, and all the land for a kilometer inland, fell into the sea in a cataclysmic collapse and displaced an equivalent volume of seawater. Setting aside the gargantuan tsunami that would savage Calais and the northern coast of France, what would happen to sea levels globally?

Would the rising waters flood low-lying areas of coastal cities? Hardly. We can see this with a simple calculation. The White Cliffs are a bit over 10 kilometers in length and roughly 100 meters high. So in our imagined collapse, we have 10 km × 1 km × 100 m = 1 billion cubic meters. Wow! It would take the Crayola company about two million years to package that much chalk.[†]

But the Earth's oceans are all connected, so this billion cubic meters of land would have to raise the water level of all the world's oceans. The surface area of these oceans is approximately 360 million square kilometers, or 360 trillion square meters. (We care about the surface area of the oceans, not the volume, because it is the surface that is raised.) So the 1 billion cubic meters of water displacement would be spread across 360 trillion square meters. The ensuing sea level rise would be 1,000,000,000 m³ / 360,000,000,000,000 m² = 0.000003 m.

---

* In one of Aesop's fables, a thirsty crow adds stones to a pitcher of water until the water level rises high enough for the bird to enjoy a drink. Unlike many of Aesop's other fables, this one may be a natural history observation rather than a moral lesson. A recent scientific study showed that crows indeed have good intuitions about what happens to the water level in a vessel when you submerge heavy objects in it.

† Crayola produces about 110 million sticks of chalk every year. If each stick weighs 10 grams, that's roughly 100 million kilograms of chalk. Chalk weighs about 2,000 kilograms per square meter, so Crayola is producing very roughly 500 cubic meters of chalk each year. At 500 cubic meters a year, it would take nearly two million years to produce the full 1,000,000,000 cubic meters of chalk that we are imagining might fall into the ocean in a White Cliffs catastrophe.

In other words, we are looking at a 3-micrometer (μm) rise in sea level. By comparison, a human hair is about 100 μm in diameter. So if the White Cliffs of Dover and thirty other comparably sized stretches of shoreline fall into the sea tomorrow, the world's oceans will rise by a hair. Literally.

In practice, when White Cliffs fall into the sea they do not do so a kilometer at a time. Rather, the average rate of erosion is about 1 cm per year. That means that each year sediment falling from the White Cliffs displaces about 10 km × 1 km × 1 cm = 100,000 cubic meters. Spread across the whole of the world's oceans, this corresponds to a sea level rise of 100,000 m³ / 360,000,000,000,000 m² = 0.0000000003 m. This is 3 angstroms—which happens to be about the size of a water molecule. So, very approximately, the annual sea level rise due to erosion from the White Cliffs is about the height of a single water molecule everywhere across the world's oceans.

Fermi estimation is useful for more than scientific problems. The same approach provides a powerful way to think about social issues. By way of example, in late 2016 the Fox News Channel's *Fox and Friends* program ran a story about food stamp fraud in the US, and framed this as a possible reason to eliminate the food stamp program (now known as SNAP). The story claimed that food stamp fraud had reached an all-time high, and that USDA statistics revealed a loss of $70 million to fraud in 2016.

Seventy million dollars! Wow, that's a lot of money. Sounds like a disastrously run program, right? Maybe even worth canceling, given that we're wasting government funds on scammers "including a state lawmaker and even a millionaire"?

Well, this is where Fermi estimation comes in handy. First of all, you may not know exactly how expansive the food stamp program is, but you could probably estimate that about 10 percent of Americans are on food stamps—or at least that it's closer to 10 percent than to 1 percent or 100 percent. (It's actually around 15 percent.) Second, you're probably aware there are about 300 million people in the country. So around 30 million people are on food stamps. The actual number is about 45 million, but our estimate is plenty close for Fermi purposes.

If you are unfamiliar with the US food stamp program, you may not have a good idea of the average benefit paid to recipients annually.

Still you could probably guess that it's closer to $1,000 than to $100 or $10,000. (In fact, it's about $1,500.)

At this point, you've got enough information to see what's wrong with Fox's argument. Using your Fermi estimates, the US invests approximately 30,000,000 people × $1,000/person = $30,000,000,000—thirty billion dollars—in its food stamp program. That means that the fraction $70,000,000 / $30,000,000,000 = 0.0023, or around 0.2 percent, is lost to fraud. Using the actual annual expenditures, the fraction turns out to be less than 0.1 percent, but your Fermi estimate is plenty good to see what's going on. If there is any substantive inefficiency in the food stamp program, it certainly isn't fraud. These figures would be the envy of any retailer; retail losses to "shrinkage" (fraud, shoplifting, employee theft, etc.) usually run around 1 to 3 percent of sales.

Based on the *Fox and Friends* story, we do not know the average amount stolen by each fraudulent user, but even if SNAP frauds are receiving no more than the average legitimate recipient, fraudulent actors represent a tiny fraction of SNAP benefit recipients. It would take an exceptionally punitive mindset to starve nine hundred and ninety-nine people in an effort to safeguard ourselves against one petty crook.

There is an entertaining postscript to this story. It turns out that *Fox and Friends* was incorrect with their figure of $70 million lost to fraud, and the US Department of Agriculture demanded a correction shortly after the story ran. The funny part is that Fox's number was not too high, it was too low. Over the period from 2009 to 2011, for example, the USDA estimated that losses to just one single form of fraud, in which food stamp recipients sell their benefits to retailers for cash, account for about $900 million annually. This loss rate is within the normal range for retail.

If you are going to make up a number out of whole cloth, be sure to make up one that actually supports your argument.

5. AVOID CONFIRMATION BIAS

Extreme claims do well on social media; so do posts that reaffirm things about the world that we already believe to be true. This brings us to our next rule of thumb for spotting bullshit: Avoid confirmation bias. *Confirmation bias* is the tendency to notice, believe, and share information that is consistent with our preexisting beliefs. When a claim confirms our beliefs about the world, we are more prone to accept it as true and less inclined to challenge it as possibly false. Our susceptibility to confirmation bias can be seen as falling under the umbrella of sociologist Neil Postman's dictum, "At any given time, the chief source of bullshit with which you have to contend is yourself."

Confirmation bias is also a significant contributor to the spread of misinformation on the Internet. Why fact-check something you "know" is true? Let's look at another example from social media, one that tripped up a number of our friends and colleagues.

In academia and industry alike, letters of recommendation provide hiring committees with an important perspective on job candidates. Studies have shown that gender stereotypes and biases commonly influence the recommendation letters that managers write for employees, professors write for students, and so forth. For example, when the candidate is a woman, letter writers are more likely to hedge in their assessments, more likely to mention the candidate's personal life, and less likely to describe the candidate as standing out above other applicants. These gender differences in recommendation letters could be driving some of the gender inequality in the academic and corporate worlds.

In this context, a friend of ours posted this message on Twitter, describing a research study in which the authors analyzed the text from nearly nine hundred letters of recommendation for faculty positions in chemistry and in biochemistry looking for systematic bias:

male associated words   female associated words

The implication of our friend's tweet was that this study had found large and systematic differences in how letter writers describe men and women as candidates. From the image that he shared, it appears that writers use words associated with exceptionalism and research ability when describing men, and words associated with diligence, teamwork, and teaching when describing women. If true, this could have huge consequences for the hiring process.

This tweet clearly struck a nerve. It was shared—retweeted—more than two thousand times, in part because it captures a truth that many people experience daily. There is indeed gender bias in academia, advantaging men over women in myriad ways. Given that the tweet confirms our preexisting notions about gender bias, why were we suspicious about it? First, we have worked hard to train ourselves to avoid confirmation bias. We aim to be particularly scrupulous in questioning claims that, like this one, reflect our preexisting notions about how the world works. Second, this claim falls afoul of one of our previous rules: If a claim seems too bad to be true, it probably is. The pattern shown in the tweet is remarkably strong. Virtually all of the words on the male side of the graphic refer to excellence or exceptionalism, while all of the words on the female side refer instead to some aspect of teamwork or diligence. In our experience, patterns based on human behavior tend to be noisy. We might expect to see a general tendency toward one or the other types of description for each gender, but we'd expect some crossover.

To check up on this claim, we traced back to the source, the original research paper. While the tweet suggests that there are shocking differences between how men and women are described, the conclusions of the paper suggest otherwise:

> Overall, the results of the current study revealed more similarity in the letters written for male and female job candidates than differences. Male and female candidates had similar levels of qualifications and this was reflected in their letters of recommendation. Letters written for women included language that was just as positive and placed equivalent emphasis on ability, achievement, and research.

So what is going on in the figure? Why does it give such a different impression? The answer is simple: The figure illustrates the *hypothesis* of the study, not its results.

Our friend got this confused. The words labeled as male-associated in the tweet are words that the researchers selected as "standout words" ("exceptional," "wonderful"), "research words" ("data," "publication"), and "ability words" ("talented," "skilled"). The words labeled as female-associated are those selected as "grindstone words" ("dependable," "hardworking") and "teaching words" ("communicate," "instruct"). The researchers had hypothesized that letter writers would use more standout words, research words, and ability words when writing letters for men, and more grindstone words and teaching words when writing for women. Instead, they found that the frequencies of ability, research, teaching, and grindstone words were comparable for both genders. Only the frequency of standout words differed. So there may be some gender differences in the text of recommendation letters, but not of the kind or at the magnitude suggested by the tweet.

6. CONSIDER MULTIPLE HYPOTHESES

In this chapter we have mainly looked how you can spot bullshit in the form of incorrect facts. But bullshit also arises in the form of incorrect explanations for true statements. The key thing to realize is that just because someone has *an* explanation for some phenomenon doesn't mean that it is *the* explanation for that phenomenon.

In May 2018, TV personality Roseanne Barr posted a racist message to Twitter. Outrage ensued and Barr apologized, blaming her actions on the sleeping medication Ambien. But it was too late; the Disney-owned ABC network canceled her sitcom despite a record-setting comeback.

Whatever one thinks about Roseanne, racism, Twitter, or Ambien, what happened next was interesting. The leading newswire service Reuters reported on Twitter that "JUST IN: Walt Disney shares down 2.5 percent after ABC cancels 'Roseanne' show." Reuters was correct that Disney stock dropped 2.5 percent that day—but the headline here implies that the *Roseanne* cancellation was somehow responsible for the decline in share price. It couldn't have been: The 2.5 percent drop occurred before, not after, the *Roseanne* announcement. Indeed, the stock market as a whole had plunged dramatically that morning. Disney's stock had actually ended its 2.5 percent slide prior to the *Roseanne* announcement in the early afternoon.

This is a powerful example of "if it seems too bad to be true, it probably is." Disney is an enormous conglomerate. *Roseanne* is a single sitcom. Disney generated about $55 billion in revenue in 2017. Season ten of *Roseanne* generated about $45 million in revenue in 2018. How could the loss of a series that generated 0.1 percent of Disney's revenue drive a 2.5 percent decline in stock price? It doesn't pass a basic plausibility check.

The problem with the Reuters tweet is that when you have a phenomenon of interest (a 2.5 percent slide in Disney's stock price) and a possible explanation for that phenomenon (*Roseanne* was canceled), your story can seem compelling. Roseanne's racist tweet was by far the most societally salient event associated with Disney's holdings at the time—television pundits, newspaper columnists, and social media posters alike were up in arms about what she wrote and about the consequences she faced for doing so. But this does not mean that this event was the most plausible explanation for the trading results.

The real point here is that in the vast majority of cases, there will be many possible explanations for any given pattern or trend, and simply being consistent with the data does not make an explanation correct. Sometimes a proposed explanation may be correct but only a small part of the causal contribution; other times the proposed explanation may be totally wrong, unconnected to the real explanation.

In order to avoid falling for these seemingly plausible but incorrect explanations, consider as many possible explanations as you can for any trend or pattern or event that you seek to understand.

SPOTTING BULLSHIT ONLINE

In chapter 2, we described how social media has changed the way that news—real or fake—spreads. When we decide what is worth sharing on Facebook, Twitter, or some other platform, we are taking on the gatekeeping role that professional editors once played. We are not only fooled ourselves by online misinformation; we are readily enlisted as vehicles to help spread it. That makes it particularly important for us to get good at spotting bullshit when it appears on the Internet or in our social media feeds. We conclude this chapter by summarizing the suggestions we've presented throughout the book for spotting online misinformation. Some of them may sound simple. But simple as they may be, the reminder is useful. We have also found that we need to continually work to cultivate our own habits of mind, including the techniques we list below.

1. Corroborate and triangulate. If you come across a surprising claim or dramatic news report from an unknown source, use a search engine to see if you can find the same claims from other sources. If not, be very suspicious. Even when one news outlet has a big scoop, other papers quickly report on the fact that the first outlet broke the story. Be sure that those reporting on the story include reliable sources. Disinformation campaigns may plant multiple versions of the same false tale in unreliable outlets.

2. Pay attention to where information comes from. If you find a piece of candy lying in the street, you are not going to eat it or share it with your friends. Unsourced information is the same. All too often, someone we don't know posts a factoid or statistic or data graphic on social media without listing its source—and we share it anyway.

3. Dig back to the origin of the story. This takes time and effort, but if you want to avoid spreading misinformation, it is effort well spent. Don't simply read a headline or tweet; read the full news story. If the news story is from an outlet that tends to sensationalize, don't stop there. Dig back to the primary article or report that the story is talking about. Or dig really deep and take a look at the data yourself.

4. Use reverse image lookup. Several search engines provide a reverse image lookup service in which you upload a picture or a few frames from a video, and the search engine tells

you where on the Web that picture or video can be found.* This is one of the more underutilized tools on the Web for fact-checking. If you are suspicious of a Twitter or Facebook account, check to see if the profile photo comes from a stock photo website.

5. Be aware of deepfakes and other synthetic media. A random stranger on the Internet could be anybody, anywhere. But while we've learned to distrust user names by themselves, we're still susceptible to people's pictures. In the past, a person's photo was pretty good proof that they existed. No longer. So-called deepfake technology makes it possible to generate photorealistic images of people who don't exist. For now, one can still spot them with a bit of practice. Learn how at our website, http://whichfaceisreal.com. It won't be long until these fakes are much more difficult to detect, so it's good to keep in mind that even if someone appears in a "photograph," he or she still might not be a real person.

6. Take advantage of fact-checking organizations. If you come across a wild story online, confirm it by visiting a fact-checking website such as Snopes.com, PolitiFact.com, or FactCheck.org. If the story is not yet documented at these websites, ask them to fact-check it. They learn what stories need to be verified or debunked from users like you.

7. Make sure you know whom you are dealing with. Like other Internet fraudsters, fake news creators try all kinds of tricks to make the information they are providing seem more legitimate than it is. A fake news story might be designed to look as if it is just one of hundreds of stories from a large newspaper or television news station—but if you were to dig deeper, you would find that no such paper or station exists. Alternatively, a fake news pusher might send a social media post with a link that says something like "view the story on cnn.com," but the link would actually direct you to a different

---

* Tineye is a standalone reverse image search engine: https://tineye.com/how.

Google provides instructions for using their reverse image search here: https://support.google.com/websearch/answer/1325808.

Bing's image match service is detailed here: https://blogs.bing.com/search/2014/03/13/find-it-faster-with-image-match/.

Web domain with pages made to look like CNN. Be aware of the web addresses you are visiting. Scammers often pick domain names that are easy to misread. Similar as they look, abc.com.co is not abc.com; faceb000k.com is not facebook. com. There are thousands of these kinds of websites that try to look legitimate. Sometimes fake news sites run ads that look like they are coming from reputable outlets but instead are traps that send you to scammers' sites.

8.   Consider a website's track record. How do you know if a website is reliable? Try to find out if the site has been known to create and push fake news sources. Wikipedia often provides an overview of media outlets; this can be a good place to start. No one gets the facts right all the time, so see if the website issues corrections. Is the site reflective about the challenges it faces in getting at the truth?

9.   Be aware of the illusory truth effect. The more often you see something, the more likely you will be to believe it. We take this very seriously when studying fake news and conspiracy content. We know that it can be disorienting to mill through fake news stories, so be cautious. Watch out for a tendency to believe something because you keep seeing it.

10.   Reduce your information intake. Take a break; be bored a few times a day and revel in "missing out" instead of being anxious about what you missed. This will enhance your ability to process information with skepticism when you are online.

Most important: When you are using social media, remember the mantra "think more, share less." The volume of information on social media, and the speed at which it allows us to interact, can be addictive. But as responsible citizens, we need to keep our information environments as clean as possible. Over the past half century people have learned not to litter the sides of the interstates. We need to do the same on the information superhighway. Online, we need to stop throwing our garbage out the car window and driving away into the anonymous night.

CHAPTER 11

Refuting Bullshit

WE BEGAN THIS BOOK BY DEFINING BULLSHIT, DISCUSSING ITS origins deep in our evolutionary history, and explaining how and why it proliferates so readily in today's digital environments. We looked at the various forms that bullshit—particularly quantitative bullshit—can take, and how to detect them. The book so far could be called *Spotting Bullshit*. But we chose to call it *Calling Bullshit*, because a solution to the ongoing bullshit epidemic is going to require more than just an ability to see it for what it is. We need to shine a light on bullshit where it occurs, and demand better from those who promulgate it.

We define *calling bullshit* as follows:

> *Calling bullshit is a performative utterance in which one repudiates something objectionable. The scope of targets is broader than bullshit alone. You can call bullshit on bullshit, but you can also call bullshit on lies, treachery, trickery, or injustice.*

This definition draws upon the concept of a performative utterance, as discussed in the philosophy of language. When we think about the purpose of language, we usually think about how we use it to make statements about ourselves or about the world. "I feel sad." "The next bus doesn't come until seven-thirty." "Many years later, as he faced the firing squad, Colonel Aureliano Buendía was to remember that distant afternoon when his father took him to discover ice."*

---

* So begins Gabriel García Márquez's *One Hundred Years of Solitude*.

Words are also useful for issuing commands: "Stop!" "Flight attendants, prepare for landing." "Honour thy father and thy mother: that thy days may be long upon the land which the Lord thy God giveth thee."

In the wryly titled book *How to Do Things with Words,* philosopher J. L. Austin noted that there is yet a third class of things that we do with speech. There are utterances that, when we make them in the appropriate circumstances, are better viewed as actions than as expressions of a proposition. These are known as performative utterances. "I dub thee Knight"; "I christen this ship the HMS *Beagle*"; "I do [take this man as my lawfully wedded husband]"; "I do solemnly swear that I will support and defend the Constitution of the United States against all enemies, foreign and domestic." In each case, the speaker is not merely reporting on her action, she is acting by means of her speech. Austin calls these sentences performative utterances, because one performs an action by uttering the expression.

Performative utterances are statements rather than questions. The subject is usually "I," and they are in the present tense rather than past or future tenses: "I resign" instead of "I resigned" or "I will resign." You could summarize all of this by saying that performative utterances tend to be expressed in the first-person singular, indicative active present tense—if you're into that sort of thing. In addition to grammatical cues, the English language even has a somewhat archaic word, "hereby," that can be used to flag a performative utterance if it is not obvious from context. We don't claim the passenger seat by shouting "I hereby call shotgun," but "hereby" remains common in legal language, where it serves to indicate that a legal document represents an official action or commitment: "I hereby accept the agreement," "I hereby renounce all claim upon the estate," "I hereby declare that the details furnished above are true and correct to the best of my knowledge and belief."

Calling bullshit is itself a performative utterance—and this observation is important for understanding what it means to call bullshit upon some claim. When I call bullshit, I am not merely reporting that I am skeptical of something you said. Rather, I am explicitly and often publicly pronouncing my disbelief. Why does this matter? Performative utterances are not idle talk. They are powerful acts, to be used with prudence. Calling bullshit is the same. Don't call bullshit carelessly—but if you can, call bullshit when necessary.

We are convinced that the world would be a better place if there were less bullshit to deal with. As the legendary journalist and political commentator Walter Lippmann noted a century ago, "There can be no liberty for a community which lacks the means by which to detect lies." Calling bullshit is crucial to the healthy functioning of a social group, be it a circle of friends, a community of academics, or the citizenry of a nation. Any group adopts wrong ideas at times, and these ideas require forceful public repudiation. But if you want to call bullshit, it is important to do so responsibly, appropriately, and respectfully. This is not an oxymoron. We the authors do this for each other on a daily basis. We understand that the proper target of calling bullshit is an idea, not a person. We realize that we will sometimes be on the producing end of bullshit. We've learned to accept and acknowledge our mistakes with a modicum of grace when bullshit is called on us.

Spotting bullshit is a private activity. Calling bullshit is a public one. If you can spot bullshit, you can keep yourself safe from its effects. If you can call bullshit, you can protect your entire community. Of course not everyone will feel comfortable calling bullshit—and that's fine. Moreover, we recognize that it might be less acceptable to do this in some cultures. There are many ways to help reduce the bullshit density of our society without sticking your neck out too far. You can learn to spot bullshit and avoid being misled yourself. You can learn to stop producing bullshit. You can learn to avoid sharing it. But we've already talked about how to do these things. For those of you who want to take the leap and call bullshit, we'll show you how to do so both effectively and appropriately.

Carelessly calling bullshit is a quick way to make enemies of strangers and strangers of friends. Because calling bullshit is a performative utterance, it is particularly important to be correct when you do so. People despise hypocrites, and being full of shit when you call bullshit is about as hypocritical as one can get. It's worse if you've called it aggressively and judgmentally. There's a thin line between being a tough-minded skeptic and a domineering jerk. We want to make sure you don't end up on the wrong side of the line.

Why did we wait until the final chapter to talk about *calling* bullshit? To spot bullshit you need to develop all of the skills and habits of mind that we've described over the past ten chapters. You need to be aware of the traps and sources of confusion, the potential misuses of numbers and data visualization and big data, the ways in which bullshit slips into not only the popular media but the scientific literature as well. To call bullshit seems comparatively easy. You simply have to open your mouth or type a few characters to say "bullshit!" But simply uttering the words is not enough. In order to call bullshit effectively, you need to know how to construct a successful refutation. The right approach will depend not only on the type of bullshit you aim to refute, but also on the audience you wish to convince. Various approaches may be best for convincing your child, your congressional representative, a stranger on an airplane, or a scientist with a background in statistics.

Now we turn to methods for refuting bullshit. Many of these should be familiar—we have been demonstrating them throughout the book.

USE *REDUCTIO AD ABSURDUM*

In the Summer Olympics of 2004, Yuliya Nesterenko won the women's hundred-meter dash in 10.93 seconds. This was not an Olympic record, but it was more than two seconds faster than the women who had run the event seventy years earlier.

Inspired by this substantial improvement over a relatively short amount of time, researchers published a short news piece in *Nature*. Comparing times for men and women, they found that over the past few decades women have been closing the gap with male sprinters. While men's times were improving, women's times were improving more rapidly. What should we expect to happen in the future? the researchers asked. Modeling the changes in winning times, the authors predicted that women will outsprint men by the 2156 Olympic Games.

It may be true that women will someday outsprint men, but this analysis does not provide a compelling argument. The authors' conclusions were based on an overly simplistic statistical model.

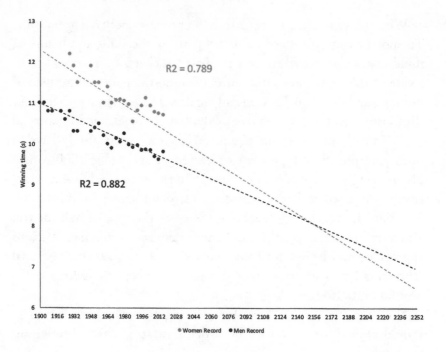

As shown above, the researchers fit a straight line through the times for women, and a separate straight line through the times for men. If you use this model to estimate future times, it predicts that women will outsprint men in the year 2156. In that year, the model predicts that women will finish the hundred-meter race in about 8.08 seconds and men will be shortly behind with times of about 8.10 seconds.

Of course, both women and men will continue to break records. However, there is something clearly wrong with the model. Many readers, including students in a high school class in Texas, caught this problem and wrote to *Nature* in reply. Our favorite response was a letter from a biostatistics professor, Ken Rice (emphasis added):

> Sir—A. J. Tatem and colleagues calculate that women may outsprint men by the middle of the twenty-second century (*Nature* 431, 525; 200410.1038/431525a). They omit to mention, however, that (according to their analysis) a far more interesting race should occur in about 2636, when times of *less than zero seconds* will be recorded. In the intervening 600 years, the authors may wish to address the obvious challenges raised for both time-keeping and the teaching of basic statistics.

This response is both humorous and highly effective. In it, Rice employed one of our favorite refutation strategies: *reductio ad absurdum*. This strategy, which dates back at least to Aristotle, shows how your opponent's assumptions can lead to ridiculous conclusions. In his *reductio,* Rice employed the same model and methods found in the *Nature* paper. Using the same model, he extrapolated further into the future and came to the preposterous conclusion that late-millennium sprinters will run the hundred-meter dash in negative times. Clearly this can't be true, so we should be skeptical of the paper's other surprising results, such as the forecasted gender reversal in winning times.

Another lesson here is to be careful about what kind of model is employed. A model may pass all the formal statistical model-fitting tests. But if it does not account for real biology—in this case, the physical limits to how fast any organism can run—we should be careful about what we conclude.

BE MEMORABLE

Functional magnetic resonance imaging (fMRI) allows neuroscientists to explore what brain regions are involved in what sorts of cognitive tasks. Researchers have looked at what areas of the brain are most active in subjects playing videogames, having sex, listening to music, engaging in exercise, or responding to other stimuli. A typical study would compare the fMRI images of afflicted patients with those of nonafflicted controls and ask why certain parts of the brain light up differently.

This technique for measuring neuronal activity has left an enormous mark on neuroscience. But the software used to detect differences in brain activity has to make assumptions about how to assess the statistical significance of these results. A recent study showed how these assumptions can sometimes make differences look more significant than they are. While scientists do not universally agree on the size of the problem, some feel the problem is serious enough to call into question the results from several thousand papers.

Years before these statistical issues came to light, a research poster presented at a neuroscience conference used *reductio ad absurdum* to present a memorable critique of fMRI technology. The title of the poster? "Neural Correlates of Interspecies Perspective Taking in the Post-mortem Atlantic Salmon: An Argument for Proper Multiple Comparisons Correction." You read correctly: a dead salmon.

This *reductio ad absurdum* came from a deliberately silly experiment. The authors placed a dead Atlantic salmon into an fMRI machine, asked the unfortunate creature the sorts of questions that researchers typically ask human subjects, and measured the activity of the deceased fish's brain. In a subsequent research paper, they described the study as follows:

> The salmon measured approximately 18 inches long, weighed 3.8 lbs, and was not alive at the time of scanning. It is not known if the salmon was male or female, but given the post-mortem state of the subject this was not thought to be a critical variable. . . . The salmon was shown a series of photographs depicting human individuals in social situations with a specified emotional valence, either socially inclusive or socially exclusive. The salmon was asked to determine which emotion the individual in the photo must have been experiencing.

It's brilliant—we have firsthand confirmation from one of the researchers that they actually spoke to the dead salmon and showed it pictures of people in different situations—and the results were striking. Several regions in the brain stem of the salmon showed higher activity when the fish was being asked about people's emotions, relative to when it was at "rest." (We can only imagine how bright the regions may have been if the salmon was asked about salmon emotions.) If these data had come out of a more straight-faced study, the researchers might have concluded that this brain stem region was involved in processing emotion. Instead, the findings highlight the risk of false positives in fMRI studies.

The authors summarized their results, in the most memorable of ways:

> Either we have stumbled onto a rather amazing discovery in terms of post-mortem ichthyological cognition, or there is something a bit off with regard to our uncorrected statistical approach.

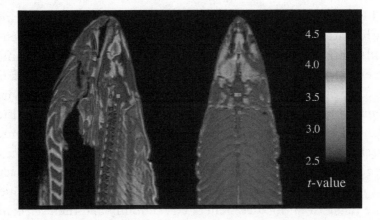

The salmon study was followed by a number of more technical and less entertaining research articles that further dissected the problem, estimated its magnitude, and proposed solutions. These projects were critical for the field to advance, but none were as effective as the original salmon study in drawing attention to the basic problem. Humor is not a requirement for *reductio ad absurdum,* but when integrated well it can be highly effective. It is memorable and spreads ideas quickly through informal conversation.

FIND COUNTEREXAMPLES

The Santa Fe Institute (SFI) is an independent scientific research center perched high above the city of Santa Fe, New Mexico, in the foothills of the Sangre de Cristo Mountains.* There, scientists from a wide range of disciplines—physics, biology, economics, sociology, computer science, mathematics, and beyond—meet to study, think, and discuss ideas over afternoon tea. It is the kind of environment where creative, big-picture thinking is encouraged and supported. But rigor is also essential, and the visitors to SFI are more than willing to point out mistakes in one's logic or holes in one's reasoning.

We heard about a great counterexample raised at a Santa Fe Institute workshop on immune systems. One physicist at the meeting

---

* Carl spent a decade on the external faculty at SFI, and Jevin has been a frequent visitor to the institute.

had learned a little bit about the immune system and had created a mathematical model to account for it. In his talk, he described his model and stressed its powerful implications. Not only are immune systems like ours useful for dealing with pathogens, he explained, but they are absolutely necessary. In order to survive in environments overrun with pathogens, he predicted, long-lived multicellular organisms such as ourselves must necessarily have immune systems with certain distinctive features. For example, the model suggested that long-lived organisms will need to have cells that detect the presence of viral infection, and other cells that produce a wide range of antibodies, generated randomly and then selected to proliferate should they match the invading pathogen. At first blush, the argument may have seemed reasonable. Plus, there was fancy mathematics behind it!

An immunologist in the room seemed unconvinced. It is at this point that someone will often raise their hand to question the assumptions of the mathematical model or ask for clarification of the analysis; extensive technical discussion and often disagreements on the mathematical details follow. The immunologist—with decades of experience designing and conducting experiments, reading and reviewing thousands of papers, and teaching courses on immunology to college students—took a different approach. Instead he asked a question that required no more than a basic education in biology. He raised his hand and asked the speaker: "But what about trees?"

Trees are multicellular organisms, and they are certainly long-lived. By most accounts, the bristlecones of the White Mountains are the oldest living organisms on the planet. But while trees have immune defenses, they have few if any of the characteristics that the speaker claimed were needed to keep a large organism alive for a long period of time.

The tree counterexample was devastating. There was basically no point in going any further with the talk or the questions. The speaker and the audience might as well have ended early and grabbed some of the delicious cookies and coffee that are always on hand for breaks.

Reductio ad absurdum can be fun and effective but nothing is as devastating to specious arguments as a simple counterexample. If someone claims that *A* implies *B*, find a case in which *A* is true but *B* is not. *A* in this case is a large, long-lived multicellular organism; *B* is having an adaptive immune system. Trees can be classified as *A,* but do not have *B;* therefore *A* does not imply *B.**

It takes practice to find good counterexamples, and few will be as effective and crushing as the tree example. If and when you do find one, please be kind. If the claims were made in earnest with no ill intent, help your target recover. We all make mistakes. Hopefully your counterexample will be instructive and will lead to better analyses with stronger claims in the future.

PROVIDE ANALOGIES

Like many large cities, Seattle has serious traffic problems. Nearly four hundred thousand vehicles commute into the city every day, and the aging infrastructure was not designed to handle anything near that volume. Making matters worse, Seattle is one of the fastest-growing cities in the US, and as the city is surrounded on both sides by water, this growth takes the form of increasing population density rather than outward expansion.

One especially problematic region is South Lake Union near Mercer Street. This once sleepy patchwork of auto body shops and small local businesses has been replaced by soaring forests of glass and steel that house Amazon's rapidly expanding headquarters and a host of

---

* Nowhere is the power of counterexample as clear as in mathematics. A single counterexample provides absolute resolution to an open conjecture. Consider Fermat's last theorem (which was not really a theorem but a conjecture, because Fermat did not provide a proof). It states that there are no three distinct integers *a, b,* and *c* such that $a^n + b^n = c^n$ for integer values of *n* greater than 2. For centuries, mathematicians tried to prove this conjecture—and failed. Finally, after years of solitary work developing major advances in several areas of mathematics, British mathematician Andrew Wiles came up with a proof drawing on recent mathematical discoveries and running 127 pages in length. It was an epic achievement, with numerous setbacks including the discovery of a mistake in the proof that set Wiles back another two years. That's what it takes to prove Fermat's last theorem true. Had the theorem been false, the proof could have been much simpler. It could have been a mere counterexample, three numeric values for *a, b,* and *c,* and a value for *n.*

Indeed, this is exactly what happened when the great eighteenth-century mathematician Leonhard Euler attempted to generalize Fermat's last theorem into what is known as the sum of powers conjecture. It says that for integers *a, b, c,* . . . , *z* and any integer *n,* if you want numbers a^n, b^n, c^n, etc., to add to some other number z^n, you need at least *n* terms in the sum. For nearly two hundred years, no one was able to prove or disprove the conjecture. Then in 1966, two mathematicians used an early computer to run through a huge list of possibilities and found a counterexample: $27^5 + 84^5 + 110^5 + 133^5 = 144^5$. No further theory is needed; from that one example we know that Euler's sum of powers conjecture is false. Counterexamples can be much easier to verify than positive proofs. There are relatively few mathematicians in the world who can verify all of Wiles's proof. But you can verify the counterexample to Euler's conjecture in a minute or so with the help of an electronic calculator.

other tech firms. Simply leaving the "Mercer Mess" and getting out onto the interstate can take the better part of an hour during the worst blockages. A few years back, the city decided to invest $74 million to improve traffic flow through this area. When the construction was finished and traffic had returned to the streets, the transportation office began measuring the travel times. The results were not what some had hoped. One local television station reported "$74 Million Later, Mercer Mess Is 2 Seconds Faster." The implication was obvious: yet another colossal waste of taxpayer money.

But was it really a waste? It is true that from the perspective of an individual driver, travel time did not decrease much. But think about why this happened. First of all, the number of people working in this area increased faster than almost anywhere in the country. Simply holding travel times constant in the face of this influx is a huge accomplishment. Second, the traffic patterns in a big city adjust themselves organically. If one route becomes substantially faster, traffic diverts from nearby routes to the faster route until travel times equilibrate for all routes. If you increase the capacity of one road, it may speed travel there only a little; the benefits are distributed across the entire traffic grid.

That seems to be precisely what happened. The Mercer corridor now handles thirty thousand more cars a day than it did before the improvement project, without any increase in travel time. The headline might have read "Seattle Road Improvement Project Allows 10 Million Extra Trips Per Year with No Increase in Travel Times." In order to measure the project's benefits, we need to consider the consequences of an improvement project across all routes in that region of the city.

Not long after we launched our Calling Bullshit course, we were asked to talk about the Mercer traffic situation on one of the local news stations. To highlight the folly of measuring travel times while ignoring trips per day, we used an analogy that resonated with Seattle-area viewers. In early 2010, the Seattle Mariners baseball team renewed the contract of pitching ace Felix Hernandez for about $78 million— comparable to the cost of the construction work on the Mercer Mess. But the Mariners' team batting average dropped from .258 in 2009 to .236 in 2010, and the number of home runs hit by Mariners players declined from 160 to 101. A local TV station could have run a headline griping that "Mariners Hitting Declines in 2010 Despite $78 Million Investment in Felix Hernandez." It's a true claim. But it's obviously a silly headline, because it couples two unrelated facts. The hitting decline has nothing to do with Hernandez. Pitchers play only every fifth game or so, they don't bat in the American League and, most important, they are not signed for their batting prowess. Pairing Hernandez's contract with the team's 2010 hitting performance implies that his salary was wasted because he didn't raise the team's batting average. Absurd, but not so different from suggesting that the Mercer Mess construction was a waste because travel times did not appreciably decrease. Each uses an irrelevant measure to evaluate the payoff of a seventy-million-dollar investment in a Seattle institution.

We use analogies often, because they help recontextualize claims that may seem reasonable at first glance. By drawing parallels between an unfamiliar situation and an example your audience intuitively understands, you encourage them to trust their own critical thinking abilities. For example, when we addressed the vaccine skeptic's dismissal of the one percentage point decrease in flu, we drew an analogy to another modern safety innovation that people understand and accept: seatbelts. We showed that she could make approximately the same claim about seatbelts as she did with the flu vaccine. Parents might feel unequipped to judge the risks associated with vaccines, but seatbelts are a matter of common sense.

REDRAW FIGURES

In chapter 7, we looked at ways in which accurate data can be displayed misleadingly. While one can point out some of the tricks that designers have used, the most effective way to refute the misleading impression is to redraw the graph in a more appropriate fashion.

In that chapter, we saw an example of this when we looked at the *National Review*'s tweet: the only climate change chart you need to see. By zooming way out and showing a temperature range from 0 to 110 degrees Fahrenheit, the designer of that graph hid the dramatic two-degree increase in temperature over the past few decades. With the exact same data, *The Washington Post* subsequently redrew the figure, zooming in to a more appropriate range. The temperature increase that leaps out of that chart tells a different story.

The Internet news site *Quartz* used this technique to strong effect when, in 2013, Apple CEO Tim Cook gave a presentation about iPhone sales. Below is a version of the graph that Cook showed:

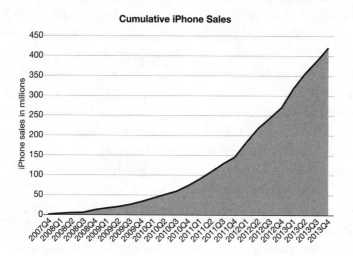

This graph looks quite impressive; it seems as if Apple is taking over the world with the iPhone as cumulative sales go up and up and up. But of course cumulative sales go up—cumulative sales can't go down! What the graph hides is the fact that quarterly iPhone sales had been declining for at least the past two quarters prior to Cook's presentation.

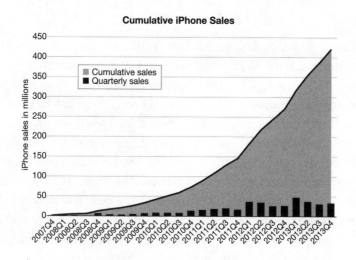

By redrawing the graph to show quarterly sales, *Quartz* was able to reveal a story that was hidden in the original line chart.

DEPLOY A NULL MODEL

Once we reach our physical peak sometime in our twenties or thirties, our performance for most physical and cognitive tasks begins to decline. Biologists call this process *senescence*.

To illustrate this lamentable fact in the evolutionary biology textbook Carl co-wrote, he plotted the world records for various field events by age. The figure below shows the average speed of world record holders in the men's 100-meter, 1,500-meter, and 10,000-meter race, with the speeds normalized so that the world record corresponds to a pace of 1.0.

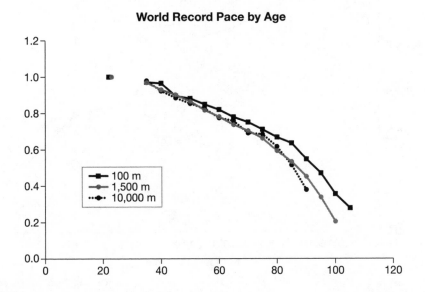

World Record Pace by Age

While teaching his course on evolution and medicine, Carl showed the students this graph. He explained that it was intended to illustrate that human physical performance declines with age, and asked them to take a few minutes to think about whether there were any problems with that argument. He anticipated that they would come up with a few objections. For example, these are world record times set by the world's best athletes. The performance curve above may not be representative of what happens to the rest of us.*

What Carl didn't anticipate, however, is that one of his students would point out a problem that he had not even considered. There are many more people running competitively in their twenties and thirties than in their seventies and eighties. The more runners you sample from, the faster you expect the fastest time to be. She was completely right. The fastest runner in a sample of a million people is likely to be much faster than the faster runner in a sample of a thousand.† We might see the same decreasing trend in speed simply as a consequence of sample size, even if runners did not get slower with age. If so, Carl's graph doesn't provide very compelling evidence for senescence.

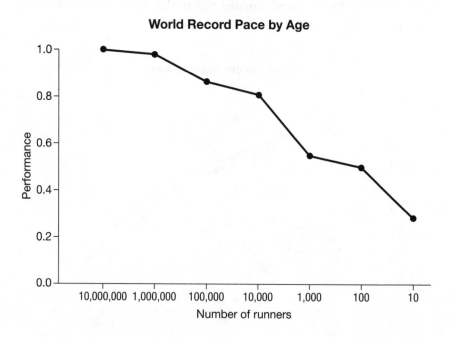

World Record Pace by Age

* Another issue with this graph is that the curve shown does not represent the performance trajectory of any single individual. Different athletes hold the records for different ages. Those who peak early may fall off faster than illustrated by the curves. Those who peak late may not have had as far to fall because they never ran at world record pace in their youth. So the curves don't really tell us about what happens to a person over time, they just tell us something about the upper bounds of human performance. Moreover, there may be "cohort effects" operating. Runners who set records in the sixty-five-and-over group trained using different techniques, diets, etc., than runners currently in their twenties. Improved training technology could have an effect on record times as well.

† If we were looking at *average speed,* the sample size wouldn't matter much. Whether we sampled a hundred, a thousand, or a million runners of a given age, we would expect the average time to be about the same. But if we are looking at the extreme outliers, the sample size matters.

To illustrate the student's point, we can create a *null model*. A null model helps us understand what we would observe in a very simple system where not much is going on. In this case we can use a computer simulation to create a pretend world where age doesn't affect running speed. Then we see if we still observe the same downward trend in physical performance simply because there are fewer runners of older ages. The graph in the previous page illustrates what we find.

Our null model generated data very much like the data that Carl presented in his textbook—without requiring any senescence. This does not mean that senescence is a myth. What it does mean is that the data Carl plotted do not provide compelling evidence of senescence, because the null model shows the same result without senescence.

That is what null models do. The point of a null model is not to accurately model the world, but rather to show that a pattern X, which has been interpreted as evidence of a process Y, could actually have arisen without Y occurring at all. In our example, the pattern X is the decreasing performance of record holders with age. The process Y is senescence: Humans run slower as they get older. Because we see decreasing performance even without senescence, our null model is a way of saying, "Sorry, you don't get to use those data as evidence for your theory." Notice here that the null model does not have to be an accurate description of the world to rob the original argument of its rhetorical force. It is enough to show that we would see the same pattern even without the process in question.

THE PSYCHOLOGY OF DEBUNKING

Myths are the most difficult to debunk when they are interwoven with a person's worldview and sense of cultural identity. We once had dinner with a zoo director who faced repeated challenges from PETA, People for the Ethical Treatment of Animals. He wanted to know how he could engage in a constructive dialogue and possibly even persuade them that his zoo plays a valuable role in conservation efforts. We explained how their views were entangled with their identities in a way that his were not. For example, if they were to convince him that keeping elephants in captivity was unethical, he would still be a scholar and zoo director. But if he were to persuade them that keeping elephants in zoos was justifiable, they could not retain their iden-

tities as PETA activists. These issues of identity made his task vastly
more difficult. Often your task won't be difficult. Help your aunt see
that she can maintain her electrolyte balance without paying eighty
dollars for a water bottle with an amethyst crystal in it. Help your
uncle see that he can still prefer a limited federal government without
denying global warming. Whatever it takes. Find ways to decouple
issues of identity from the matter you are trying to debunk.

In the previous chapter we discussed being aware of our own confirmation biases, which arise because we tend to search for, believe,
and recall information that aligns with our own worldviews. Recognize that others suffer from confirmation bias as well. Once an idea is
entrenched it is difficult to replace with a better supported idea, no
matter how hard you try. In addition to the methods we've discussed
so far, here are some time-tested tips for debunking myths:

1.   Keep it simple. One advantage that falsehood has over
truth is that the truth is often complicated whereas falsehoods
can be crafted to be simple. Look for ways to make your story
as simple as possible without distorting it. Focus on your core
points and let the rest go. Scoring rhetorical points on tangential technicalities doesn't convince anyone, it just pisses people
off.

2.   Take it offline. Take your conversations offline if you
can. No one likes to be called out in public. If you're going to
call bullshit on your brother-in-law, do so on a quiet walk, not
at the Thanksgiving table. If you're going to call out someone
online, consider doing so in a private message rather than on
someone's public Twitter feed. (Admittedly, this is complicated
by a need to protect others from being deceived.) When called
out publicly, most of us dig in and try to defend our previous
statements rather than considering objections in good faith. Privately, people are often more open to critique.

3.   Find common ground. The less antagonistic your interaction is, the more likely someone will seriously consider your
ideas. One of the best ways to soften your words is to first establish a point of common ground. When talking to someone
who is skeptical about vaccine safety, don't start out saying "I
can't believe you're dumb enough to fall that for that stupid

hippie BS." Instead, try the common-ground approach. "Wow, it's really hard to know how to do right by our kids. I worry about it all the time myself . . ."

4. Don't overemphasize the myth. Familiarity increases the stickiness of myth. If a reference to the myth is necessary, precede with explicit warnings. Some research suggests that people's beliefs in misinformation can be strengthened if you reiterate the myth before you debunk it.

5. Fill in knowledge gaps with alternative explanations. It is not enough to simply debunk a myth; you need to replace it with an alternative account. People don't like incomplete stories in which events lack explanation. Your argument against a myth may seem convincing now, but if you don't replace it with a new narrative, your audience may fall back on the same old misinformation in the future. Good defense lawyers know this. Instead of just explaining to a jury why their defendant is *not guilty,* they will point to other suspects or circumstances that can fill the void if their client is not the perpetrator.

Now that we have given you some pointers to spot and refute bullshit, you're almost ready to go. But before you go out there and start calling bullshit willy-nilly, we would like to conclude with a few thoughts about how to do so in an ethical and constructive manner.

Be correct

The students who take our course on calling bullshit gain confidence in their ability to spot and refute it. We want to instill a sense of humility as well. It should go without saying, but it needs to be said: If you are going to call bullshit, be correct.

Make sure you have the facts at hand—don't skimp on the background research—and then double-check them. Mountaineers learn to check and double-check and then check their safety gear one more time. Just as you don't want to have your locking carabiner fly open during a forty-foot fall, you don't want to have your facts wrong when you're trying to drive home a point. Also, run your argument by a friend or colleague. We have been doing this for each other for fifteen years. If one of us gets excited about a new research result, he asks the other to try to undermine it. We've saved each other from embarrassment a number of times.

Be charitable

Twitter has been compared to a nation of television viewers yelling back at their TV sets, encouraged by a faint hope that the people on the TV might hear them. This seems an apt description of a lot of public discourse today. In a combative environment like this, it is easy to demonize those who disagree with us. When we hear something that we think we know is wrong, we are tempted to invoke malice or even conspiracy as the reason for the falsehood. Consider a few alternatives:

- You might be wrong. You may think this is unlikely, but at least be mindful of the possibility. It could be that you misheard the statement or misinterpreted an argument.
- Don't impute malice when incompetence is a sufficient explanation. Most people who write foolish things on the Internet or anywhere else do not have a nefarious underlying motive. They simply don't know what they are talking about.
- Don't assume incompetence when an honest mistake can account for error. We all make honest mistakes and say stupid things at times; it doesn't mean that we are stupid or that we are incompetent.

Being charitable is about keeping your friends, but it is also about focusing your refutation on the argument itself. To call bullshit in a civil way, attack the argument, rather than the person. Your neighbor may have good intentions in telling you about a study they found linking autism to the MMR vaccine. I can almost guarantee that your neighbor isn't aiming to harm children. They may not know that the paper they saw was written by the disgraced researcher Andrew Wakefield, nor that it was retracted and is now considered fraud by most of the medical community. Instead of assuming malice, consider that perhaps your neighbor made an honest mistake. Though in some cases you would be right, this principle will help you save face when you end up being wrong.

Admit fault

Humility is a virtue. We all make mistakes. When you do make a mistake, own it and admit fault swiftly and graciously. The first rule of arguing on the Internet seems to be "Always double down on your own stupidity," but we strongly discourage this practice. It doesn't move us forward, it wastes everyone's time, and it jams up what could have been a productive venue for discussion. Such acts of defiance and childishness tarnish your credibility—and your credibility has to be worth more than the outcome of one argument.

Be clear

Imagine that you're flying across the country and your seatmate engages you in a conversation about immigration or race relations or abortion or global warming. (We don't recommend this, but it happens!) Your seatmate may be wrong; you know it; the person on the other side of them knows it; the flight attendant knows it. If there is any hope of convincing this individual, you need to be clear. A deluge of unordered facts never convinced anyone to abandon their previous beliefs. Your arguments need to be clear, understandable, persuasive, and preferably free of jargon. This usually requires as much effort, often far more effort, than it took to spot the bullshit in the first place.

For more serious rebuttals in your professional life, the presentation is as important as the argument. As we tell our students, effective refutation is hard work. For us, creating a clear presentation often requires creating and refining visualizations, developing a null model, creating a synthetic data set, testing the argument with friends, and double-checking to be sure we are not missing anything. The good news is that we can all get better at these things. The bad news is that we can't possibly do this for every piece of bullshit that we find. Pick your battles. And when you have found your battle, make sure you win it. Do your homework in advance, and be clear in expressing your rationale.

Be pertinent

When we teach our students to call bullshit, we want to avoid creating a legion of "well, actually" guys. What's a well-actually guy? It's the guy who interrupts a conversation to demonstrate his own cleverness by pointing out some irrelevant factoid that renders the speaker incorrect on a technicality.*

Let's take an example. I'm talking to a friend of mine over lunch, and I say: "It's interesting. There are lots of birds that trick other species into raising their offspring. Cuckoos, cowbirds, honeyguides, even some ducks. But mammals never do this. I wonder why not."

She thinks for a moment, and then observes, "I suspect it is because mammals don't lay eggs. That makes it a lot harder to sneak a baby in there!"

"Well, actually," I respond, "*some* mammals *do* lay eggs. Echidnas and platypuses, collectively known as monotremes and found only in Australia and Papua New Guinea, are both oviparous."

Let's face it, that was a totally annoying thing to do. And it had nothing to do with calling bullshit. Why not? Let's look at some of the factors that distinguish a caller of bullshit from a well-actually guy.

- Relevance. When you do a good job of calling bullshit, you undermine a claim in a fundamental way. Your objections negate the argument the speaker is trying to make. A well-actually guy doesn't move the discussion forward at all. Instead, he offers a pedantic or tangential objection that does not have much bearing on the core claims. When I objected about monotremes and eggs, I was not wrong, but my objection was almost entirely immaterial to the conversation we were having. There are a few egg-laying mammals, but my friend was right about 99.9 percent of mammal species.† In the end, my friend's statement "mammals don't lay eggs" isn't universally true. But her idea sounds right, and my objection does nothing to undermine it.

---

* "Hey, wait. 'Guy' is a gendered term," you object. "Actually, women sometimes do this too. . . ." They do. But in our experience, they do so far less often than men do. Congratulations. You're the "well, actually . . ." guy.

† Even the two exceptions conform to her rule. Though echidnas lay eggs, they never afford anyone an opportunity to slip in an egg of their own, because they lay them right in their own pouches. Platypuses don't have pouches, but the female seals herself into her tunnel before laying her eggs and doesn't emerge until after they have hatched. Again, there is no opportunity for anyone to slip in their own offspring.

- Speaker's intention. Typically, a caller of bullshit refutes someone who is intentionally bullshitting or being deceptive. A well-actually guy is different. He doesn't hesitate to contradict someone who is engaging in a dialogue in good faith. When I griped about monotremes, I fell on the wrong side of this line. My friend's suggestion was made in good faith. She wasn't trying to impress anyone. She wasn't trying to mislead anyone. She was simply trying to help me by answering my question.

- Objector's motivations. A well-actually guy doesn't care so much about where the argument is going as he does about demonstrating his own intellectual superiority. I didn't mention monotremes because they had any bearing on my friend's idea; I brought them up in order to make it clear that I'm better versed in matters zoological than she is—and possibly for the opportunity to use the word "oviparous" in conversation. Calling bullshit is not a way to signal your intelligence. Get a MENSA card if that sort of thing is important to you.

- Audience. When you call bullshit, you are usually trying to prevent a bullshitter or liar from misleading his audience. A well-actually guy doesn't care about protecting an audience, he is merely interested in demonstrating his own cleverness. When I objected about monotremes, no one else was even part of the conversation.

- Power dynamics. When you call bullshit, you may find yourself speaking truth to power. A well-actually guy isn't speaking truth to power. He's often punching down. His motivation is to put the speaker in her place while raising himself up.

- Judiciousness. A caller of bullshit makes a careful decision about whether it is worthwhile to speak up, derail a conversation, risk a confrontation, or make someone feel defensive. A well-actually guy simply cannot help himself. He hears something he believes he can contradict and doesn't have the self-control to think first about whether it is helpful to do so.

In the end, a well-actually guy has more in common with a bullshitter than he does with a caller of bullshit. A bullshitter disregards truth or logical coherence in order to impress or overwhelm an audience.

That's the well-actually guy. He doesn't care about advancing truth, or about the logical coherence of his objections. He is simply trying to impress or intimidate someone with his knowledge. Calling bullshit is not about making yourself look or feel smarter. If that is your goal, you are missing the point of this chapter, and indeed the whole point of this book. Effective bullshit calling is about making *others* smarter. This should be your barometer of success—and requires an extra level of social finesse.

Spotting bullshit is not easy, especially with the daily onslaught of misinformation. It takes practice and deliberate effort. Remember, calling bullshit is more than a claim. It's a powerful action, and can easily be misused. But if you make an effort to be clear and correct and to remain reasonably civil, most people will respect you.

Before you publicly refute a claim, ask yourself who your audience is—and whether that audience is worth your time. Some people are so entrenched in their beliefs that they will never be convinced, no matter how cogent the argument and how airtight the facts. Spend your time and effort on people who are willing to engage.

Above all, remember Neil Postman's dictum: "At any given time, the chief source of bullshit with which you have to contend is yourself." Confirmation bias can make us more confident than we ought to be, and humility is an important corrective. Self-reflection and an appreciation for the difficulty of getting to the truth: These are the marks of a mature thinker worth trusting. Sure, we want to keep the rest of the world honest—but for everyone's sake, let's start with ourselves.

Calling bullshit is more than a party trick, a confidence booster, or a way to sound impressive in front of your boss. It is a moral imperative. As we note in the opening line of the book, the world is awash with bullshit—from clickbait to deepfakes. Some of it is innocuous, some is a minor annoyance, and some is even funny. But a lot of the bullshit out there has serious consequences for human health and prosperity, the integrity of science, and democratic decision making.

The rise of misinformation and disinformation keeps us up at night. No law or fancy new AI is going to solve the problem. We all have to be a little more vigilant, a little more thoughtful, a little more careful when sharing information—and every once in a while, we need to call bullshit when we see it.

Acknowledgments

THIS BOOK COULD NOT HAVE BEEN WRITTEN WITHOUT THE HELP of many, many people.

First of all, we thank our wives, Holly Bergstrom and Heather West, for reading draft chapters and calling bullshit where necessary. Without their help, this book would have 83 percent more bullshit than it does. (We can get away with this one made-up statistic, because neither spouse will read this prior to publication.) We thank our children, Helen and Teddy, and Braylen and Camryn, for their patience when we were preoccupied with our writing, and for showing us that the ideas in this book do not require a college education to absorb.

We thank the hundreds of students and thousands of colleagues who have listened to us lecture about this material. Their attention, enthusiasm, questions, comments, suggestions, and challenges have been invaluable in helping us refine our message. We thank the Powers That Be at the University of Washington for initially tolerating and later enthusiastically promoting our vision for the Calling Bullshit course. Those we follow and those who follow us on Twitter have suggested numerous examples—many of which appear in this book—and they have kept us feeling just hip enough that we continue to embarrass ourselves in front of Generation Z. We are grateful to our friends who listened to us talk about bullshit *ad nauseum*, contributed their own views on the subject, and told us when we were pushing more bullshit than we were debunking. And we are grateful to our friends who helped us get away from the project at times, whether on the tennis courts or hiking trails.

Our friend, colleague, and coauthor, Jennifer Jacquet, provided the early encouragement we needed to even think of turning our ideas into a book, and provided valuable support along the way. Our agent, Max Brockman, helped us develop a loose set of ideas about bullshit into the concept for this book. Our editor at Random House, Hilary Redmon, took a poorly arranged draft and restructured it into the book you hold in your hands. Her editorial talents sliced out a hundred or more pages that you are blessed not to have read, and softened our natural dialect—tedious academic prose—into what you find here. Molly Turpin at Random House kept the entire project running and on schedule, while handling the logistical nightmares associated with producing over a hundred figures for a trade book. The beautiful text design you see here is the work of Barbara Bachman. Publicity manager London King, with assistance from marketer Ayelet Gruenspecht, guided us as we worked to reach a broad audience with the ideas we have developed in the book. Production manager Katie Zilberman, production editor Jennifer Rodriguez, and managing editor Rebecca Berlant somehow managed to pull the entire project together despite our best efforts to miss deadlines and make changes long after it was reasonable to even contemplate doing so. Our editor at Penguin Press, Casiana Ionita, shared our vision for the book from the start and was a wonderful source of enthusiastic support throughout the process. With her team—publicity manager Matt Hutchinson, marketer Julie Woon, production manager Sandra Fuller, and copy editor Stephanie Barrett—she developed the U.K. edition of the book. Pete Garceau designed the U.S. cover, and Richard Green designed the U.K. cover. Joel Klemenhagen, Matthew Brady, and the crew at The Shambles provided us with a home-away-from-home where we could discuss and develop the ideas in this book.

We are proud to serve as faculty members at one of the great public universities, the University of Washington. Our role at the University is not only to teach the students enrolled there. Our mission is to serve the people of our state, our country, and our world by helping to inform, educate, and cultivate the clarity of thought that will lead us all toward a world of greater truth and justice.

Bibliography

PREFACE

Frankfurt, Harry G. *On Bullshit*. Princeton, N.J.: Princeton University Press, 2009.

Galeotti, Mark. "Putin Is Waging Information Warfare. Here's How to Fight Back." *The New York Times*. December 14, 2016.

Horne, Alistair. *Harold Macmillan, 1894–1956*. London: Macmillan, 1988.

CHAPTER I: BULLSHIT EVERYWHERE

Afzal, M. A., E. Armitage, S. Ghosh, L. C. Williams, and P. D. Minor. "Further Evidence of the Absence of Measles Virus Genome Sequence in Full Thickness Intestinal Specimens from Patients with Crohn's Disease." *Journal of Medical Virology* 62 (2000): 377–82.

Biss, Eula. *On Immunity: An Inoculation*. Minneapolis: Graywolf Press, 2014.

Boseley, Sarah. "Andrew Wakefield Struck Off Register by General Medical Council." *The Guardian*. May 24, 2010.

Bugnyar, T., S. A. Reber, and C. Buckner. "Ravens Attribute Visual Access to Unseen Competitors." *Nature Communications* 7 (2016): 10506.

Cavazuti, Lisa, Christine Romo, Cynthia McFadden, and Rich Schapiro. " 'Zone Rouge': An Army of Children Toils in African Mines." NBC News. November 18, 2019.

Deer, Brian. "How the Case against the MMR Vaccine Was Fixed." *British Medical Journal* 342 (2011): c5347.

———. "How the Vaccine Crisis Was Meant to Make Money." *British Medical Journal* 342 (2011): c5258.

———. "MMR Doctor Fixed Data on Autism." *The Sunday Times* (London). February 8, 2009.

Del Vicario, M., et al. "The Spreading of Misinformation Online." *Proceedings of the National Academy of Sciences* 113 (2016): 554–59.

Editors of the *British Medical Journal*. "BMJ Declares MMR Study 'an Elaborate

Fraud'—Autism Claims Likened to " 'Piltdown Man' Hoax." Press release. June 26, 2012.

Editors of *The Lancet*. "Retraction—Ileal-Lymphoid-Nodular Hyperplasia, Non-specific Colitis, and Pervasive Developmental Disorder in Children." *The Lancet* 375 (2010): 445.

Fanelli, Uriel. "La teoria della montagna di merda." *Niente Stronzate* [No Bullshit]. March 26, 2010. https://nientestronzate.wordpress.com/2010 /03/26/la-teoria-della-montagna-di-merda/.

Friggeri, Adrien, L. A. Adamic, D. Eckles, and J. Cheng. "Rumor Cascades." *Proceedings of the Eighth International AAAI Conference on Weblogs and Social Media*. May 16, 2014. Pages 101–10.

Gino, Francesca. "There's a Word for Using Truthful Facts to Deceive: Paltering." *Harvard Business Review*. October 5, 2015.

Godlee, F., J. Smith, and H. Marcovitch. "Wakefield's Article Linking MMR Vaccine and Autism Was Fraudulent." *British Medical Journal* 342 (2011): c7452.

Grice, Paul. *Studies in the Way of Words*. Cambridge, Mass.: Harvard University Press, 1991.

Groening, Matt. *The Simpsons*.

Honda, H., Y. Shimizu, and M. Rutter. "No Effect of MMR Withdrawal on the Incidence of Autism: A Total Population Study." *Journal of Child Psychology and Psychiatry* 46 (2005): 572–79.

Lo, N. C., and P. J. Hotez. "Public Health and Economic Consequences of Vaccine Hesitancy for Measles in the United States." *JAMA Pediatrics* 171 (2017): 887–92.

Madsen, K. M., A. Hviid, M. Vestergaard, D. Schendel, J. Wohlfahrt, P. Thorsen, J. Olsen, and M. Melbye. "A Population-Based Study of Measles, Mumps, and Rubella Vaccination and Autism." *The New England Journal of Medicine* 347 (2002): 1477–82.

Mäkelä, A., J. P. Nuorti, and H. Peltola. "Neurologic Disorders after Measles-Mumps-Rubella Vaccination." *Pediatrics* 110 (2002): 957–63.

Murch, S. H., A. Anthony, D. H. Casson, M. Malik, M. Berelowitz, A. P. Dhillon, M. A. Thompson, A. Valentine, S. E. Davies, and J. A. Walker-Smith. "Retraction of an Interpretation." *The Lancet* 363 (2004): 750.

Salmon, D. A., M. Z. Dudley, J. M. Glanz, and S. B. Omer. "Vaccine Hesitancy: Causes, Consequences, and a Call to Action." *Vaccine* 33 (2015): D66–D71.

Schauer, Frederick, and Richard Zeckhauser. "Paltering." In *Deception: From Ancient Empires to Internet Dating,* edited by Brooke Harrington, 38–54. Stanford, Calif.: Stanford University Press, 2009.

Sun, Lena H. "Anti-Vaccine Activists Spark a State's Worst Measles Outbreak in Decades." *The Washington Post*. May 5, 2017.

Swift, Jonathan. "Political Lying." *The Examiner*. September 11, 1710.

Taylor, B., E. Miller, C. P. Farrington, M. C. Petropoulos, I. Favot-Mayaud, J. Li, and P. A. Waight. "Autism and Measles, Mumps, and Rubella Vaccine: No Epidemiological Evidence for a Causal Association." *The Lancet* 353 (1999): 2026–29.

Taylor, L. E., A. L. Swerdfeger, and G. D. Eslick. "Vaccines Are Not Associated with Autism: An Evidence-Based Meta-analysis of Case-Control and Cohort Studies." *Vaccine* 32 (2014): 3623–29.

Wakefield, A. J., S. H. Murch, A. Anthony, J. Linnell, D. M. Casson, M. Malik, . . . and A. Valentine. "RETRACTED: Ileal-Lymphoid-Nodular Hyperplasia, Non-specific Colitis, and Pervasive Developmental Disorder in Children." *The Lancet* 351 (1998): 637–41.

CHAPTER 2: MEDIUM, MESSAGE, AND MISINFORMATION

Blair, A. "Reading Strategies for Coping with Information Overload, ca. 1550–1700." *Journal of the History of Ideas* 64 (2003): 11–28.

Blom, J. N., and K. R. Hansen. "Click Bait: Forward-Reference as Lure in Online News Headlines." *Journal of Pragmatics* 76 (2015): 87–100.

Brant, Sebastian. Ca. 1500. Quoted in John H. Lienhard. "What People Said about Books in 1498." Lecture presented at the Indiana Library Federation Annual Conference, Indianapolis. April 7, 1998. http://www.uh.edu /engines/indiana.htm.

BuzzSumo (blog). "We Analyzed 100 Million Headlines. Here's What We Learned (New Research)." Rayson, Steve. June 26, 2017. http://buzzsumo .com/blog/most-shared-headlines-study.

Carey, James W. "A Cultural Approach to Communication." In *Communication as Culture: Essays on Media and Society*. Revised edition. New York: Routledge, 2009, 11–28.

Conger, Kate. "Twitter Will Ban All Political Ads, C.E.O. Jack Dorsey Says." *The New York Times*. October 30, 2019.

de Strata, Filipo. 1474. Quoted in Jeremy Norman. "Scribe Filipo de Strata's Polemic against Printing." Jeremy Norman's History of Information. Accessed February 19, 2020. http://www.historyofinformation.com /expanded.php?id=4741.

Dodda, Tejeswi Pratima, and Rakesh Dubbudu. *Countering Misinformation in India: Solutions & Strategies*. Factly Media & Research and The Internet and Mobile Association of India, 2019. https://2nafqn3o0l6kwfofi3ydj9li -wpengine.netdna-ssl.com/wp-content/uploads//2019/02/Countering -Misinformation-Fake-News-In-India.pdf.

Donath, Judith. "Why Fake News Stories Thrive Online." *CNN*. November 20, 2016. http://www.cnn.com/2016/11/20/opinions/fake-news-stories -thrive-donath/index.html.

Fleishman, Glenn. "FCC Chair Ajit Pai Admits Millions of Russian and Fake Comments Distorted Net Neutrality Repeal." *Fortune*. December 5, 2018. http://fortune.com/2018/12/05/fcc-fraud-comments-chair-admits/.

Garber, Megan. "Common Knowledge: Communal Information in a Fragmented World." *Columbia Journalism Review*. September 8, 2009. https:// archives.cjr.org/the_news_frontier/common_knowledge.php.

Goldman, Russell. "Reading Fake News, Pakistani Minister Directs Nuclear Threat at Israel." *The New York Times*. December 24, 2016.

Grimaldi, James V. "New York Attorney General's Probe into Fake FCC Com-

ments Deepens." *The Wall Street Journal*. October 16, 2018. https://www
.wsj.com/articles/new-york-attorney-general-probes-fake-comments-on
-net-neutrality-1539729977.

Guess, Andrew M., Brendan Nyhan, and Jason Reifler. "Exposure to Untrustworthy Websites in the 2016 U.S. Election." *Nature Human Behaviour* (in
press). http://www.dartmouth.edu/~nyhan/fake-news-2016.pdf.

*Hearing Before the United States Senate Committee on the Judiciary Subcommittee on
Crime and Terrorism: Testimony of Colin Stretch, General Counsel, Facebook.*
October 31, 2017. 115th Congress. https://www.judiciary.senate.gov/imo
/media/doc/10-31-17%20Stretch%20Testimony.pdf.

Hitlin, Paul, Kenneth Olmstead, and Skye Toor. "Public Comments to the Federal Communications Commission about Net Neutrality Contain Many In-
accuracies and Duplicates." Pew Research Center. November 29, 2017.
https://www.pewinternet.org/2017/11/29/public-comments-to-the
-federal-communications-commission-about-net-neutrality-contain-many
-inaccuracies-and-duplicates/.

Ingraham, Nathan. "Facebook Removed over 1.5 Billion Fake Accounts in the
Last Six Months." *Engadget*. November 15, 2018. https://www.engadget
.com/2018/11/15/facebook-transparency-report-fake-account-removal/.

Kasparov, Garry (@kasparov63). "The point of modern propaganda isn't only
to misinform or push an agenda. It is to exhaust your critical thinking, to
annihilate truth." Twitter, December 13, 2016, 2:08 P.M. https://twitter
.com/kasparov63/status/808750564284702720?lang=en.

Martin, G. J., and A. Yurukoglu. "Bias in Cable News: Persuasion and Polariza-
tion." *American Economic Review* 107 (2017): 2565–99.

Nicas, Jack. "How YouTube Drives People into the Internet's Darkest Corners." *The Wall Street Journal*. February 7, 2018.

Paul, Christopher, and Miriam Matthews. *The Russian "Firehose of Falsehood"
Propaganda Model: Why It Might Work and Options to Counter It*. Santa
Monica, Calif.: RAND Corporation, 2016. https://www.rand.org/pubs
/perspectives/PE198.html.

Postman, Neil. "Bullshit and the Art of Crap-Detection." Paper presented at
the National Convention for the Teachers of English, Washington, D.C.,
November 28, 1969.

Qin, B., D. Strömberg, and Y. Wu. "Why Does China Allow Freer Social
Media? Protests versus Surveillance and Propaganda." *Journal of Economic
Perspectives* 31 (2017): 117–40.

Rely on Common Sense (blog). "Our Democracy Has Been Hacked." Jenna
Abrams. November 8, 2017. https://jennabrams.wordpress.com/2017/11
/08/our-democracy-has-been-hacked/.

Ritchie, Hannah. "Read All about It: The Biggest Fake News Stories of 2016."
CNBC. December 30, 2016. https://www.cnbc.com/2016/12/30/read-all
-about-it-the-biggest-fake-news-stories-of-2016.html.

Roberts, David. "Donald Trump and the Rise of Tribal Epistemology." *Vox*.
May 19, 2017. https://www.vox.com/policy-and-politics/2017/3/22
/14762030/donald-trump-tribal-epistemology.

Rose-Stockwell, Tobias. "This Is How Your Fear and Outrage Are Being Sold for Profit." *Medium*. July 14, 2017. https://medium.com/@tobiasrose/the-enemy-in-our-feeds-e86511488de.

Shahbaz, Adrian. "Fake News, Data Collection, and the Challenge to Democracy." In *Freedom on the Net 2018*. Washington, D.C.: Freedom House, 2018. https://freedomhouse.org/report/freedom-net/freedom-net-2018/rise-digital-authoritarianism.

Silverman, Craig, Lauren Strapagiel, Hamza Shaban, Ellie Hall, and Jeremy Singer-Vine. "Hyperpartisan Facebook Pages Are Publishing False and Misleading Information at an Alarming Rate." *BuzzFeed*. October 20, 2016. https://www.buzzfeednews.com/article/craigsilverman/partisan-fb-pages-analysis.

Somaiya, Ravi. "The Junk Cycle." *Columbia Journalism Review*. Fall 2019.

Sonnad, Nikhil. "How a Bot Made 1 Million Comments against Net Neutrality Look Genuine." *Quartz*. November 28, 2017. https://qz.com/1138697/net-neutrality-a-spambot-made-over-a-million-anti-net-neutrality-comments-to-the-fcc/.

"Study: 70% of Facebook Users Only Read the Headline of Science Stories before Commenting." *The Science Post*. March 5, 2018. http://thesciencepost.com/study-70-of-facebook-commenters-only-read-the-headline/.

Subramanian, Samanth. "Inside the Macedonian Fake-News Complex." *Wired*. February 15, 2017. https://www.wired.com/2017/02/veles-macedonia-fake-news/.

Szathmary, Eörs, and John Maynard Smith. *The Major Transitions in Evolution*. Oxford; New York: Oxford University Press, 1995.

Tufekci, Zeynep. "YouTube, the Great Radicalizer." *The New York Times*. March 10, 2018.

Vance, Ashlee. "This Tech Bubble Is Different." *Bloomberg Businessweek*. April 14, 2011. https://www.bloomberg.com/news/articles/2011-04-14/this-tech-bubble-is-different.

Wiseman, Cale Guthrie. "Hyper-Partisan Content Is Still the Best Performing on Facebook." *Fast Company*. February 1, 2018. https://www.fastcompany.com/40525289/hyper-partisan-content-is-still-the-best-performing-on-facebook.

The Wrap. "Here's a Completely Fake Pro-Trump Twitter Account Created by Russian Trolls." Sean Burch. November 3, 2017. https://www.thewrap.com/fake-pro-trump-twitter-troll-russian-jenna-abrams/.

CHAPTER 3: THE NATURE OF BULLSHIT

Biddle, Sam. "Troubling Study Says Artificial Intelligence Can Predict Who Will Be Criminals Based on Facial Features." *The Intercept*. November 18, 2016.

Cohen, G. A. "Deeper into Bullshit." In *Contours of Agency: Essays on Themes from Harry Frankfurt*, edited by Sarah Buss and Lee Overton, 321–39. Cambridge, MA: MIT Press, 2002.

Crews, Frederick. *Freud: The Making of an Illusion*. New York: Profile Books, 2017.

Emerging Technology from the arXiv. "Neural Network Learns to Identify Criminals by Their Faces." *MIT Technology Review.* November 22, 2016.

Gunnell, J. J., and S. J. Ceci. "When Emotionality Trumps Reason: A Study of Individual Processing Style and Juror Bias." *Behavioral Sciences & the Law* 28 (2010): 850–77.

Latour, Bruno. *Pandora's Hope: Essays on the Reality of Science.* Cambridge, Mass.: Harvard University Press, 1999.

———. *Science in Action.* Cambridge, Mass.: Harvard University Press, 1987.

Littrell, S., E. F. Risko, and J. A. Fugelsang. "The Bullshitting Frequency Scale: Development and Psychometric Properties." 2019. PsyArXiv preprint: 10.31234/osf.io/dxzqh.

Lombroso, Cesare. *L'Uomo Delinquente.* 1876.

Smagorinsky, P., E. A. Daigle, C. O'Donnell-Allen, and S. Bynum. "Bullshit in Academic Writing: A Protocol Analysis of a High School Senior's Process of Interpreting Much Ado about Nothing." *Research in the Teaching of English* 44 (2010): 368–405.

Sullivan, Ben. "A New Program Judges if You're a Criminal from Your Facial Features." *Vice.* November 18, 2016.

Turpin, M. H., et al. "Bullshit Makes the Art Grow Profounder." *Judgment and Decision Making* 14 (2019): 658–70.

Wu, X., and X. Zhang. "Automated Inference on Criminality Using Face Images." 2016. arXiv: 1611.04135.

CHAPTER 4: CAUSALITY

Adamczyk, Alicia. "Build the Skill of Delayed Gratification." *Lifehacker.* February 7, 2018. https://twocents.lifehacker.com/build-the-skill-of-delayed-gratification-1822800199.

Banks, Emily, et al. "Tobacco Smoking and All-Cause Mortality in a Large Australian Cohort Study: Findings from a Mature Epidemic with Current Low Smoking Prevalence." *BMC Medicine* 13 (2015): 38.

Beck, A. L., M. Heyman, C. Chao, and J. Wojcicki. "Full Fat Milk Consumption Protects against Severe Childhood Obesity in Latinos." *Preventive Medicine Reports* 8 (2017): 1–5.

Begley, Sharon. "Does Exercise Prevent Cancer?" *Stat.* May 16, 2016. https://www.statnews.com/2016/05/16/exercise-prevent-cancer/.

Beil, Laura. "The Brain May Clean Out Alzheimer's Plaques during Sleep." *Science News.* July 15, 2018. https://www.sciencenews.org/article/sleep-brain-alzheimers-plaques-protein.

Benes, Ross. "This Chart Shows Which College Football Teams Have the Most Success per Dollar." *SB Nation.* March 24, 2016. https://www.sbnation.com/college-football/2016/3/24/11283338/ncaa-football-teams-costs-spending-expenses.

Bourne, P. A., A. Hudson-Davis, C. Sharpe-Pryce, I. Solan, and S. Nelson. "Suicide and Marriage Rates: A Multivariate Analysis of National Data from 1970–2013 in Jamaica." *International Journal of Emergency Mental Health and Human Resilience* 17 (2015): 502–8.

Davis. Josh. "How (and Why) to Master the Habit of Delaying Gratification." *Fast Company*. January 17, 2017. https://www.fastcompany.com/3067188 /how-and-why-to-master-the-habit-of-delaying-gratification.

Doctorow, Cory. "Correlation between Autism Diagnosis and Organic Food Sales." *Boing Boing*. January 1, 2013. https://boingboing.net/2013/01/01 /correlation-between-autism-dia.html.

Doll, R., R. Peto, J. Boreham, and I. Sutherland. "Mortality in Relation to Smoking: 50 Years' Observations on Male British Doctors." *British Medical Journal* 328 (2004): 1519.

Esposito, Lisa. "Health Buzz: Exercise Cuts Cancer Risk, Huge Study Finds." *U.S. News & World Report*. May 16, 2016. https://health.usnews.com /wellness/articles/2016-05-16/exercise-cuts-cancer-risk-huge-study-finds.

Fisher, Sir Ronald A. *Smoking. The Cancer Controversy: Some Attempts to Assess the Evidence*. Edinburgh and London: Oliver and Boyd, 1959.

Gajanan, Mahita. "The Cost of Raising a Child Jumps to $233,610." *Money*. January 9, 2017. http://time.com/money/4629700/child-raising-cost -department-of-agriculture-report/.

Geller, E. S., N. W. Russ, and M. G. Altomari. "Naturalistic Observations of Beer Drinking among College Students." *Journal of Applied Behavior Analysis* 19 (1986): 391–96.

"The Great American Smoke Out." Mike Pence for Congress website. 2000. http://web.archive.org/web/20010415085348/http://mikepence.com /smoke.html.

Haber, N., E. R. Smith, E. Moscoe, K. Andrews, R. Audy, W. Bell, . . . and E. A. Suarez. "Causal Language and Strength of Inference in Academic and Media Articles Shared in Social Media (CLAIMS): A Systematic Review." *PLOS One* 13 (2018): e0196346.

Hasday, J. D., K. D. Fairchild, and C. Shanholtz. "The Role of Fever in the Infected Host." *Microbes and Infection* 2 (2000): 1891–904.

Healy, Melissa. "Exercising Drives Down Risk for 13 Cancers, Research Shows." *Los Angeles Times*. May 16, 2016. http://www.latimes.com /science/sciencenow/la-sci-sn-exercising-cancer-20160516-story.html.

Lefkowitz, E. S., R. Wesche, and C. E. Leavitt. "Never Been Kissed: Correlates of Lifetime Kissing Status in U.S. University Students." *Archives of Sexual Behavior* 47 (2018): 1283–93.

Mackie, John. *The Cement of the Universe: A Study of Causation*. Oxford: Oxford University Press, 1980.

McCandless, David. "Out of Your Hands." Knowledge Is Beautiful. 2015. https://informationisbeautiful.net/visualizations/out-of-your-hands/.

Moore, S. C., I.-M. Lee, E. Weiderpass, P. T. Campbell, J. N. Sampson, C. M. Kitahara, S. K. Keadle et al. "Leisure-Time Physical Activity and Risk of 26 Types of Cancer in 1.44 Million Adults." *JAMA Internal Medicine* 176 (2016): 816–25.

Mumford, Stephen, and Rani Lill Anjum. *Causation: A Very Short Introduction*. Oxford: Oxford University Press, 2013.

Park, Alice. "Exercise Can Lower Risk of Some Cancers by 20%." *Time*. May 16, 2016. http://time.com/4330041/reduce-cancer-risk-exercise/.

Passy, Jacob. "Another Adverse Effect of High Home Prices: Fewer Babies." MarketWatch. June 9, 2018. https://www.marketwatch.com/story /another-adverse-effect-of-high-home-prices-fewer-babies-2018-06-06.

Schaffer, Jonathan. "The Metaphysics of Causation." Stanford Encyclopedia of Philosophy. 2016. https://plato.stanford.edu/entries/causation-meta physics/.

Shoda, Y., W. Mischel, and P. K. Peake. "Predicting Adolescent Cognitive and Self-regulatory Competencies from Preschool Delay of Gratification: Identifying Diagnostic Conditions." *Developmental Psychology* 26 (1990): 978.

Sies, Helmut. "A New Parameter for Sex Education." *Nature* 332 (1988): 495.

Sumner, P., S. Vivian-Griffiths, J. Boivin, A. Williams, C. A. Venetis, A. Davies et al. "The Association between Exaggeration in Health Related Science News and Academic Press Releases: Retrospective Observational Study." *British Medical Journal* 349 (2014): g7015.

Tucker, Jeff. "Birth Rates Dropped Most in Counties Where Home Values Grew Most." Zillow. June 6, 2018. https://www.zillow.com/research /birth-rates-home-values-20165/.

Vigen, Tyler. "Spurious Correlations." 2015. http://www.tylervigen.com /spurious-correlations.

Watts, T. W., G. J. Duncan, and H. Quan. "Revisiting the Marshmallow Test: A Conceptual Replication Investigating Links between Early Delay of Gratification and Later Outcomes." *Psychological Science* 29 (2018): 1159–77.

Zoldan, Ari. "40-Year-Old Stanford Study Reveals the 1 Quality Your Children Need to Succeed in Life." *Inc.* February 1, 2018.

CHAPTER 5: NUMBERS AND NONSENSE

Binder, John. "2,139 DACA Recipients Convicted or Accused of Crimes against Americans." *Breitbart*. September 5, 2017. http://www.breitbart .com/big-government/2017/09/05/2139-daca-recipients-convicted-or -accused-of-crimes-against-americans/.

Bogaert, A. F., and D. R. McCreary. "Masculinity and the Distortion of Self-Reported Height in Men." *Sex Roles* 65 (2011): 548.

Campbell, D. T. "Assessing the Impact of Planned Social Change." *Evaluation and Program Planning* 2 (1979): 67–90.

Camper, English. "How Much Pappy Van Winkle Is Left after 23 Years in a Barrel?" Alcademics. January 15, 2014. http://www.alcademics.com/2014 /01/how-much-pappy-van-winkle-is-left-after-23-years-in-a-barrel-.html.

Center for Science in the Public Interest. "Caffeine Chart." December 2016. https://cspinet.org/eating-healthy/ingredients-of-concern/caffeine-chart.

Centers for Disease Control and Prevention. "Disease Burden of Influenza." 2018. https://www.cdc.gov/flu/about/disease/burden.htm.

Cimbala, John M., and Yunus A. Çengel. "Dimensional Analysis and Modeling," Section 7-2: "Dimensional Homogeneity." In *Essential of Fluid Mechanics: Fundamentals and Applications*. New York: McGraw-Hill, 2006.

Drozdeck, Steven, and Lyn Fisher. *The Trust Equation*. Logan, Utah: Financial Forum Publishing, 2005.

Ellenberg, Jordan. *How Not to Be Wrong: The Power of Mathematical Thinking.* New York: Penguin Press, 2014.

Garfield, Eugene. "I Had a Dream . . . about Uncitedness." *The Scientist.* July 1998.

Goodhart, Charles. "Problems of Monetary Management: The U.K. Experience." In *Inflation, Depression, and Economic Policy in the West,* edited by Anthony S. Courakis, 111–46. Lanham, MD: Rowman & Littlefield.

Gordon, Dr. Deborah. *2015 Flu Season.* https://www.drdeborahmd.com/2015 -flu-season.

Hamilton, D. P. "Publishing by—and for?—the Numbers." *Science* 250 (1990): 1331–32.

———. "Research Papers: Who's Uncited Now?" *Science* 251 (1991): 25.

Heathcote, Elizabeth. "Does the Happiness Formula Really Add Up?" *Independent.* June 20, 2010. https://www.independent.co.uk/life-style/health-and -families/features/does-the-happiness-formula-really-add-up-2004279 .html.

Hines, Nick. "The Amount of Scotch Lost to the Angel's Share Every Year Is Staggering." *Vinepair.* April 11, 2017. https://vinepair.com/articles/what -is-angels-share-scotch/.

Howell, Elizabeth. "How Many Stars Are in the Universe?" *Space.com.* May 18, 2017. https://www.space.com/26078-how-many-stars-are-there.html.

International Whaling Commission. "Population (Abundance) Estimates." 2018. https://iwc.int/estimate.

Jago, Arthur G. "Can It Really Be True That Half of Academic Papers Are Never Read?" *Chronicle of Higher Education.* June 1, 2018.

Jefferson, T., C. Di Pietrantonj, A. Rivetti, G. A. Bawazeer, L. A. Al-Ansary, and E. Ferroni. "Vaccines for Preventing Influenza in Healthy Adults." *Cochrane Library* (2010). https://doi.org/10.1002/14651858.CD001269.pub6.

The Keyword (blog). "Our Latest Quality Improvements for Search." Ben Gomes. Google. April 25, 2017. https://blog.google/products/search/our -latest-quality-improvements-search/.

Kutner, Max. "How to Game the College Rankings." *Boston.* August 26, 2014.

"*The Lancet*: Alcohol Is Associated with 2.8 Million Deaths Each Year Worldwide." Press release. American Association for the Advancement of Science. August 23, 2018. https://www.eurekalert.org/pub_releases/2018-08/tl -tla082218.php.

Molinari, N-A. M., I. R. Ortega-Sanchez, M. L. Messonnier, W. W. Thompson, P. M. Wortley, E. Weintraub, and C. B. Bridges. "The Annual Impact of Seasonal Influenza in the US: Measuring Disease Burden and Costs." *Vaccine* 25 (2007): 5086–96.

National Highway Traffic Safety Administration. "Seat Belts." 2016. https:// www.nhtsa.gov/risky-driving/seat-belts.

National Safety Council. "NSC Motor Vehicle Fatality Estimates." 2017. https://www.nsc.org/portals/0/documents/newsdocuments/2017/12 -month-estimates.pdf.

NCD Risk Factor Collaboration. "A Century of Trends in Adult Human Height." *eLife* 5 (2016): e13410.

Pease, C. M., and J. J. Bull. *Think Critically*. Ebook. Biology for Business, Law and Liberal Arts (Bio301d) course, University of Idaho. https://bio301d .com/scientific-decision-making/.

Reuter, P. "The (Continued) Vitality of Mythical Numbers." *The Public Interest* 75 (1984): 135.

Silversin, J., and G. Kaplan. "Engaged Physicians Transform Care." Presented at the 29th Annual National Forum on Quality Improvement in Health Care. Slides at http://app.ihi.org/FacultyDocuments/Events/Event-2930/Presen tation-15687/Document-12690/Presentation_Q6_Engaged_Physicians _Silversin.pdf.

Spiegelhalter, David. "The Risks of Alcohol (Again)." *Medium*. August 24, 2018. https://medium.com/wintoncentre/the-risks-of-alcohol-again-2ae8 cb006a4a.

Tainer, H. A., et al. "Science, Citation, and Funding." *Science* 251 (1991): 1408–11.

Tefft, B. C., A. F. Williams, and J. G. Grabowski. "Teen Driver Risk in Rela- tion to Age and Number of Passengers, United States, 2007–2010." *Traffic Injury Prevention* 14 (2013): 283–92.

Todd W. Schneider (blog). "Taxi, Uber, and Lyft Usage in New York City." Schneider, Todd. April 5, 2016. http://toddwschneider.com/posts/taxi -uber-lyft-usage-new-york-city/.

"Truthiness." Dictionary.com. http://www.dictionary.com/browse/truthiness.

"Use this Equation to Determine, Diagnose, and Repair Trust." *First Round Re- view*. 2018. http://firstround.com/review/use-this-equation-to-determine -diagnose-and-repair-trust/.

Van Noorden, Richard. "The Science That's Never Been Cited." *Nature* 552 (2017): 162–64.

Vann, M. G. "Of Rats, Rice, and Race: The Great Hanoi Rat Massacre, an Epi- sode in French Colonial History." *French Colonial History* 4 (2003): 191–203.

Welsh, Ashley. "There's 'No Safe Level of Alcohol,' Major New Study Con- cludes." CBS News. August 23, 2018. https://www.cbsnews.com/news /alcohol-and-health-no-safe-level-of-drinking-major-new-study-concludes/.

West, Jevin. "How to Improve the Use of Metrics: Learn from Game Theory." *Nature* 465 (2010): 871–72.

CHAPTER 6: SELECTION BIAS

Aldana, S. G. "Financial Impact of Health Promotion Programs: A Compre- hensive Review of the Literature." *American Journal of Health Promotion* 15 (2001): 296–320.

Baicker, K., D. Cutler, and Z. Song. "Workplace Wellness Programs Can Gen- erate Savings." *Health Affairs* 29 (2010): 304–11.

Carroll, Aaron E. "Workplace Wellness Programs Don't Work Well. Why Some Studies Show Otherwise." *The New York Times*. August 6, 2018.

Chapman, L. S. "Meta-Evaluation of Worksite Health Promotion Economic Return Studies: 2005 Update." *American Journal of Health Promotion* 19 (2005): 1–11.

"Class Size Distributions Interactive Report." Office of Institutional Research and Analysis, Marquette University. 2019. https://www.marquette.edu /oira/class-size-dash.shtml.

"Digital Are the Channels of Choice for Today's Auto Insurance Shopper; Digital Leaders Setting the Pace for Premium Growth, Says J.D. Power Study." Press release. J.D. Power. April 29, 2016. http://www.jdpower.com/press -releases/2016-us-insurance-shopping-study.

Ellenberg, Jordan. *How Not to Be Wrong: The Power of Mathematical Thinking.* New York: Penguin Press, 2014.

"Every Single Auto Insurance Ad." Truth in Advertising. March 26, 2014. https://www.truthinadvertising.org/every-single-auto-insurance-ad/.

Feld, S. L. "Why Your Friends Have More Friends Than You Do." *American Journal of Sociology* 96 (1991): 1464–477.

Frakt, Austin, and Aaron E. Carroll. "Do Workplace Wellness Programs Work? Usually Not." *The New York Times*. September 11, 2014.

Henrich, J., S. J. Heine, and A. Norenzayan. "The Weirdest People in the World?" *Behavioral and Brain Sciences* 33 (2010): 61–83.

Hernán, M. A., S. Hernández-Díaz, and J. M. Robins. "A Structural Approach to Selection Bias." *Epidemiology* 15 (2004): 615–25.

Jackson, Kirabo (@KiraboJackson). "A difference in average SAT scores among admitted students IS NOT evidence of preferential treatment or lower standards for any group." Twitter, August 3, 2017, 6:47 P.M. https://twitter .com/KiraboJackson/status/893241923791663104.

Jones, D., D. Molitor, and J. Reif. "What Do Workplace Wellness Programs Do? Evidence from the Illinois Workplace Wellness Study." Working paper no. 24229, National Bureau of Economic Research. January 2018, revised June 2018. http://www.nber.org/workplacewellness/s/IL_Wellness_Study _1.pdf.

Kenny, Dianna Theadora. "Music to Die For: How Genre Affects Popular Musicians' Life Expectancy." *The Conversation*. March 22, 2015. https:// theconversation.com/music-to-die-for-how-genre-affects-popular -musicians-life-expectancy-36660.

Kenny, Dianna, and Anthony Asher. "Life Expectancy and Cause of Death in Popular Musicians: Is the Popular Musician Lifestyle the Road to Ruin?" *Medical Problems of Performing Artists* 31 (2016): 37–44.

Morse, Robert, and Eric Books. "A More Detailed Look at the Ranking Factors." *U.S. News & World Report*. September 8, 2019. https://www.usnews .com/education/best-colleges/articles/ranking-criteria-and-weights.

Moyer, Justin Wm. "Over Half of Dead Hip-Hop Artists Were Murdered, Study Finds." *The Washington Post*. March 25, 2015.

Norvig, Peter. "How Computers Learn." Vienna Gödel Lecture. 2015. https:// www.youtube.com/watch?v=T1O3ikmTEdA; discussion: Bernhardsson, Erik. "Norvig's Claim That Programming Competitions Correlate Negatively with Being Good on the Job." April 4, 2015. https://erikbern.com /2015/04/07/norvigs-claim-that-programming-competitions-correlate -negatively-with-being-good-on-the-job.html.

"SF1.1: Family Size and Household Composition." Social Policy Division, Directorate of Employment, Labour and Social Affairs, OECD Family Database. June 12, 2016. https://www.oecd.org/els/family/SF_1_1_Family _size_and_composition.pdf.

Stephens-Davidowitz, Seth. *Everybody Lies: Big Data, New Data, and What the Internet Can Tell Us About Who We Really Are.* New York: HarperCollins, 2017.

Ugander, J., B. Karrer, L. Backstrom, and C. Marlow. "The Anatomy of the Facebook Social Graph." 2011. arXiv: 1111.4503.

"U.S. Survey Research: Collecting Survey Data." Pew Research Center. December 2019. http://www.pewresearch.org/methods/u-s-survey-research /collecting-survey-data/.

CHAPTER 7: DATA VISUALIZATION

Alden, Lori. "Statistics Can Be Misleading." Econoclass.com. 2008. http:// www.econoclass.com/misleadingstats.html.

Antoniazzi, Alberto. "Rock'n'Roll Metro Map." https://society6.com/prod uct/rocknroll-metro-map_print.

Brendan Nyhan (blog). "The Use and Abuse of Bar Graphs." Nyhan, Brendan. May 19, 2011. https://www.brendan-nyhan.com/blog/2011/05/the-use -and-abuse-of-bar-graphs.html.

Bump, Philip. "Why This National Review Global Temperature Graph Is So Misleading." *The Washington Post.* December 14, 2015. https://www.wash ingtonpost.com/news/the-fix/wp/2015/12/14/why-the-national-reviews -global-temperature-graph-is-so-misleading.

Chan, Christine. "Gun Deaths in Florida." Data visualization. Reuters. February 16, 2014.

——— (@ChristineHHChan). "@john_self My inspiration for the graphic: http://www.visualisingdata.com/blog/wp-content/uploads/2013/04 /IRAQ.jpg . . ." Twitter, April 25, 2014, 12:31 A.M. https://web.archive .org/web/20180604180503/https:/twitter.com/ChristineHHChan /status/455971685783441408.

Ciolli, Joe. "Facebook's Earnings Disaster Erased $120 Billion in Market Value—The Biggest Wipeout in US Stock-Market History." *Business Insider.* July 26, 2018. https://www.businessinsider.com/facebook-stock -price-earnings-report-market-value-on-pace-for-record-drop-2018-7.

Clarke, Conor. "Daily Chart: Tax the Rich to Pay for Healthcare?" *The Atlantic.* July 13, 2009. https://www.theatlantic.com/daily-dish/archive/2009 /07/daily-chart-tax-the-rich-to-pay-for-health-care/198869/.

Clinton, Hillary (@hillaryclinton). Instagram, April 12, 2016. http://www .instagram.com/p/BEHAc8vEPjV/.

Deisher, T. A., N. V. Doan, K. Koyama, and S. Bwabye. "Epidemiologic and Molecular Relationship between Vaccine Manufacture and Autism Spectrum Disorder Prevalence." *Issues in Law and Medicine* 30 (2015): 47–70.

Donahoo, Daniel. "The Periodic Table of Periodic Tables." *Wired.* March 29, 2010. https://www.wired.com/2010/03/the-periodic-table-of-periodic -tables/.

Engel, Pamela. "This Chart Shows an Alarming Rise in Florida Gun Deaths After 'Stand Your Ground' Was Enacted." *Business Insider*. February 18, 2014.

Environmental Protection Agency. "Estimated Animal Agriculture Nitrogen and Phosphorus from Manure." 2013. https://www.epa.gov/nutrient -policy-data/estimated-animal-agriculture-nitrogen-and-phosphorus -manure.

Geiger, A. W., and Gretchen Livingston. "8 Facts about Love and Marriage in America." Pew Research Center. February 13, 2019. http://www.pew research.org/fact-tank/2018/02/13/8-facts-about-love-and-marriage/.

Goo, Sarah Kehaulani. "The Art and Science of the Scatterplot." Pew Research Center. September 16, 2015. https://www.pewresearch.org/fact-tank/2015 /09/16/the-art-and-science-of-the-scatterplot/.

Hayward, Steven. "The Only Global Warming Chart You Need from Now On." *Powerline*. October 21, 2015. http://www.powerlineblog.com /archives/2015/10/the-only-global-warming-chart-you-need-from -now-on.php.

Lorch, Mark. "The Underground Map of the Elements." September 3, 2013. https://www.theguardian.com/science/blog/2013/sep/03/underground -map-elements-periodic-table.

Mason, Betsy. "Why Scientists Need to Be Better at Data Visualization." *Knowable Magazine*. November 12, 2019. https://www.knowablemagazine.org /article/mind/2019/science-data-visualization.

Max Woolf's Blog. "A Thoughtful Analysis of the Most Poorly-Designed Chart Ever." Woolf, Max. January 20, 2014. http://minimaxir.com/2014/01 /more-language-more-problems/.

National Center for Health Statistics. "Birth Rates for Females by Age Group: United States." Centers for Disease Control and Prevention. 2020. https:// data.cdc.gov/NCHS/NCHS-Birth-Rates-for-Females-by-Age-Group -United-S/yt7u-eiyg.

Pelletier, F., and D. W. Coltman. "Will Human Influences on Evolutionary Dynamics in the Wild Pervade the Anthropocene?" *BMC Biology* 16 (2018): 7. https://bmcbiol.biomedcentral.com/articles/10.1186/s12915-017 -0476-1.

Potter, Andrew. "How a Snowstorm Exposed Quebec's Real Problem: Social Malaise." *Maclean's*. March 20, 2017.

Random Axis (blog). "A Subway Map of Maps That Use Subway Maps as a Metaphor." Andy Proehl. October 16, 2012. http://randomaxis.blogspot. com/2012/10/a-subway-map-of-maps-that-use-subway.html.

Robinson-Garcia, N., R. Costas, K. Isett, J. Melkers, and D. Hicks. "The Unbearable Emptiness of Tweeting—about Journal Articles." *PLOS One* 12 (2017): e0183551.

Scarr, Simon. "Iraq's Deadly Toll." Data visualization. *South China Morning Post*. December 17, 2011. https://www.scmp.com/infographics/article /1284683/iraqs-bloody-toll.

Science-Based Medicine (blog). " 'Aborted Fetal Tissue' and Vaccines: Combining Pseudoscience and Religion to Demonize Vaccines.' " David Gorski. Au-

gust 17, 2015. https://sciencebasedmedicine.org/aborted-fetal-tissue-and
-vaccines-combining-pseudoscience-and-religion-to-demonize-vaccines-2/.

Swanson, N. L., A. Leu, J. Abrahamson, and B. Wallet. "Genetically Engineered
Crops, Glyphosate and the Deterioration of Health in the United States of
America." *Journal of Organic Systems* 9 (2014): 6–37.

Trilling, Bernie, and Charles Fadel. *21st Century Skills: Learning for Life in Our
Times.* San Francisco: Wiley, 2009. Via van der Zee, Tim (@Research_Tim).
"There are bad visualizations, and then there's the 'bicycle of education.'"
Twitter, May 31, 2016, 5:26 P.M. https://twitter.com/Research_Tim
/status/737757291437527040.

Tufte, Edward. *The Visual Display of Quantitative Information.* Cheshire, Conn.:
Cheshire Press, 1983.

Venturi, Robert, Denise Scott Brown, and Steven Izenour. *Learning from Las
Vegas.* Cambridge, Mass.: MIT Press, 1972.

Woods, Christopher J. "The Periodic Table of the London Underground." The
Chemogenesis Web Book: Internet Database of Periodic Tables. 2015.
https://www.meta-synthesis.com/webbook/35_pt/pt_database.php?PT
_id=685.

Zaveri, Mihir. "Monsanto Weedkiller Roundup Was 'Substantial Factor' in
Causing Man's Cancer, Jury Says." *The New York Times.* March 19, 2019.

CHAPTER 8: CALLING BULLSHIT ON BIG DATA

"Advances in AI Are Used to Spot Signs of Sexuality." *The Economist.* September 9, 2017.

Anderson, Chris. "The End of Theory: The Data Deluge Makes the Scientific
Method Obsolete." *Wired.* June 23, 2008.

Babbage, Charles. *Passages from the Life of a Philosopher.* London: Longman and
Co., 1864.

Bloudoff-Indelicato, Mollie. "Have Bad Handwriting? The U.S. Postal Service
Has Your Back." *Smithsonian.* December 23, 2015.

Bradley, Tony. "Facebook AI Creates Its Own Language in Creepy Preview of
Our Potential Future." *Forbes.* July 31, 2017.

Domonoske, Camila. "Elon Musk Warns Governors: Artificial Intelligence
Poses 'Existential Risk.'" National Public Radio. July 17, 2017.

Emery, David. "Did Facebook Shut Down an AI Experiment Because Chatbots
Developed Their Own Language?" *Snopes.com.* August 1, 2017.

Ginsberg, J., et al. "Detecting Influenza Epidemics Using Search Engine Query
Data." *Nature* 457 (2009): 1012–14.

LaFrance, Adrienne. "An Artificial Intelligence Developed Its Own Non-
Human Language." *The Atlantic.* June 15, 2017.

Lazer, David, and Brian Kennedy. "What We Can Learn from the Epic Failure
of Google Flu Trends." *Wired.* October 1, 2015.

Leuner, John. "A Replication Study: Machine Learning Models Are Capable of
Predicting Sexual Orientation from Facial Images." Unpublished master's
thesis. 2018. arXiv: 1902.10739v1.

Levin, Sam. "New AI Can Tell Whether You Are Gay or Straight from a Photograph." *The Guardian*. September 7, 2017.

Markoff, John. "Brain-Like Computers, Learning from Experience." *The New York Times*. December 28, 2013.

———. "Microsoft Finds Cancer Clues in Search Queries." *The New York Times*. June 8, 2016.

Naughton, John. "Google and the Flu: How Big Data Will Help Us Make Gigantic Mistakes." *The Guardian*. April 5, 2014.

"New Navy Device Learns by Doing." *The New York Times*. July 8, 1958.

Pritchard, Duncan. *Epistemology*. New York: Palgrave Macmillan, 2016.

Ribeiro, M. T., S. Singh, and C. Guestrin. " 'Why Should I Trust You?' Explaining the Predictions of any Classifier." Proceedings of the 22nd ACM SIGKDD International Conference on Knowledge Discovery and Data Mining, San Francisco, August 2016.

Salzberg, Steven. "Why Google Flu Is a Failure." *Forbes*. March 23, 2014.

Wang, Y., and M. Kosinski. "Deep Neural Networks Are More Accurate Than Humans at Detecting Sexual Orientation from Facial Images." *Journal of Personality and Social Psychology* 114 (2018): 246–57.

Weinberger, David. "Our Machines Now Have Knowledge We'll Never Understand." *Wired*. April 18, 2017.

Wilson, Mark. "AI Is Inventing Languages Humans Can't Understand. Should We Stop It?" *Fast Company*. July 14, 2017.

Zech, J. R., M. A. Badgeley, M. Liu, A. B. Costa, J. J. Titano, and E. K. Oermann. "Variable Generalization Performance of a Deep Learning Model to Detect Pneumonia in Chest Radiographs: A Cross-Sectional Study." *PLOS Medicine* 15 (2018): e1002683.

CHAPTER 9: THE SUSCEPTIBILITY OF SCIENCE

Angwin, Julia, Jeff Larson, Surya Mattu, and Lauren Kirchner. "Machine Bias." *ProPublica*. May 23, 2016.

Bacon, Francis. Preface to the *Instauratio Magna*. In *Famous Prefaces*. The Harvard Classics, vol. 39. New York: Little, Brown, 1909.

Balsamo, Michael, Jonathan J. Cooper, and Gillian Flaccus. "Earlier Search for California Serial Killer Led to Wrong Man." Associated Press. April 28, 2018.

Begley, C. G., and Ellis, L. M. "Raise Standards for Preclinical Cancer Research." *Nature* 483 (2012): 531–33.

Booth, Robert. "Police Face Calls to End Use of Facial Recognition Software." *The Guardian*. July 3, 2019.

Camerer, C. F., A. Dreber, E. Forsell, T-H. Ho, J. Huber, M. Johannesson, M. Kirchler et al. "Evaluating Replicability of Laboratory Experiments in Economics." *Science* 351 (2016): 1433–36.

Dastin, J. "Amazon Scraps Secret AI Recruiting Tool That Showed Bias against Women." Reuters. October 9, 2018.

Davenas, E., F. Beauvais, J. Amara, M. Oberbaum, B. Robinzon, A. Miadonnai,

A. Tedeschi et al. "Human Basophil Degranulation Triggered by Very Dilute Antiserum against IgE." *Nature* 333 (1988): 816–18.

Dumas-Mallet, E., A. Smith, T. Boraud, and F. Gonon. "Poor Replication Validity of Biomedical Association Studies Reported by Newspapers." *PLOS One* 12 (2017): e0172650.

Fanelli, D. "Negative Results Are Disappearing from Most Disciplines and Countries." *Scientometrics* 90 (2012): 891–904.

Fleischmann, Martin, Stanley Pons, and Marvin Hawkins. "Electrochemically Induced Nuclear Fusion of Deuterium." *Journal of Electroanalytical Chemistry* 261 (1989): 301–8.

Hignett, Katherine. "Scott Kelly: NASA Twins Study Confirms Astronaut's DNA Actually Changed in Space." *Newsweek*. March 9, 2018.

Ioannidis, John P. A. "Why Most Published Research Findings Are False." *PLOS Medicine,* August 30, 2005.

Kelly, Scott (@StationCDRKelly). "What? My DNA changed by 7%! Who knew? I just learned about it in this article. This could be good news! I no longer have to call @ShuttleCDRKelly my identical twin brother anymore." Twitter, March 10, 2018, 6:47 P.M. https://twitter.com/Station CDRKelly/status/972620001340346368.

Kitcher, Philip. *The Advancement of Science: Science without Legend, Objectivity without Illusions.* New York: Oxford University Press, 1995.

Koren, Marina. "How Did Astronaut DNA Become 'Fake News'?" *The Atlantic*. March 16, 2018.

Lapp, Joseph (@JosephTLapp). "How to read a news report about a scientific finding. I wrote this in response to a friend who posted news of a study concluding canola oil is bad for us. (Note: my point is independent of the truth about canola oil.)" Twitter, December 9, 2017, 8:51 P.M. https://twitter.com/JosephTLapp/status/939673813272363008.

Leung, P. T. M, E. M. Macdonald, M. B. Stanbrook, I. A. Dhalla, and D. N. Juurlink. "A 1980 Letter on the Risk of Opioid Addiction." *The New England Journal of Medicine* 376 (2017): 2194–95.

Lippincott, E. R., R. R. Stromberg, W. H. Grant, and G. L. Cessac. "Polywater." *Science* 164 (1969): 1482–87.

Manthorpe, Rowland, and Alexander J. Martin. "81% of 'Suspects' Flagged by Met's Police Facial Recognition Technology Innocent, Independent Report Says." *Sky News*. July 4, 2019.

McCool, John H. "Opinion: Why I Published in a Predatory Journal." *The Scientist*. April 6, 2017.

Merton, R. K. "Priorities in Scientific Discovery: A Chapter in the Sociology of Science." *American Sociological Review* 22 (1957): 635–59.

"Mortgage Algorithms Perpetuate Racial Bias in Lending, Study Finds." Press release. University of California, Berkeley. November 13, 2018.

"NASA Twins Study Confirms Preliminary Findings." Press release. National Aeronautics and Space Administration. January 31, 2018. https://www.nasa.gov/feature/nasa-twins-study-confirms-preliminary-findings.

NORC General Social Survey. 2017. Data compiled by the Pew Research Center.

Open Science Collaboration. "Estimating the Reproducibility of Psychological Science." *Science* 349 (2015): aac4716.

Pauling, L., and R. B. Corey. "A Proposed Structure for the Nucleic Acids." *Proceedings of the National Academy of Sciences* 39 (1953): 84–97.

Pauling, Linus. *Vitamin C and the Common Cold.* 1st edition. San Francisco: W. H. Freeman, 1970.

Porter, J. and H. Jick. "Addiction Rare in Patients Treated with Narcotics." *The New England Journal of Medicine* 302 (1980): 123.

Prior, Ryan. "A 'No-Brainer Nobel Prize': Hungarian Scientists May Have Found a Fifth Force of Nature." *CNN.* November 23, 2019.

Scutti, Susan. "Astronaut's DNA No Longer Matches That of His Identical Twin, NASA Finds." *CNN.* March 15, 2018.

Shen, C., and B.-C. Björk. "'Predatory' Open Access: A Longitudinal Study of Article Volumes and Market Characteristics." *BMC Medicine* 13 (2015): 230.

Simmons, J. P., L. D. Nelson, and U. Simonsohn. "False-Positive Psychology: Undisclosed Flexibility in Data Collection and Analysis Allows Presenting Anything as Significant." *Psychological Science* 22 (2011): 1359–66.

Stapel, Diedrich. *Faking Science: A True Story of Academic Fraud.* Translation by Nicholas J. L. Brown of Dutch edition *Ontsporing (Derailed).* Amsterdam: Prometheus Books, 2012. https://errorstatistics.files.wordpress.com/2014/12/fakingscience-20141214.pdf.

Stump, Scott, and Marguerite Ward. "After Year in Space, Astronaut Scott Kelly No Longer Has Same DNA as Identical Twin." *Today.* March 15, 2018.

Sumner, P., S. Vivian-Griffiths, J. Boivin, A. Williams, C. A. Venetis et al. "The Association between Exaggeration in Health Related Science News and Academic Press Releases: Retrospective Observational Study." *British Medical Journal* 349 (2014): g7015.

Sumner, P., S. Vivian-Griffiths, J. Boivin, A. Williams, L. Bott et al. "Exaggerations and Caveats in Press Releases and Health-Related Science News." *PLOS One* 11 (2016): e0168217.

Than, Ker. "'God Particle' Found? 'Historic Milestone' from Higgs Boson Hunters." *National Geographic.* July 4, 2012. https://news.nationalgeographic.com/news/2012/07/120704-god-particle-higgs-boson-new-cern-science/.

Turner, E. H., A. M. Matthews, E. Linardatos, R. A. Tell, and R. Rosenthal. "Selective Publication of Antidepressant Trials and Its Influence on Apparent Efficacy." *The New England Journal of Medicine* 358 (2008): 252–60.

van Nostrand, M., J. Riemenschneider, and L. Nicodemob. "Uromycitisis Poisoning Results in Lower Urinary Tract Infection and Acute Renal Failure: Case Report." *Urology & Nephrology Open Access Journal* 4 (2017): 00132.

Vinson, J. A., B. R. Burnham, and M. V. Nagendran. "Retracted: Randomized, Double-Blind, Placebo-Controlled, Linear Dose, Crossover Study to Evaluate the Efficacy and Safety of a Green Coffee Bean Extract in Overweight Subjects." *Diabetes, Metabolic Syndrome and Obesity: Targets and Therapy* 5 (2012): 21–27.

CHAPTER 10: SPOTTING BULLSHIT

Allen, Ron. "Survey Finds Foreign Students Aren't Applying to American Colleges." NBC News. March 25, 2017. https://www.nbcnews.com/nightly -news/survey-finds-foreign-students-aren-t-applying-american-colleges -n738411.

Baysinger, Tim. " 'Roseanne' Could Have Earned $60 Million in Ad Revenue Next Season." *The Wrap*. 2018. https://www.thewrap.com/roseanne-60 -million-ad-revenue-channing-dungey-barr-valerie-jarrett/.

Bump, Philip. "Fox News Wonders Whether We Should Cancel Food Stamps Because 0.09% of Spending Is Fraudulent." *The Washington Post*. December 28, 2016.

"FBI Releases 2015 Crime Statistics." Press release. FBI. September 26, 2016. https://www.fbi.gov/news/pressrel/press-releases/fbi-releases-2015-crime -statistics.

"Food Stamp Fraud at All-Time High: Is It Time to End the Program?" Fox News. December 27, 2016. Archived at https://web.archive.org/web /20161228144917/http://insider.foxnews.com/2016/12/27/food-stamp -fraud-all-time-high; "UPDATE: Fox & Friends Corrects Report about Food Stamp Fraud." Fox News. December 27, 2016. http://insider .foxnews.com/2016/12/27/food-stamp-fraud-all-time-high.

Galbi, Douglas A. "Long Term Trends in Personal Given Name Frequencies in the UK." July 20, 2002. https://www.galbithink.org/names.htm.

"The Goop Medicine Bag." Goop. https://shop.goop.com/shop/products/the -goop-medicine-bag?country=USA; "8 Crystals for Better Energy." Goop. https://goop.com/wellness/spirituality/the-8-essential-crystals/.

"How Many People in the UK Share Your Name?" *The Press* (York, United Kingdom). February 10, 2017. http://www.yorkpress.co.uk/news /15085294.How_many_people_in_the_UK_share_your_name_/.

Koblin, John. "After Racist Tweet, Roseanne Barr's Show Is Canceled by ABC." *The New York Times*. May 29, 2018. https://www.nytimes.com /2018/05/29/business/media/roseanne-barr-offensive-tweets.html.

Lee, Bruce Y. "This Is How Disgusting Airport Security Trays Are." *Forbes*. September 5, 2018.

Parker, Laura. "We Made Plastic. We Depend On It. Now We're Drowning in It." *National Geographic*. June 2018. Pages 40–69.

Postman, N. "Bullshit and the Art of Crap-Detection." Paper presented at the Annual Convention of the National Council of Teachers of English, Washington, D.C., November 28, 1969. *College English* 17: 2008.

Sauter, Michael, Samuel Stebbins, and Thomas C. Frohlich. "The Most Dangerous Cities in America." *24/7 Wall St*. January 13, 2016. https://247wallst .com/special-report/2016/09/27/25-most-dangerous-cities-in-america/.

Schmader, T., J. Whitehead, and V. H. Wysocki. "A Linguistic Comparison of Letters of Recommendation for Male and Female Chemistry and Biochemistry Job Applicants." *Sex Roles* 57 (2007): 509–14.

Stopera, Dave. "12 Reasons Why Sam, the Cat with Eyebrows, Should Be Your

New Favorite Cat." *BuzzFeed*. January 29, 2013. https://www.buzzfeed
.com/daves4/12-reasons-why-sam-the-cat-with-eyebrows-should.

"Style Rituals: Meet Colleen [McCann]." 2015. http://www.stylerituals.com
/about-avenue/.

Weinstein, Lawrence, and John A. Adam. *Guesstimation*. Princeton, N.J.:
Princeton University Press, 2008.

Wemple, Erik. "Agriculture Department Seeks Correction from Fox News on
Food-Stamp Fraud Report." *The Washington Post*. December 29, 2016.

Wittes, Benjamin (@benjaminwittes). "Information is like candy obtained in
public. Ask yourself this question: if this were candy and I were walking
down the street, would I eat this? And would I give it to my kids and
friends?" Twitter, June 16, 2019, 8:45 A.M. https://twitter.com/benjamin
wittes/status/1140238942698135559.

CHAPTER II: REFUTING BULLSHIT

Austin, John Langshaw. *How to Do Things with Words*. Oxford: Clarendon Press,
1975.

Bennett, C. M., A. A. Baird, M. B. Miller, and G. L. Wolford. "Neural Correlates of Interspecies Perspective Taking in the Post-mortem Atlantic
Salmon: An Argument for Multiple Comparisons Correction." Poster, Organization for Human Brain Mapping Annual Meeting, San Francisco, June
15, 2009, *NeuroImage* 47 (2009), Suppl. 1: S125.

Bergstrom, Carl T., and Lee Alan Dugatkin. *Evolution*. 2nd edition. New York:
W. W. Norton and Co., 2012, 2016.

Eklund, A., T. E. Nichols, and H. Knutsson. "Cluster Failure: Why fMRI Inferences for Spatial Extent Have Inflated False-Positive Rates." *Proceedings of
the National Academy of Sciences* 113 (2016): 7900–7905.

Hendren, Jon (@fart). "the big reason twitter is popular is becuase its the same
thing as yelling back at the tv except they might actually see it." Twitter,
July 12, 2019, 10:10 P.M. https://twitter.com/fart/status/11498635344
71200769.

Lippmann, Walter. *Liberty and the News*. Mineola, N.Y.: Dover, 1919, 2010.

Markovich, Matt. "$74 Million Later, Mercer Mess Is 2 Seconds Faster."
KOMO News. October 17, 2016. https://komonews.com/news/local
/mercer-mess.

Rice, Kenneth. "Sprint Research Runs into a Credibility Gap." *Nature* 432
(2004): 147. https://doi.org/10.1038/432147b.

Ryan, John. "Driving in Downtown Seattle? You May Soon Have to Pay a
Toll." *KUOW*. April 4, 2018. https://kuow.org/stories/driving-down
town-seattle-you-may-soon-have-pay-toll/.

Tatem, A. J., C. A. Guerra, P. M. Atkinson, and S. I. Hay. "Athletics: Momen-
tous Sprint at the 2156 Olympics?" *Nature* 431 (2004): 525.

Yanofsky, David. "The Chart Tim Cook Doesn't Want You to See." *Quartz*.
September 10, 2013. https://qz.com/122921/the-chart-tim-cook-doesnt
-want-you-to-see/.

Index

ABOUT THE AUTHORS

CARL T. BERGSTROM is an evolutionary biologist and professor in the Department of Biology at the University of Washington, where he studies how epidemics spread through populations and how information flows through biological and social systems at scales—from the intracellular control of gene expression to the spread of misinformation on social media.

Twitter: @CT_Bergstrom

JEVIN D. WEST is an associate professor in the Information School at the University of Washington. He is the director of UW's Center for an Informed Public and co-director of its DataLab, where he studies the science of science and the impact of technology on society. He also coordinates data science education at UW's eScience Institute.

Twitter: @jevinwest

callingbullshit.org

Facebook.com/callinBS

Twitter: @callin_bull